The
Psych
101
Series

James C. Kaufman, PhD, Series Editor
Neag School of Education
University of Connecticut

Robert Youdin, PhD, is an independent scholar at the Princeton Research Forum. He has been a private practitioner for the past 31 years and practices in Princeton, New Jersey. For 20 years, Dr. Youdin was an adjunct associate professor at the Fordham University Graduate School of Social Service in New York City. In 2007–2008, he was a project director for a Gero Innovations Grant for the Master's Advanced Curriculum Project funded by the John A. Hartford Foundation and Council on Social Work Education. In 2005–2007, Dr. Youdin was a participant in the Curriculum Development Institute (Gero-Ed) sponsored by the John A. Hartford Foundation and Council on Social Work Education. He is a past assistant research scientist of the Biometrics Unit of the New York State Psychiatric Institute in New York City. In 1977, he was elected as member of Sigma Xi, the Scientific Research Society of North America. In addition, he has appeared on numerous public service radio programs discussing older adult substance abuse and eating disorder problems. Dr. Youdin enjoys creating an existential oasis of peace and serenity when playing jazz piano. Dr. Youdin's website can be visited at www.youdin.net.

Psychology of Aging 101

Robert Youdin, PhD

SPRINGER PUBLISHING COMPANY

NEW YORK

Springer Publishing Company, LLC
11 West 42nd Street
New York, NY 10036
www.springerpub.com

Acquisitions Editor: Sheri W. Sussman
Composition: S4Carlisle Publishing Services

ISBN: 978-0-8261-3012-9
e-book ISBN: 978-0-8261-3013-6

16 17 18 19 20 / 5 4 3 2 1

The author and the publisher of this Work have made every effort to use sources believed to be reliable to provide information that is accurate and compatible with the standards generally accepted at the time of publication. The author and publisher shall not be liable for any special, consequential, or exemplary damages resulting, in whole or in part, from the readers' use of, or reliance on, the information contained in this book. The publisher has no responsibility for the persistence or accuracy of URLs for external or third-party Internet websites referred to in this publication and does not guarantee that any content on such websites is, or will remain, accurate or appropriate.

Library of Congress Cataloging-in-Publication Data

Names: Youdin, Robert, author.
Title: Psychology of aging 101 / Robert Youdin.
Description: New York : Springer, [2016] | Includes bibliographical references and index.
Identifiers: LCCN 2015038173 | ISBN 9780826130129
Subjects: LCSH: Aging—Psychological aspects. | Older people—Psychology.
Classification: LCC BF724.55.A35 Y68 2016 | DDC 155.67—dc23 LC record available at http://lccn.loc.gov/2015038173

Special discounts on bulk quantities of our books are available to corporations, professional associations, pharmaceutical companies, health care organizations, and other qualifying groups. If you are interested in a custom book, including chapters from more than one of our titles, we can provide that service as well.

For details, please contact:
Special Sales Department, Springer Publishing Company, LLC
11 West 42nd Street, 15th Floor, New York, NY 10036-8002
Phone: 877-687-7476 or 212-431-4370; Fax: 212-941-7842
E-mail: sales@springerpub.com

Printed in the United States of America by Gasch Printing.

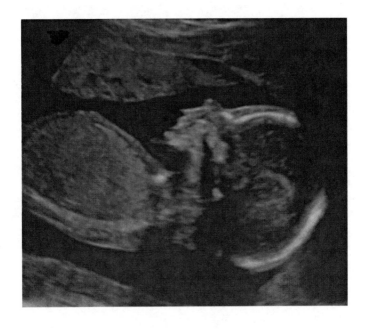

To my grandson Charlie, who is beginning his life journey
at the time I am beginning the end of my life journey

Contents

CONTENTS

Acknowledgments

I am most grateful to Sheri W. Sussman, my editor at Springer Publishing Company, who gave me the wonderful opportunity to write this book introducing the exciting field of aging to psychology students and professors. Her support and guidance, and, yes, sometimes criticism, created an environment of inspiration and humanism consistent with my experiences with the wonderful staff at Springer.

I would like to acknowledge the many psychologists and psychiatrists who were my mentors, professors, and friends, who through the years have encouraged me and supported my academic and clinical endeavors. I am forever grateful to Samuel Sutton, Arnold Mordkoff, Donald Spence, Nancy Hemmes, Benito Mustine, Milton Erickson, Sidney Rosen, Rhea Tuxen, Ted Coons, Paul Wachtel, and Bob Holt. In addition, I would like to acknowledge the many students I have had the privilege of teaching who consistently impressed me with their intellectual curiosity and highly motivated desire for learning. And, last but not least, I would like to acknowledge the many older adults I have encountered in my clinical practice who allowed me the privilege to enter their lives for brief moments and taught me the richness of their lives, shared their struggles with the trials and tribulations of late life, and taught me life lessons about being vital, interesting, and dignified while aging.

ACKNOWLEDGMENTS

This book would not have been possible without the extraordinary support and love from my wife, Naomi Browar. She sacrificed many hours of having my companionship without complaint, always offering encouragement and insightful advice from her clinical practice. In addition, I thank Yoni Youdin for his consistent support and companionship while I was writing this text.

Creativity 101
James C. Kaufman, PhD

Genius 101
Dean Keith Simonton, PhD

IQ Testing 101
Alan S. Kaufman, PhD

Leadership 101
Michael D. Mumford, PhD

Anxiety 101
Moshe Zeidner, PhD
Gerald Matthews, PhD

Psycholinguistics 101
H. Wind Cowles, PhD

Humor 101
Mitch Earleywine, PhD

Obesity 101
Lauren M. Rossen, PhD, MS
Eric A. Rossen, PhD

Emotional Intelligence 101
Gerald Matthews, PhD
Moshe Zeidner, PhD
Richard D. Roberts, PhD

Personality 101
Gorkan Ahmetoglu, PhD
Tomas Chamorro-Premuzic, PhD

Giftedness 101
Linda Kreger Silverman, PhD

Evolutionary Psychology 101
Glenn Geher, PhD

Psychology of Love 101
Karin Sternberg, PhD

Intelligence 101
Jonathan Plucker, PhD
Amber Esping, PhD

Depression 101
C. Emily Durbin, PhD

History of Psychology 101
David C. Devonis, PhD

Psychology of Trauma 101
Lesia M. Ruglass, PhD
Kathleen Kendall-Tackett, PhD, IBCLC, FAPA

Memory 101
James Michael Lampinen, PhD
Denise R. Beike, PhD

Media Psychology 101
Christopher J. Ferguson, PhD

Positive Psychology 101
Philip C. Watkins, PhD

Psychology of Aging 101
Robert Youdin, PhD

Creativity 101, Second Edition
James C. Kaufman, PhD

Introduction

The most beautiful people we have known are those who have known defeat, known suffering, known struggle, known loss, and have found their way out of the depths. These persons have an appreciation, a sensitivity, and an understanding of life that fills them with compassion, gentleness, and a deep loving concern. Beautiful people do not just happen.

Elisabeth Kübler-Ross (1975)

When discussing the psychology of aging, it is important to define whom we are discussing. Most psychologists accept that an older person is 65 years of age or older. This is an important distinction because the terms *older, older people, older adults, elder people, elder adults, seniors,* and so forth may indicate different age cohorts depending on whom you are talking to when discussing an older adult. For example, if talking to a middle school student, he or she may feel that you are talking about someone in high school who is looked upon as an older person. There are no clear guidelines for what is a correct label for a person 65 years of age or older. In this book, for purpose of clarity, the terms *older person, older people,* or *older adult* are the adjectival labels of choice, unless referring to works of other authors using other labels.

1

GEROPSYCHOLOGY

The field of aging in psychology is called *geropsychology* (American Psychological Association, 2010), and is now a recognized subfield of psychology. Geropsychology encompasses all of the subfields of psychology, such as clinical psychology, community psychology, neuropsychology, developmental psychology, research, policy, and environmental psychology, as they relate to older adults. The importance of the field of geropsychology is seen in the ever-increasing demographics of older adults. Walker (2005) cautions that with the retiring baby boomers, there is a coming *demographic tidal wave* or *tsunami* that, once arrived, will never depart. As a relevant metaphor, think of the recent tsunami that occurred in Japan and how it overwhelmed the resources of the country, with profound effects on the population of Japan.

Psychologists practicing with older adults are engaging in a rapidly growing field. This rapid growth is a consequence of the increasing population of older adults. According to Potter (2010), by 2020, there will be more than 53 million people over the age of 65 and about 7 million over the age of 85. Jungers and Slagel (2009) indicate that between 2008 and 2050, the American population over the age of 85 is expected to more than triple, from 5.4 to 19 million. In addition, starting in 2012, an average of 10,000 older adults from the baby-boom cohort began retiring each day. These older adults are more likely than previous cohorts to seek counseling from psychologists due to their higher level of education and greater acceptance of psychotherapy devoid of the stigma felt by older cohorts regarding mental health services. Conflicts addressed by psychologists arise from issues caused by retirement, living longer, financial stressors, psychological problems, coping with chronic illness (and, in some cases, multiple chronic illnesses), dementia, sexual issues, substance abuse, and, of course, death and dying.

Given this aging population trend, training in geropsychology is important because the members of the current cohort of people entering the older category, the baby boomers, represent a new trend of aging adults who are accustomed to accessing psychological services, and thus being familiar with aging issues is now a necessity for psychologists (Koenig, George, & Schneider, 1994). Clinicians will need a knowledge base of issues unique to older adults. These include the different developmental perspective of late life, issues with multiple chronic illnesses, complications of multiple medications prescribed by multiple providers, unique aspects of psychological problems in later life, the ability to differentiate cognitive impairments, the understanding of sensory impairments and their effects on functioning, issues of loss, and the different issues and complications of changing family systems.

A CONTEMPORARY CHANGE IN HOW PSYCHOLOGISTS PERCEIVE OLDER ADULTS

Historically, psychologists shied away from the clinical importance of treating older adults based on an orientation postulated by Sigmund Freud (1900/1953). Freud indicated that adults age 50 or greater were not candidates for psychoanalysis because learning stops at age 50. Obviously, if psychologists today followed this model, there would be no treatment for older adults. Consistent with Freud's attitude toward older adults, many post-Freudian psychotherapy theories were oriented toward younger and middle-aged adults, adolescents, or children, and then were extrapolated to older adults by psychologists seeking some guidelines for treating an older adult.

This trend changed when a discovery was made by Eriksson et al. (1998). They found that *neurogenesis* (the creation of new neurons) occurs in the hippocampus, a structure in the midbrain. This discovery disproved the prevailing theory at that time that the nervous system was a fixed, hard-wired system incapable of generating new neurons. Based on this discovery, the concept of *neuroplasticity* arose, which describes a phenomenon whereby the brain has the capacity to change as a product of interpersonal (Badenoch, 2008; Siegel, 2006) and intrapersonal memories that are disconfirmed by existential interpersonal experiences (Toomey & Ecker, 2009).

This concept of neuroplasticity became a component of mindfulness theory in the discovery of how meditation techniques and psychotherapy change and enhance neurocircuitry in the human brain (Lazar et al., 2005). Mindfulness theory is based on interpersonal neurobiology, first described by Siegel (1999). Interpersonal neurobiology explains how interpersonal relationships that occur throughout one's life span shape brain circuitry (neuroplasticity) into an ever-changing narrative of experiences and emotions that creates both healthy self-concepts and psychological problems (Schore, 2003a, 2003b). Therefore, an older adult is amenable to therapeutic change through the clinical intervention of a psychologist (see Chapter 3).

Rosen and Erickson (1991) indicate that "the optimal therapeutic relationship is not what is often called *positive transference*. Rather, it is one in which there is a state of *rapport* between therapist and patient" (pp. 44–45). The ideal therapeutic person is the psychologist performing psychotherapy. Any psychologist is a gestalt of his or her history, training, and current life situation. The therapeutic alliance works based on the idea that the psychologist is a willing participant whose primary concern is to provide support to an older adult patient's effort for desired change.

Knight (2004) finds that interpersonal psychotherapy is an effective method to help older adults adjust to the many health and social challenges that they confront. The relationship between the psychologist and older adult patient is a reciprocal process that entails the psychologist understanding the older adult patient and the older adult feeling a positive sense of recognition (Eriksen, Sundfor, Karlsson, Raholm, & Arman, 2012). This reciprocal relationship allows a shared experience in which the older adult has a greater degree of understanding of subsequent treatment, and the psychologist has the ability to comprehensively share his or her expertise (Clark, 2010; Hain & Sandy, 2013). Neuropsychology explains that mirror neurons are a neuronal mechanism that enables a person to internalize the nervous system, body sensations, and brain experience of another person (Badenoch, 2008; Iacoboni, 2009; Siegel, 2007). This enables a person to have an internalized representation of another person through an interpersonal interaction. This internalized representation gives the psychologist the opportunity to understand the patient's feelings and perceptions during interactions within a psychotherapy session. This understanding leads to an empathic understanding of the patient, which in turn helps change the negative self-representations held by the older adult patient. With repeated exposure to the psychologist, an internalized positive empathic representation becomes a permanent representation within the older adult patient, helping the older adult to correct distorted self-representations.

OPPORTUNITIES TODAY IN GEROPSYCHOLOGY

Opportunities to work with older adults are increasing with the exponential rise in the older adult population. The American Psychological Association (2015) reports that "psychologists provide more than 50,000 hours of care each week to older adults, and 70% of practicing psychologists provide some services to older adults" (p. 1). Psychology students can expect many career opportunities in a variety of clinical settings. These include hospitals, psychiatric facilities, community mental health facilities, forensic institutions, group practices, private practices, continuing care facilities, assisted living facilities, hospice in home and facility settings, and in-home service delivery for aging-in-place older adults. Within these settings, psychologists may work independently, or be part of an interprofessional collaborative team.

REFERENCES

American Psychological Association. (2010). *Public description of profes-sional geropsychology.* Retrieved from http://www.apa.org/ed/graduate/specialize/gero.aspx

American Psychological Association. (2015). Psychologists make a sig-nificant contribution. *Psychology and Aging.* Retrieved from http://www.apa.org/pi/aging/resources/guides/aging.pdf

Badenoch, B. (2008). *Being a brain-wise therapist: A practical guide to inter-personal neurobiology.* New York, NY: W. W. Norton.

Clark, A. J. (2010). Empathy: An integral model in the counseling pro-cess. *Journal of Counseling & Development, 88,* 348–356.

Eriksen, K. A., Sundfor, B., Karlsson, B., Raholm, M.-B., & Arman, M. (2012). Recognition as a valued human being: Perspectives of men-tal health service users. *Nursing Ethics, 19*(3), 357–368. doi:10.1177/0969733011423293

Eriksson, P. S., Perfilieva, E., Bjork-Eriksson, T., Alborn, A. M., Nordborg, C., Peterson, D. A., & Gage, F. H. (1998). Neurogenesis in the adult hu-man hippocampus. *Nature Medicine, 4,* 1313–1317.

Freud, S. (1953). On psychotherapy. In J. Strachey (Ed. & Trans.), *The standard edition of the complete psychological works of Sigmund Freud* (Vol. 6, pp. 249–263). London, England: Hogarth Press. (Original work published 1900)

Hain, D. J., & Sandy, D. (2013). Partners in care: Patient empowerment through shared decision-making. *Nephrology Nursing Journal, 40*(2), 153–157.

Iacoboni, M. (2009). *Mirroring people: The science of empathy and how we connect with others.* New York, NY: Picador.

Jungers, C. M., & Slagel, L. (2009). Crisis model for older adults: Spe-cial considerations for an aging population. *Adultspan Journal, 8*(2), 92–101.

Knight, B. G. (2004). Grief work with older adults. In *Psychotherapy with older adults* (3rd ed., pp. 139–159). Thousand Oaks, CA: Sage.

Koenig, H. G., George, L. K., & Schneider, R. (1994). Mental health care for older adults in the year 2000: A dangerous and avoided topic. *The Gerontologist, 34,* 674–679.

Kübler-Ross, E. (1975). *Death: The final stage of growth.* New York, NY: Simon & Schuster.

Lazar, S. W., Wasserman, C. E., Gray, J. R., Greve, D. N., Treadway, M. T., McGarvey, M., . . . Fisch, B. (2005). Meditation experience is associated with increased cortical thickness. *NeuroReport, 16*(17), 1893–1897.

Potter, J. F. (2010). Aging in America: Essential considerations in shaping senior care policy. *Aging Health, 6*(3), 289–299.

Rosen, S., & Erickson, M. H. (1991). *My voice will go with you: The teaching tales of Milton H. Erickson, M.D.* New York, NY: W. W. Norton.

Schore, A. N. (2003a). *Affect dysregulation and disorders of the self.* New York, NY: W. W. Norton.

Schore, A. N. (2003b). *Affect regulation and the repair of the self.* New York, NY: W. W. Norton.

Siegel, D. J. (1999). *The developing mind: How relationships and the brain interact to shape who we are.* New York, NY: Guilford Press.

Siegel, D. J. (2006). An interpersonal neurobiology approach to psychotherapy: Awareness, mirror neurons, and neuroplasticity in the development of well-being. *Psychiatric Annals, 36*(4), 247–258.

Siegel, D. J. (2007). *The mindful brain: Reflection and attunement in the cultivation of well-being.* New York, NY: W. W. Norton.

Toomey, B., & Ecker, B. (2009). Competing visions of the implications of neuroscience for psychotherapy. *Journal of Constructivist Psychology, 22*(2), 95–140.

Walker, D. M. (2005, December 12). *A look at our future: When baby boomers retire.* 2005 White House Conference on Aging. Retrieved from http://www.gao.gov/cghome/whitehousewalker1205/walker_whitehouse1212.pdf

Older Adults Are Not All the Same

Now this is not the end. It is even not the beginning of the end.
But it is, perhaps, the end of the beginning.
Winston Churchill, 1942 Lord Mayors
Luncheon (London, Scriven, & Lalani, 2006)

In order for a psychologist to recognize the conflicts with which an older adult is struggling, as well as the recognition of strengths inherent in the older adult, the psychologist needs to understand the various life stages that define the many different cohorts of older adults.

This understanding facilitates appropriate psychological interventions that enable an older adult to enjoy the benefits and positive aspects of his or her respective life stage, and to reduce psychopathology and morbidity. Unfortunately, historically, older adults have been underserved by psychologists (Gatz & Smyer, 2001).

CHAPTER 1

Psychologists work with micro-level and macro-level orientations. Clinical psychologists with a micro-level orientation focus on individuals, families, and small groups when performing psychotherapy. Community psychologists have a macro-level orientation. They focus on developing techniques and strategies for governments, civic organizations, and vocational organizations to expand help for older adults beyond traditional psychotherapy. Both orientation levels interact with each other. The macro-level orientation initiates policies that affect clinical practice, and the micro-level orientation informs community psychologists on the need for more policy directives to guide clinical practice.

The aging population presents many opportunities for psychologists, both those engaged in scholarship and those working clinically with older adults, and for community psychologists addressing issues relating to social structures and organized communities of older adults, economic issues such as poverty and access to medical services, and issues relating to senior housing (Cheng & Heller, 2009). Psychologists are seeing increasing presentations of older adults for counseling services (Myers & Harper, 2004). Contemporary theory indicates that it is equally important for psychologists working with older adults to focus on the positive aspects of aging (Morrow-Howell, Tang, Kim, Lee, & Sherraden, 2005) when addressing the psychopathological problems older adults are experiencing (see Chapter 3). Community psychologists are involved in program planning and evaluation, consultation to local and federal government agencies, and training initiatives for those psychologists working with older adults. Therefore, for those psychologists working on a macro level, knowledge of older life stages is as critical as for those psychologists working on a micro/clinical level.

OLDER ADULT LIFE STAGES

Even though age ranges categorize older adult life stages, it must be understood that these life stages are not static and are constantly changing as older adults age. For example, the young-old life stage began to dramatically change with the baby-boom generation turning age 65 in 2011, bringing large numbers of older adults into the young-old life stage.

Young-Old Adults (65–74 Years of Age)

Older adults who are of the young-old cohort are relatively healthy, have virtually no cognitive impairments, and have few, if any, disabilities (Darton et al., 2011). This cohort is going through a differentiation from previous young-old adults who are still in the young-old life stage, or have recently moved on to the middle-old life stage. The *baby-boom generation* consists of people born between 1946 and 1964 (Radner, 1998). The baby-boomer generation began turning 65 in 2011 (Caffrey, Sengupta, Moss, Harris-Kojetin, & Valverde, 2011).

The baby-boom generation brings to the young-old life stage a significant problem of substance abuse, a phenomenon that has not existed in prior cohorts (Duncan, Nicholson, White, Bradley, & Bonaguro, 2010). Many researchers have indicated that the newly arriving baby boomers will show an exponential increase in prescription drug abuse from 1.2% in 1999 to 2.4% in 2020 (Menninger, 2002; Pennington, Butler, & Eagger, 2000; Rigler, 2000). As baby boomers continue to enter the young-old life stage, it is projected that the number of older adults experiencing substance abuse problems will increase to 5 million in 2020 compared to 2.5 million in 1999 (Gfoerer, Penne, Pemberton, & Folson, 2008). This is a consequence of the "sex, drugs, and rock 'n' roll" culture of the 1960s (Cottrell, 2015; Willis, 2015). Psychologists must be alert to this new incidence of substance abuse because the commonly held notion that substance abuse does not affect older adults, or is rarely seen, is no longer valid (see Chapter 6).

Those in the baby-boom generation of older adults are showing a pattern of working past the traditional retirement age of 65 because people are living longer and need continuing income to supplement Social Security benefits and, in some cases, the lack of pensions. In addition, the baby-boom cohort is more educated than prior cohorts and is able to continue working in jobs that are less physically demanding. Women in the baby-boom generation are used to participating in the workforce and often wish to continue working. Most older adults working past age 65 feel a need for additional training to transition from one career to another. Recognizing this need, community colleges began outreach to older adults who require retraining and education in order to find jobs as they cycle in and out of working and periods of retirement (Hoover, 2009). While being vocationally active, baby-boom adults are, in addition, sexually active (see Chapter 5), continuing the *free-love* sexual traditions of the 1960s that enabled the baby-boom generation to break the sexual inhibitions seen in prior cohorts (Cottrell, 2015). These older adults feel that sexual activity "strengthens bones and muscles, boosts the immune system, prevents wrinkles around the eyes, and is the exercise equivalent of walking up two flights of stairs" (Gulli, 2010, p. 64).

Fear of falling, not actual falls, becomes a significant risk factor for young-old adults and an increasing risk factor for subsequent age stages. This fear heralds the reality that one is aging, despite the relatively healthy experience of this age stage. For the first time, some young-old adults begin to experience some minor disability in functioning. Fear of falling causes some disability in activities of daily living (ADLs), and, subsequently, a poor health status (Lach, 2005; Martin, Hart, Spector, Doyle, & Harari, 2005; Nourhashemi, Andrieu, & Gillette-Guyonnet, 2001). ADLs include bathing, feeding, grooming, maintaining continence, putting on clothes, selecting proper attire, toileting, and walking and/ or transferring (moving from bed to wheelchair or chair). ADLs should not be confused with instrumental activities of daily living (IADLs), which include handling transportation (driving or public transportation), taking care of housework and home maintenance, managing finances, managing medications, preparing meals, shopping, and using the telephone/cell phone.

Fear of falling is an interesting problem for the psychologist to treat because it does not manifest itself as a psychological problem. Instead, an older adult presents with a disability in one or more of the ADLs, but the etiology is psychological rather than medical/physical. By carefully assessing an older adult, a psychologist can determine if a deficit in ADL functioning needs to be addressed by teaching an older adult how to manage the anxiety related to falling. More often than not, the older adult will present in good health, with a significant increase in lower limb weakness and a significant slowing in walking speed, consequences of a maladaptive strategy to prevent falling (Brouwer, Musselman, & Culham, 2004; Li, Fisher, Harmer, McAuley, & Wilson, 2003).

Middle-Old Adults (75–84 Years of Age)

Clinical psychologists and community psychologists recognize that middle-old adults become at risk for social isolation (Cornwell, Laumann, & Schumm, 2008). Social isolation is caused by lack of social network diversity (Barefoot, Gronback, Jensen, Schnohr, & Prescott, 2005), and infrequent social contact (Brummett et al., 2001). Isolation often occurs when an older adult is experiencing grieving, develops a disability, or experiences relocation, psychological problems, or a debilitating medical problem. Places of social contact that middle-old adults tend to frequent less often are centers offering social activities to older adults; churches, mosques, and synagogues that offer worship activities; and volunteer opportunities that offer social contact. Consequences of social isolation are increasing incidences of depression, cardiovascular problems, and inflammation (Cacioppo, Hughes, Waite, Hawkley, & Thisted, 2006; Hawkley, Masi, Berry, & Cacioppo, 2006; Steptoe, Owen, Kunz-Ebrecht, & Brydon, 2004). In addition, *social disconnectiveness* is caused by the loss of a partner/spouse, and/or retirement (Cornwell et al., 2008; Weiss, 2005).

Middle-old adults may become vulnerable to co-occurring chronic and/or acute illnesses. Co-occurring illness is a phenomenon in which two or more medical illnesses occur at the same time, or when psychopathologies such as anxiety or depression occur with one or more medical illnesses. An older adult experiencing co-occurring illnesses has an increased risk for disability and mortality, a considerably higher risk than that from any one medical illness (Cacioppo et al., 2002; Holt-Lunstad, Smith, & Layton, 2010). Disability occurs when an older adult has difficulty with, or loses the ability to independently engage in, ADLs (Nagi, 1991). Disability is a multidimensional phenomenon that takes place in the intersection of social, medical, economic, and psychological forces (Fried & Guarlnik, 1997; Stuck et al., 1999). In addition, disability sets the stage for future functional and medical complications. Psychologists are needed to help these older adults cope with the newly acquired illness, the consequences of dying, and/or the death of a loved one (see Chapter 9) by teaching positive coping skills. In addition, psychologists are often needed to intervene with family members and/or caregivers because the distress of co-occurring illnesses affects not only the older adult who is ill, but also the family members/caregivers who are assisting in the care of the older adult.

Old-Old Adults (85–99 Years of Age)

The population of old-old adults is expected to increase to 153 million by the year 2025, from 70 million old-old adults in the year 2000 (Potter, 2010). Functional changes, experience with illness, and psychological problems increase with this cohort as compared with previous cohorts of older adults (Zeng & Vaupel, 2002). Understanding how old-old adults are fundamentally different from younger cohorts is another example of the importance of psychologists learning the differences of older cohorts and, through this understanding, how to adapt clinical interventions for older adults in their respective life stages (Smith, Borchelt, Maier, & Jopp, 2002). This understanding creates an opportunity for a psychologist working with an old-old adult to reframe the older adult's perspective from a negative view of his or her life to a new understanding of the positive aspects of healthy aging (McCarthy, Ling, & Carini, 2013).

Centenarians (100–109 Years of Age)

The United Nations (2006, 2007) projects that the centenarian population or oldest-old worldwide will increase exponentially by approximately sevenfold by the year 2050. Such increases were preceded by increases in the oldest-old populations in the last 50 years in the United States (Kestenbaum & Ferguson, 2005), Canada (Bourbeau & Lebel, 2000), and France (Vallin & Meslé, 2001). These greater populations of oldest-old adults increase the probability of older adults living to be centenarians. Centenarians are mostly women living in their own homes (25%), senior housing (37%), or nursing homes (38%) (Wilson, Crawford, & Shabot, 2000). Because these older adults have achieved such a long life span, studies are often performed to discover how they achieved this. Was it genetics? The food they eat? Where they live? Unfortunately, most of these studies are on centenarians who are compared with comparable younger people (Franceschi et al., 2007). Comparing a centenarian, or group of centenarians, with a younger contemporary cohort is criticized as an inaccurate comparison due to varying fertility rates, selective migration, and mortality rates (Canudas-Romo, 2010). However, this criticism does not discount the importance of studying the oldest of older adults, whose resilience in aging teaches lessons about maintaining happiness and a sense of life satisfaction, coping with disease and trauma (both past and present), and improving one's nutrition for a better experience of older age (Poon & Cohen-Mansfield, 2011).

A curious phenomenon is occurring in Japan that is considered to be a form of institutional ageism (see Chapter 2) directed against centenarians. For an as-yet-to-be-discovered reason, centenarians are not being recognized by Japanese municipal governments, causing a group of *missing centenarians* (Ebihara, Freeman, Ebihara, & Kohzuki, 2010). Because municipal governments do not track centenarians, these older adults lack essential psychological and social services and become isolated, and their isolation promotes psychological and medical health problems for these missing centenarians (Hawkley, Burleson,

Berntson, & Cacioppo, 2003; Sorkin, Rook, & Lu, 2002; Step-toe et al., 2004). In addition, the traditional Japanese family value of caring for older parents seems to be declining. This causes many centenarians in Japan to live on their own and be independent of family. Consistent with the declining family values in Japan is the phenomenon in which many deaths of centenarians are not being reported so that family members can fraudulently continue to receive benefits from the government (Hall, 2010). The predominant mental health problem in these centenarians is depression (Cacioppo et al., 2006; Heikkinen & Kauppinen, 2004; Mehta, Yaffe, & Covinsky, 2002). Another consequence of not keeping track of centenarians is that this neglect of census validation may distort research studies on the longevity of centenarians and *super-centenarians* (110 years and older) because the populations being studied may not truly represent the overall populations of these age groups (Saito, 2010).

Centenarian Psychologists, a Centenarian Psychiatrist, and a Centenarian Psychopharmacologist

Older adults achieving centenarian status usually excite the imagination of many people who ascribe a special social status to these individuals because they have lived so long. Several centenarians have made significant contributions to the field of psychology, as follows:

- Martin S. Bergmann (1913–2014), who was a professor of psychology at New York University and taught and wrote about psychoanalysis, the Holocaust, and the phenomenology of love and child sacrifice. In addition, he played the role of a philosopher in the movie *Crimes and Misdemeanors* (Fox, 2014).
- Heinz Ansbacher (1904–2006), who was an expert on and scholar of the psychological theories of Alfred Adler (Noble, 2006). He is the author of *The Individual Psychology of Alfred Adler* (Ansbacher & Ansbacher, 1964).

- Sidney W. Bijou (1908–2009), who was a pioneer in the establishment of using rewards in behavioral therapy with children with autism and attention deficit disorder (Carey, 2009).
- Rudolf Arnheim (1904–2007), who was an expert on the cognitive basis of art, its interpretation, and its symbolic meaning in understanding the world (Fox, 2007).
- Henri Baruk (1897–1999), who was a proponent of *moral psychiatry* (Baruk, 1978).
- Albert Hofmann (1906–2008), who synthesized lysergic acid diethylamide (LSD), psilocybin, and psilocin. His discoveries generated over 10,000 scientific publications in psychology, psychiatry, and medicine (Hofmann, 2013).

Super-Centenarians (110+ Years of Age)

The study of super-centenarians is fraught with difficulty because most countries do not have accurate or readily available records for researchers (Canudas-Romo, 2010; Saito, 2010). This is an invaluable opportunity for psychologists to initiate census data collection for subsequent research studies that will enable researchers to locate centenarians for qualitative interviews that would enrich psychologists' understanding of super-centenarians. In addition, more accurate medical and psychological health information can be gleaned for comparative studies with centenarians to determine if being a super-centenarian is significantly different than being a centenarian. Or, conversely, is the distinction between centenarians and super-centenarians just an arbitrary divide?

ERIKSON'S STAGE THEORY

Erikson's stage theory is a social theory indicating that crises are resolved through interpersonal interaction. Successful interaction involves achieving trust in others, and a sense of personal identity and one's place in society. A major contribution of this theory is the notion that personality development occurs throughout the life span. This is a theory that is linear, meaning that one's personality is developed in a predetermined order, successfully resolving one life stage to advance to the next life stage. This is called the *epigenic principle* (Erikson, 1982).

Erikson's *stage theory* (Erikson, 1982) originally had seven stages: basic trust versus basic mistrust; autonomy versus shame and doubt; initiative versus guilt; industry versus inferiority; identity versus role confusion; intimacy versus isolation; and generativity versus stagnation. Each of these stages is about the development of an individual. Erikson postulates that psychological development occurs throughout one's lifetime by making successful adjustments to psychological, biological, and social environments at eight different stages in life through an intergenerational process. Each stage is grounded in previous stages. In order for an individual to transition from one stage to the next, he or she must experience acceptance of the strength of the stage and release conflicted aspects of the respective stage.

Resolution of each stage is derived from interpersonal, intergenerational interaction. This intergenerational interaction facilitates the accomplishment of a successful resolution of his or her life stage. The direction of the intergenerational interaction is from the individual's stage position to others in an older stage. For example, an infant achieving a successful resolution of the stage of basic trust versus basic mistrust cannot do so without an adult caretaker who has successfully left a self-centered stage of youth and is able to provide the nurturing and validation needed by the infant. In the ideal world, the older person of the intergenerational interaction has successfully resolved previous stages in order to facilitate resolution in the younger person's stage of development.

In the real world, there are many confounding factors that make stage resolution less than ideal. These include environmental influences outside of and in addition to interpersonal interaction. For example, environmental factors such as war, disease, physical deformity, and poverty may interfere with nurturing and validation. Therefore a psychologist needs to integrate *person-in-environment theory* (see Chapter 3) when assessing an older adult's life-stage history, or current life-stage conflict.

Unlike the previous seven life stages, the eighth stage of Erikson's theory requires the opposite intergenerational interaction; that is, the direction of interaction is from the older adult to a younger person rather than a young person to an older adult. This requires an older person to focus on the needs of a younger person, rather than a more symbiotic focus on having another meet his or her need. Thus, gratification of the needs of a younger person facilitates resolution of this eighth stage. This occurs on micro and macro levels, with family, friends, and community. As in the previous seven life stages, environmental factors such as war, disease, physical deformity, and poverty confound conflict resolution within this eighth life stage.

Erikson and Erikson (1997) later indicated that *spiritual transcendence* is the ninth life stage that is subsequent to the stage of ego integrity versus despair. In this final stage, transcendence is created in the ego, body, and role of the older adult, whereby the older adult moves to acceptance of his or her self-worth rather than engaging in preoccupation with disease and disability, and a loss of professional self. This is accomplished by focusing retrospectively, identifying satisfaction with one's life accomplishments. This is not to say that life satisfaction and acceptance of one's accomplishments are not evidenced in successful aging throughout the prior life stages (McCarthy, 2011; McCarthy et al., 2013). This is consistent with the theory of *gerotranscendence* (Hyse & Tornstam, 2009), which states that an older adult experiences an existential redefinition of self, while simultaneously examining his or her interpersonal relationships, resulting in a phenomenon of becoming more exacting in his or her social relationships and activities. This occurs in harmony with an older adult achieving balance in psychological, social, and biological systems, as seen in *Roy's adaptation model of successful aging* (Saleem, 2011).

A psychologist addresses this despair as an existential dilemma in the older adult, and helps the older adult move toward a more positive reframing of his or her life successes, failures, and conflicts, in order to balance the tension between integrity and despair experienced by the older adult. This achieves what Aserr, Milillo, Long, and Horne-Moyer (2004) indicate as an older adult's experiencing lower levels of anxiety about death when compared to younger adults.

LIMITATIONS OF LIFE STAGES AND ERIKSON'S STAGE THEORY

Viewing differences in older adults through the lens of life stages or the lens of Erikson's stage theory is not all encompassing. Within each life stage and developmental stage is a heterogeneity that is more diverse than in younger age groups (Crowther & Zeiss, 2003). Learning the aspects of this diversity is essential for a psychologist, who must understand the biases and stereotyped views (see Chapter 2) of older adults that he or she might hold (Jackson & Samuels, 2011; Williams & Mohammed, 2009).

The Office on Aging (2010) indicates the statistics on the diversification of subgroups in the current cohort of older adult Americans shown in Table 1.1. What is readily seen is that as

TABLE 1.1 Diversified Subgroups of Older Adult Americans, 2010 to 2050

	2010	2050
Non-Hispanic Whites	45,942,504	64,360,470
Hispanics	4,274,333	22,642,470
Blacks	4,942,504	13,020,151
American Indians and Native Alaskans	309,189	837,328
Asians	2,014,022	9,488,038
Native Hawaiians and Pacific Islanders	51,338	216,295
Mixed racial older adults	382,474	1,472,535

each cohort ages and moves up the life stages, the diversity of older adult Americans dramatically increases. Therefore, by 2050 Jackson and Samuels (2011) indicate that 20% (1 in 5 Americans) will be from a multiracial background.

REFERENCES

Ansbacher, H. L., & Ansbacher, R. R. (Eds.). (1964). *The individual psychology of Alfred Adler: A systematic presentation in selections from his writings*. New York, NY: Harper Perennial.

Aserr, L., Milillo, D., Long, S., & Horne-Moyer, H. (2004). The relationship between social desirability and death anxiety in elders. *The Gerontologist, 44*(1), 135.

Barefoot, J. C., Gronback, M., Jensen, G., Schnohr, P., & Prescott, E. (2005). Social network diversity and risks of ischemic heart disease and total mortality: Findings from the Copenhagen City Heart Study. *American Journal of Epidemiology, 161*, 960–967.

Baruk, H. (1978). *Patients are people like us: The experiences of half a century in neuropsychiatry*. New York, NY: Morrow.

Bourbeau, R., & Lebel, A. (2000). Mortality statistics for the oldest-old: An evaluation of Canadian data. *Demographic Research, 2*(2), 1–36.

Brouwer, B., Musselman, K., & Culham, E. (2004). Physical function and health status among seniors with and without a fear of falling. *Gerontology, 50*, 131–141.

Brummett, B. H., Barefoot, J. C., Siegler, I. C., Clapp-Channing, N. E., Lytle, B. L., Bosworth, H. B., . . . Mark, D. B. (2001). Characteristics of socially isolated patients with coronary artery disease who are at elevated risk for mortality. *Psychosomatic Medicine, 63*, 267–272.

Cacioppo, J. T., Hawkley, L. C., Crawford, E., Ernst, J. M., Burleson, M. H., Kowalewski, R. B., . . . Berntson, G. C. (2002). Loneliness and health: Potential problems. *Psychosomatic Medicine, 64*, 407–417.

Cacioppo, J. T., Hughes, M. E., Waite, L. J., Hawkley, L. C., & Thisted, R. A. (2006). Loneliness as a specific risk factor for depressive symptoms: Cross-sectional and longitudinal analyses. *Psychology and Aging, 21*, 140–151.

Caffrey, C., Sengupta, M., Moss, A., Harris-Kojetin, L., & Valverde, R. (2011). *Home health care and discharged hospice care patients: United States, 2000 and 2007*. Retrieved from http://www.cdc.gov/nchs/data/

Canudas-Romo, V. (2010). Three measures of longevity: Time trends and record values. *Demography, 47*(2), 299–312.

Carey, B. (2009). Sidney W. Bijou, child psychologist, is dead at 100. *Science.* Retrieved March 22, 2015, from http://www.nytimes.com/2009/07/22/science/22bijou.html?_r=1

Cheng, S.-T., & Heller, K. (2009). Global aging: Challenges for community psychology. *American Journal of Community Psychology, 44*, 161–173.

Cornwell, B., Laumann, E. O., & Schumm, L. P. (2008). The social connectedness of older adults: A national profile. *American Sociological Review, 73*, 185–203.

Cottrell, R. C. (2015). *Sex, drugs, and rock 'n' roll: The rise of America's 1960s counterculture.* Lanham, MD: Rowman & Littlefield.

Crowther, M. R., & Zeiss, A. M. (2003). Aging and mental health. In J. S. Mio & G. Y. Iwamasa (Eds.), *Culturally diverse mental health: The challenge of research and resistance* (pp. 309–322). New York, NY: Brunner-Routledge.

Darton, R., Baumker, T., Callaghan, L., Holder, J., Netten, A. N. N., & Towers, A.-M. (2011, January). The characteristics of residents in extra care housing and care homes in England. *Health and Social Care in the Community, 20*(1), 87–96.

Duncan, D. F., Nicholson, T., White, J. B., Bradley, D. B., & Bonaguro, J. (2010). The baby boomer effect: Changing patterns of substance abuse among adults ages 55 and older. *Journal of Aging & Social Policy, 22*(3), 237.

Ebihara, S., Freeman, S., Ebihara, T., & Kohzuki, M. (2010). Missing centenarians in Japan: A new ageism. *The Lancet, 376*(9754), 1739.

Erikson, E. H. (1982). *The life cycle completed: A review.* New York, NY: W. W. Norton.

Erikson, E. H., & Erikson, J. M. (1997). *The life cycle completed: Extended version with new chapters on the ninth state of development.* New York, NY: W. W. Norton.

Fox, M. (2007). Rudolf Arnheim, 102, psychologist and scholar of art and ideas, dies. *The New York Times.* Retrieved March 22, 2015, from http://www.nytimes.com/2007/06/14/obituaries/14arnheim.html?_r=2&oref=slogin&oref=slogin

Fox, M. (2014). Martin S. Bergmann, psychoanalyst and an on-screen philosopher, dies at 100. *The New York Times.* Retrieved March 22, 2015, from http://www.nytimes.com/2014/01/27/movies/martin-s-bergmann-psychoanalyst-and-woody-allens-on-screen-philosopher-dies-at-100.html?_r=2

Franceschi, C., Bezrukov, V., Blanché, H., Bolund, L., Christensen, K., de Benedictis, G., . . . Vaupel, J. W. (2007). Genetics of healthy aging in Europe: The EU-Integrated Project GEHA (GEnetics of Healthy Aging). *Annals of the New York Academy of Sciences, 1100,* 21–45.

Fried, I. P., & Guarlnik, J. M. (1997). Disability in older adults: Evidence regarding significance, etiology, and risk. *Journal of the American Geriatrics Society, 45,* 92–100.

Gatz, M., & Smyer, M. A. (2001). Mental health and aging at the outset of the twenty-first century. In J. F. Birren & K. W. Schaie (Eds.), *Handbook of the psychology of aging* (5th ed., pp. 523–544). San Diego, CA: Academic Press.

Gfoerer, J. C., Penne, M. A., Pemberton, M. R., & Folson, J. R. E. (2008). The aging baby boom cohort and future prevalence of substance abuse. In S. P. Korper & C. L. Council (Eds.), *Substance use by older adults: Estimates of future impact on the treatment system* (DHHS Publication No. SMA 03-3763, OAS Analytic Series A-21; pp. 71–94). Rockville, MD: Substance Abuse and Mental Health Services Administration.

Gulli, C. (2010, September 13). Health: Forever young boomer health: Part 1 of 3: The "boom boom" generation: Baby boomers are proving that getting older actually makes for a more satisfying sex life. *Maclean's, 123,* 64.

Hall, K. (2010). Japan's centenarians falling through the cracks. *Los Angeles Times.* Retrieved from http://articles.latimes.com/2010/sep/05/world/la-fg-japan-centenarians-20100905

Hawkley, L. C., Burleson, M. H., Berntson, G. G., & Cacioppo, J. T. (2003). Loneliness in everyday life: Cardiovascular activity, psychosocial context, and health behaviors. *Journal of Personality and Social Psychology, 85,* 105–120.

Hawkley, L. C., Masi, C. M., Berry, J. D., & Cacioppo, J. T. (2006). Loneliness is a unique predictor of age-related differences in systolic blood pressure. *Psychology and Aging, 21,* 152–164.

Heikkinen, R.-L., & Kauppinen, M. (2004). Depressive symptoms in late life: A 10-year follow-up. *Archives of Gerontology and Geriatrics, 38*(3), 239–250.

Hofmann, A. (2013). *LSD: My problem child. Insights/outlooks* (J. Ott, Trans.). Oxford, England: Oxford University Press/Beckley Foundation Press.

Holt-Lunstad, J., Smith, T. B., & Layton, J. B. (2010). Social relationships and mortality risk: A meta-analytic review. *PLoS Medicine, 7*(7), 1–19.

Hoover, E. (2009). Community colleges anticipate boom in baby-boomer students. *The Chronicle of Higher Education, 55*(32). Retrieved from http://chronicle.com/article/Community-Colleges-Anticipate/47160

Hyse, K., & Tornstam, L. (2009). *Recognizing aspects of oneself in the theory of gerotranscendence.* Retrieved from http://www.diva-portal.org/smash/record.jsf?pid=diva2%3A175132&dswid=1303

Jackson, K. F., & Samuels, G. M. (2011). Multiracial competence in social work: Recommendations for culturally attuned work with multiracial people. *Social Work, 56*(3), 235–245.

Kestenbaum, B., & Ferguson, B. R. (2005, March 31–April 2). *Numbers of centenarians in the United States 01/01/1990, 01/01/2000, 01/01/2010 based on improved Medicare data.* Paper presented at the Population Association of America, Philadelphia, PA.

Lach, H. W. (2005). Incidence and risk factors for developing fear of falling in older adults. *Public Health Nursing, 22*, 45–52.

Li, F., Fisher, K. J., Harmer, P., McAuley, E., & Wilson, N. L. (2003). Fear of falling in elderly persons: Association with falls, functional ability, and quality of life. *Journal of Gerontology Series B: Psychological Sciences and Social Sciences, 58*, 283–290.

London, C., Scriven, A., & Lalani, N. (2006). Sir Winston Churchill: Greatest Briton used as an anti-stigma icon. *Journal of the Royal Society for the Promotion of Health, 126*(4), 163–164.

Martin, F. C., Hart, D., Spector, T., Doyle, D. V., & Harari, D. (2005). Fear of falling limiting activity in young-old women is associated with reduced functional mobility rather than psychological factors. *Age and Ageing, 34*, 281–287.

McCarthy, V. L. (2011). A new look at successful aging: Exploring a midrange nursing theory among older adults in a low-income retirement community. *Journal of Theory Construction & Testing, 15*, 17–21.

McCarthy, V. L., Ling, J., & Carini, R. M. (2013). The role of self-transcendence: A missing variable in the pursuit of successful aging? *Research in Gerontological Nursing, 6*(3), 178–186.

Mehta, K. M., Yaffe, K., & Covinsky, K. E. (2002). Cognitive impairment, depressive symptoms, and functional decline in older people. *Journal of the American Geriatrics Society, 50*, 1045–1050.

Menninger, J. A. (2002). Assessment and treatment of alcoholism and substance-related disorders in the elderly. *Bulletin of the Menninger Clinic, 66*, 166–184.

Morrow-Howell, N., Tang, F., Kim, J., Lee, M., & Sherraden, M. (2005). Maximizing the productive engagement of older adults. In M. L. Wykle,

P. J. Whitehouse, & D. L. Morris (Eds.), *Successful aging through the life span* (pp. 19–53). New York, NY: Springer Publishing Company.

Myers, J. E., & Harper, M. (2004). Evidence-based effective practices with older adults. *Journal of Counseling & Development, 82*, 207–219.

Nagi, S. Z. (1991). *Disability concepts revisited: Implications for prevention.* Washington, DC: National Academies Press.

Noble, H. B. (2006). Heinz Ansbacher, 101, Adlerian psychology expert, dies. *The New York Times.* Retrieved March 22, 2015, from http://www.nytimes.com/2006/06/24/us/24ansbacher.html?_r=0

Nourhashemi, F., Andrieu, S., & Gillette-Guyonnet, H. (2001). Instrumental activities of daily living as a potential marker of frailty: A study of 7364 community-dwelling elderly women (the EPIDOS study). *Journals of Gerontology Series A: Biological Sciences and Medical Sciences, 56*, 448–453.

Office on Aging. (2010). *Projected future growth of the older population by race and Hispanic origin.* Washington, DC: Office on Aging, Department of Health and Human Services.

Pennington, H., Butler, R., & Eagger, S. (2000). The assessment of patients with alcohol disorders by an old age psychiatric service. *Aging & Mental Health, 4*, 182–185.

Poon, L. W., & Cohen-Mansfield, J. (Eds.). (2011). *Understanding well-being in the oldest old.* New York, NY: Cambridge University Press.

Potter, J. F. (2010). Aging in America: Essential considerations in shaping senior care policy. *Aging Health, 6*(3), 289–299.

Radner, D. B. (1998). The retirement prospects of the baby boom generation. *Social Security Bulletin, 61*, 3–19.

Rigler, S. K. (2000). Alcoholism in the elderly. *American Family Physician, 61*, 1710–1716.

Saito, Y. (2010). Supercentenarians in Japan. In H. Maier, J. Gampe, B. Jeune, J.-M. Robine, & J. W. Vaupel (Eds.), *Supercentenarians. Demographic research monographs* (pp. 75–99). Berlin, Germany: Springer-Verlag.

Saleem, T. K. (2011). Roy's adaptation model. *Nursing Theories: A companion to nursing theories and models.* Retrieved from http://currentnursing.com/nursing_theory/Roy_adaptation_model.html

Smith, J., Borchelt, M., Maier, H., & Jopp, D. (2002). Health and well-being in the young and oldest old. *Journal of Social Issues, 58*, 715–732.

Sorkin, D., Rook, K. S., & Lu, J. L. (2002). Loneliness, lack of emotional companionship, and the likelihood of having a heart condition in an elderly sample. *Annals of Behavioral Medicine, 24*, 290–298.

Steptoe, A., Owen, N., Kunz-Ebrecht, S. R., & Brydon, L. (2004). Loneliness and neuroendocrine, cardiovascular, and inflammatory stress responses in middle-age men and women. *Psychoneuroendocrinology*, *29*, 593–611.

Stuck, A. E., Walthert, J. M., Nikolaus, T., Bula, C. J., Hollmann, C., & Beck, J. C. (1999). Risk factors for functional status decline in community-living elderly people: A systematic literature review. *Social Science & Medicine, 48*, 445–469.

United Nations, Population Division of the Department of Economic and Social Affairs of the United Nations Secretariat. (2006). *World urbanization prospects: The 2005 revision*. Retrieved from http://www.un.org/esa/population/publications/WUP2005/2005WUPHighlights_Final_Report.pdf

United Nations, Population Division of the Department of Economic and Social Affairs of the United Nations Secretariat. (2007). *World population prospects: The 2006 revision*. Retrieved from http://www.un.org/esa/population/publications/wpp2006/English.pdf

Vallin, J., & Meslé, F. (2001). Vivre au-delà de 100 ans. *Population & Sociétes, 365*, 1–4.

Weiss, R. (2005). Retirement, marriage, and social isolation. *Illness, Crisis, and Loss, 13*, 75–84.

Williams, D. R., & Mohammed, S. A. (2009). Discrimination and racial disparities in health: Evidence and needed research. *Journal of Behavioral Medicine, 32*, 20–47.

Willis, J. (2015). *1960s counterculture: Documents decoded*. Santa Barbara, CA: ABC-CLIO.

Wilson, M. T., Crawford, K. L., & Shabot, M. M. (2000). Intensive care unit outcomes of surgical centenarians: The "oldest old" of the new millennium. *The American Surgeon, 66*(9), 870–873.

Zeng, Y., & Vaupel, J. W. (2002). Functional capacity and self-evaluation of health and life of the oldest old in China. *Journal of Social Issues, 58*, 733–748.

Ageism and Stigma

There is no need to be afraid of death. It is not the end of the
physical body that should worry us. Rather, our concern must be to
live while we're alive—to release our inner selves from the spiritual
death that comes with living behind a façade designed to conform
to external definitions of who and what we are.
Elisabeth Kübler-Ross (1975, p. 164)

A psychologist must confront many prejudices against older adults that are manifested in most people in non–older adult cohorts (see Chapter 1). Many caregivers and spouses/partners of older adults also hold these negative perceptions of older adults. Most importantly, a psychologist has a professional imperative to recognize any prejudices he or she may have toward older adults that would subsequently interfere with his or her ability to render care to older adults.

Clinical psychologists specializing in geropsychology work with individual older adults; family members of older adults, including spouses/partners, siblings, and adult children; and caregivers when treating the psychological problems experienced by older adults and dealing with issues of caregiving to older adults experiencing mental illness (see Chapter 3), dementia (see Chapter 4), and/or psychological reactions to co-occurring medical illnesses.

Unlike clinical psychologists, community psychologists help older adults by developing techniques and strategies for governments, civic organizations, and vocational organizations to expand help for older adults beyond traditional psychotherapy. They do this in the capacity of policy developers, program evaluators, researchers in community organizations, professors in university settings, consultants and researchers for government organizations, and program directors.

Community psychologists engage in research with the goal of developing effective action-oriented strategies to develop programs, to facilitate the implementation of programs, and to develop means to evaluate programs for their effectiveness in fighting oppression and social inequalities that effect marginalized populations in the workplace and institutions serving older adults, and to train health care professionals, first responders, police, and other public professionals serving older adults. These programs are designed to solve social and psychological problems on a community level rather than the individual/family/group level seen in clinical psychology.

Unfortunately, despite the fact that older adults are affected by the forces of ageism and stigma, and the fact that community psychologists strive to understand and improve social inequalities and to enable empowerment of marginalized people, there is a significant dearth of research in the field of community psychology (Cheng & Heller, 2009). Cheng and Heller found that when using the publication search engine PsycINFO with the keywords *elderly, older adults*, and *aging*, they were only able to locate fewer than 80 articles. This search is in sharp contrast to other searches these authors performed looking for articles on *race, gender, sexism,* and *ethnic diversity*, social forces that dramatically affect other disadvantaged groups. *Race* and *gender* produced over 450 articles. The authors found that special journal issues represented the topics of sexism and ethnic diversity. This lack of evidence-based research about older adults indicates that a community psychologist most likely will have a deficit of knowledge about older adult communities. Therefore, an opportunity is present for community psychologists interested in research to address this dearth of research studies.

AGEISM

The overriding theory that explains the underlying types of ageism is *terror management theory*. Terror management theory (Greenberg, Solomon, & Pyszczynski, 1997) is based on a theory first described by Becker (1973) called the *theory of generative death anxiety*. This theory indicates that the anxiety experienced by people knowing that their death is inevitable causes people to engage unconsciously in behaviors to avoid any perception of their ultimate mortality. Therefore, older adults become an obvious target (Martens, Goldenberg, & Greenberg, 2005) of these anxieties because older adults represent, to many, a life stage of dying and death (see Chapter 9).

Death anxiety is a clinical issue of importance to psychologists because death anxiety is the most chronic anxiety experienced by people across all life stages (Greenberg & Arndt, 2011). Most anxieties treated by psychologists (see Chapter 3) are experienced consciously. Conscious experience means that the person suffering from anxiety is aware that he or she is anxious and is aware of the fear and discomfort being felt. Anxiety disorders affecting older adults include panic disorder, agoraphobia, generalized anxiety disorder, adjustment disorder with anxiety, and obsessive-compulsive disorder. Death anxiety is experienced unconsciously and is considered to be an existential anxiety (Winkielman & Berridge, 2004). Existential anxiety that relates to death occurs when a person experiences a heightened awareness of his or her mortality. This is often repressed (becomes unconscious) and is displaced onto older adults who represent dying and death. This displacement causes a person experiencing death anxiety to act in a biased and negative manner toward older adults.

Greenberg et al. (1990) feel that a person experiencing death anxiety develops a prejudice called *in-group bias/out-group prejudice*. In-group bias/out-group prejudice is a phenomenon whereby a person favors people in a group he or she belongs to over those who are so-called out-group members. People identifying with an in-group tend to give positive attributions to events and behaviors within the in-group and, conversely, to give negative attributions to events and behaviors within the out-group. With regard to a person experiencing death anxiety who is not an older adult, older adults are seen as an out-group that symbolically represents the end stage of life, whose finality is death. Therefore, a person experiencing death anxiety will deflect existential anxiety about his or her fear of mortality by producing negative, prejudicial attitudes toward older adults, and by acting out negative behaviors toward older adults. This deflection of anxiety is called *ageism*.

Psychologists also experience death anxiety. Psychologists may exhibit prejudice toward older adults due to their own defense against the fear of their mortality. This causes many people entering the field of psychology, and some already trained as psychologists, to be reluctant to treat older adults based on the false assumption that older adults are rigid in their ways, and consequently are unable to change (Lee, Volans, & Gregory, 2003). In addition, older psychologist cohorts may still hold the ageist view of Sigmund Freud, who felt that adults age 50 or greater are not candidates for psychoanalysis because learning stops at age 50 (Freud, 1900/1953).

Another aspect a psychologist must be vigilant about is using patronizing speech when communicating with an older adult. This type of speech is known as *elder speak* or *secondary baby talk* (Kemper, Otrhick, Gerhing, Gubarchuk, & Billington, 1998; Miller, 2009; Ruscher, 2001; Williams & Nussbaum, 2001). This speech pattern is common when a younger adult speaks to an older adult and is similar to when one speaks to an individual with disabilities (Giles & Gasiorek, 2011; Hummert & Ryan, 2001).

Less patronizing communication to an older adult from a younger adult is shown to have positive effects on the psychological well-being of an older adult (Giles, McCann, Ota, & Noels, 2002). This type of positive communication is called *symbiotic niceness*, whereby an older adult and a psychologist each benefit by creating a positive relationship (Li, 2004). By restructuring communication with an older adult, a psychologist creates a communication environment that leads to equality in decision making (Daveson et al., 2013; Haggstrom, Mamhidir, & Kihlgren, 2010; Hain & Sandy, 2013). This symbiotic niceness can also be taught by the psychologist to spouses/partners, caregivers, and relatives who are involved with caregiving activities to an older adult. This positive change in communication is an important intervention that helps prevent the older adult abuse (see Chapter 7) that is perpetrated on many older adults by caregivers.

Types of Ageism

There are four types of ageism: personal, institutional, intentional, and unintentional (Anti-aging Task Force, 2006). *Personal ageism* occurs when non-older people view older people as incompetent or incapable of functioning properly. This form of ageism intersects with stigmatized aspects of older adults (see the following section on stigma). *Institutional ageism* occurs when institutions create policies that discriminate against older people. An egregious example of institutional ageism occurred in Japan, where it was found that municipal governments failed to keep track of where centenarians (see Chapter 1) were residing (Ebihara, Freeman, Ebihara, & Kohzuki, 2010). This failure put these older adults at risk by not providing needed social/medical/psychological services. This institutional trend in Japan led to the term *missing centenarians*.

Institutional ageism often occurs in nursing homes. An older adult who is a resident in a nursing home is often abused by staff members when he or she complains in a hostile manner, or is experiencing dementia (Burgess, Dowdel, & Prentky, 2000; Burgess & Morgenbesser, 2005). This abuse may be verbal, physical, or sexual (see Chapter 7). Many of the older adults abused in nursing homes have a history of being abused by caregivers prior to admission to a nursing home (Dong & Simon, 2013). Older adult residents in nursing homes who are cognitively free of dementia often have a higher incidence of verbal abuse that causes anxiety and depressive disorders (Begle et al., 2011; Tatara, 2001).

Another example of institutional ageism is found in social and governmental policies in the United States. In a classic policy analysis, Callahan (1987) warns of an ongoing health care system crisis that will escalate as more and more of the baby-boom generation passes 65 years of age. Callahan describes that this is caused by the increasingly high utilization of health care and psychiatric care services by older Americans. Likewise, Peterson (1999) indicates that advocates for children blame older Americans who receive government funding and benefits for subsequently causing inadequate funding for food, housing, and education for children. This trend of policy antagonisms may inspire an intergenerational war in developed countries.

For psychologists, this causes a dilemma. Due to the pressure to decrease funding for Medicare and Medicaid recipients (Kakani, 2011; Moffit & Senger, 2013), psychological services available to older adults are in serious jeopardy. This may occur because any increase in spending for Medicare and Medicaid increases the national debt. Critics of Medicare and Medicaid feel that increased spending for health care causes a decrease in spending for other domestic needs, causing an eventual economic stagnation. Campbell (2003) feels that this age bias is driven by younger policymakers who are demonizing older adults even though the policies currently supporting older adults' mental health and health care needs are successful.

Intentional ageism occurs when attitudes and rules that discriminate against older people are maintained even though they are recognized as age-biased. Examples of intentional ageism are when an older person is denied employment simply because of his or her age, and the practice in some hospitals whereby some emergency room staff members who are reluctant to treat an older adult often label the older adult a *GOMER* ("get out of my emergency room"). *Unintentional ageism* occurs when there is no recognition that attitudes and rules are discriminating against older people. An example would be a planned community in which older adults reside with younger people, but elevators and ramps are lacking or nonexistent in the community. More often than not, references in broadcast and print media favor youth and are disparaging of older adults.

ADDITIONAL CLASSIC THEORIES OF AGEISM

Butler (1969) was the first to introduce the phenomenon called *ageism*. Butler described ageism as when a person has a negative attitude toward an older adult based on numerous negative stereotypes of older adults. These negative attitudes based on biased stereotypes of older adults are experienced continuously across all of a person's developmental stages. This chronic experience of negative reactions to older adults is cumulative, creating greater negativity toward older adults as people age. The majority of older adults have experienced age discrimination and stigmatization at some time after the age of 65 (Palmore, 2001). This negativity is most acutely expressed by adult men and younger people (Palmore, Branch, & Harris, 2005). Butler (Butler, 1975, 1995) indicates that according to *social identity theory*, younger people distance themselves from older adults by identifying exclusively with their own age group and reducing older adults to being other than fellow human beings. This dehumanization of older adults can be extended to a model developed for gender inequality described as *benign condescension* (Glick & Fiske, 2001). Conversely, Rupp, Vodanovich, and Crede (2005) report that as one ages, the level of ageism held by the older adult decreases. Therefore, older adults hold more positive attitudes toward older target groups than do younger adults.

The New Ageism

Another foundational study of ageism led to the theory described by Kalish (1979) as the *new ageism*. This theory explains how older professionals, even if they are advocates for older adults, will display age bias to the patients/clients they serve. In the case of a psychologist treating an older adult, the older psychologist may view his or her patient as less capable, less healthy, and less alert because the older adult is seeking help. When the psychologist compares the older adult to himself or herself, this prejudice is exacerbated because the psychologist is *healthy* and is treating an *unhealthy* person.

This phenomenon can happen whether the psychologist is treating psychopathologies such as depressive disorders and anxiety disorders, or giving supportive advice for life events the older adult is experiencing. These may include coping with a serious illness, having problems adjusting to a new neighborhood, being confused about managing finances, and experiencing *disenfranchised grief* (Doka, 2002). Disenfranchised grief occurs when an older adult experiences a loss that appears insignificant to others, such as the loss of a pet. The older adult becomes isolated in his or her grief and suffers emotional distress similar to what others feel when they lose a loved one. Bodner and Lazar (2009) indicate that this type of discrimination between an older adult (healthy psychologist) to an older adult (unhealthy patient/client) is an indication of prejudice toward older adults by the discriminator that has been brought forward from earlier developmental stages to his or her current life stage as an older adult. This is a form of intragenerational ageism in which older adults are biased toward fellow older adults when a group identity is labeled as *old age* (Kite & Wagner, 2002).

The Incompetence Model

Kalish (1979) extended the new ageism theory to the macro level of institutional-level ageism. In this model, institutions that advocate for older adults, and provide funding for older adults, do so while ironically arguing that older adults are incompetent and therefore need the help of the respective institution. The programs created by this funding highlight the fact that older adults are incompetent in their social and psychological functioning, as evidenced by their need for help. This argument of older adult incompetence distorts the needs of a minority group of older adults who are the least independent and competent of older adults, by representing that such incompetency is typical of the whole of older adults. This facilitates and promotes the ageism that ultimately leads to biased treatment of older adults.

The Geriactivist Model

In this model, Kalish (1979) describes how older professionals who advocate for and/or treat older adults identify with younger professionals, and consequently bias treatment decisions for the older adults they are trying to help. This psychological collusion may happen when an older psychologist is treating an older adult, or participating on a treatment team treating an older adult, when the older psychologist joins with the ageist views of younger colleagues. It has been known for many years, and to this day, that the ageist views of mental health professionals often cause older adults not to be diagnosed with depression or to be misdiagnosed with dementia (Lambert & Bieliaukas, 1993). The overriding concern of the consequence of ageist views of older adults by treating psychologists is resulting inadequate treatment that further exacerbates psychological disorders (Cuddy & Fiske, 2002).

STIGMA

Stigma is a concept first described by Goffman (1963). Goffman indicates that stigma is a process that reduces vulnerable people (in this book, older adults) to a negative status of having *spoiled identities*. Spoiled identities cause a minority group

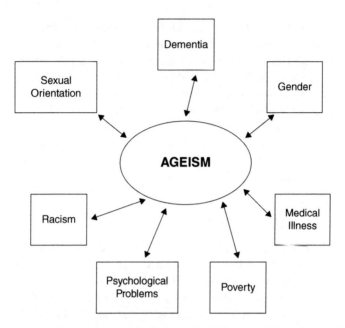

FIGURE 2.1 Intersection of stigmatized labels of older people with ageism.

Adapted from Youdin (2014).

(older adults) to aggregate together based on negative attributes (Burke, Martens, & Fauchner, 2010). This aggregation is the point of intersection (Figure 2.1) where ageism joins different stigmatized labels created by the majority against the minority (Cavelti, Kvrgic, Beck, Rusch, & Vauth, 2012).

OTHER TYPES OF STIGMA

Self-Stigma

When the non–older adult majority stigmatizes older adults, many of these older adults identify with this stigma. The identification with the stigmatized view of how others see them causes many older adults to internalize the stigma directed at them. This process of internalization is called *self-stigma*. Paradoxically, this internalized process in turn becomes a validation of the stigma directed by others to older adults (Cavelti et al., 2012).

Corrigan, Watson, and Barr (2006) describe three subtypes of self-stigma: *stereotype agreement, self-concurrence,* and *self-esteem decrement.* Of these three subtypes, self-esteem is a key indicator of the severity of self-stigma that an older adult may experience (Schmeichel et al., 2009). If the older adult has a strong intact sense of self, the incidence of self-stigma will be attenuated as compared with an older adult who has a reduced sense of self.

Courtesy Stigma

The many labels used by the majority of non-older adults cause older adults to be devalued and marginalized. These labels exacerbate the stigma of being old by adding other stigmatized concepts, such as gender, race, poverty, sexual orientation, and medical/psychological illness. Goffman (1963) indicates that for stigmatized individuals, the stigma is not restricted to the individual (older adult). By being associated with the stigmatized older adult, spouses/partners, caregivers, adult children, siblings, other relatives, and friends become stigmatized by association. This is called *courtesy stigma.*

STIGMATIZED LABELS OF OLDER ADULTS THAT INTERSECT WITH AGEISM

There are a diverse number of stigmatized social constructs that influence how a psychologist views an older adult. Unfortunately, these concepts may bias a psychologist, consequently putting an older adult at risk for inadequate and inaccurate psychological interventions or, in some cases, no psychological services at all. As discussed, older adults may internalize the biases held by a psychologist (self-stigma), thus exacerbating the negative treatment of a psychologist, or, in some cases prematurely termi-nating treatment. Consequently, there is a need for psychologists to engage in evidence-based studies to identify means to prevent the stigma of older adults harbored by psychologists and to ex-plore how to develop respectful relationships with older adult clients (Satorius et al., 2010; Weiss & Ramakrishna, 2006). Results of such research will contribute to supporting ethical mandates in psychology and enhance professional competence.

Dementia

The fear of experiencing dementia (see Chapter 4) and its con-sequent effects on independent functioning is the greatest dread of older adults as well as adults approaching old age (Rowe & Kahn, 1998). These fears drive many older adults to be hyper-vigilant about their memory functioning. Such fears of memory functioning are contributory to the stigmatization of older adults experiencing dementia. In addition, when older adults verbalize these fears to others who are facilitating courtesy stigma of family members, spouses/partners, caregivers, and friends of the older adult, they in turn feel that stigma of dementia. An example of this fear of dementia is described by Lachman (2000), who found that 39% of people across the adult age spectrum of 25 to 75 years of age reported noticing a problem with their memory at least one time per week. The fear of dementia is also explained by the theory of *stereotype threat* (Eich, Murayama, Castel, & Knowlton, 2014). This theory explains that an older person is at risk for becom-ing, or for confirming, the negative stereotypes attributed to older adults. In this case, the stigmatization effect is that older people have memory problems and/or dementia (Barber & Mather, 2013, 2014; Hess, Hinson, & Hodges, 2009).

Gender

The issue of gender as a stigmatizing concept usually brings to mind classic issues relating to the power differential between men and women. Calasanti and Kiecolt (2007) indicate that inequalities that exist in wealth, authority, and labor between men and women are supported by the patriarchal notion of men's power privilege in vocational and social settings (Dixon, Levine, Reicher, & Durrheim, 2012). This patriarchal attitude experienced by a person throughout his or her development promotes and supports ageism of older adult women. Stahl and Metzer (2012) find that college undergraduates report negative attitudes toward older adults, with males showing the most ageist behavior. Women who experience high levels of discrimination in their lives consequently have a lower sense of eudemonic well-being (Ryff, Keyes, & Hughes, 2003). This causes reduction in feelings of growth, mastery, autonomy, and self-acceptance. In addition, older women are more likely to be widowed, living alone, and financially stressed, and to have a lower level of formal education, as compared with older men (Darkwa & Mazibuko, 2002). Once widowed, women often are denied inheritance and burial rights, and face home eviction, physical abuse, loss of social status, marginalization, and poverty (DiGiacomo, Davidson, Byles, & Nolan, 2013).

Whereas the evidence just cited is characteristic of the gender dichotomy between men and women, another gender subgroup of older adults exists, and that is transgender older adults. All too often, when assessing an older adult in a clinical setting, a psychologist will label an older adult as male or female, neglecting to investigate whether the older adult is transgender.

In research, transgender older adults are often not focused on, or are equated with older gay male or lesbian adults (Davies, Greene, Macbridge-Stewart, & Sheperd, 2009). When research psychologists dichotomize gender categories to male and female, transgender older adults are relegated to a no-gender status, which in turn causes their unique problems to be underserved by psychologists (Bockting, Robinson, & Rosser, 1998; Burke, 2011; Kenagy, 2005).

Psychologists studying gender differences would benefit by extending the *intersectionality theory* (Cronin & King, 2010) to the study of gender differences between male, female, and transgender older adults. Intersectionality theory describes that in research on lesbian, gay male, and bisexual (LGB) older adults, there are significant cultural, social, and psychological differences within each subcategory of LGB older adults. Curiously, this theory rightly looks at differences in sexual orientation, yet it avoids the transgender category, which has its own sexual orientation differences as well as being a third gender category (see Chapter 5). Therefore, when discussing gender influences in stigma, differences need to be identified for each of the three gender subtypes.

Medical Illness

As discussed previously, Callahan (1987) warns of a *demographic, economic, and medical avalanche* that may bankrupt health care resources for younger adults and children. This demonization of older adults serves to increase the stigma of adults experiencing medical illnesses, which in turn may cause the phenomenon of underservice of older adults by prejudiced health care providers, and as a result of older adults avoiding presenting for medical care. Putting older adults at greater risk for more acute and chronic health care problems increases the burden on the health care system and casts inappropriate blame on older adults for the crisis in the health care system (Lee, Hatzenbuehler, Phelan, & Link, 2013). This is a paradox because by discriminating against older adults who have medical problems, the situation that Callahan advocated becomes facilitated by such stigmatization (Williams & Mohammed, 2009).

Psychological Problems

Older adults experiencing psychological problems (see Chapter 3) encounter the stigma of mental illness, along with their relatives, spouses/partners, and caregivers who experience courtesy stigma (see earlier discussion) (Corrigan, 2007; Ostman & Kjellin, 2002; Shrivastava, Bureau, Rewari, & Johnston, 2013). The stigma of experiencing psychological problems exacerbates the psychological problems an older adult encounters, sabotaging the older adult's ability to return to a normal status (Shrivastava et al., 2013).

When compared to a more acceptable disease such as diabetes, the stigma of a mental illness is significantly worse (Lee, Lee, Chiu, & Kleinman, 2005).

A serious consequence of stigmatizing an older adult who is experiencing psychological problems is that it can exacerbate self-blame in the older adult, leading an older adult to attempt or complete suicide (Miranda et al., 2005; Pompili, Mancinelli, & Tararelli, 2003). According to the National Institute of Mental Health, older adults, who comprise 12% of the overall adult population in the United States, account for 16% of deaths by suicide (2007). Unfortunately, the stigma of an older adult experiencing psychological problems often prevents the older adult from seeking treatment with a psychologist (Bayer & Peay, 1997; Bucholz & Robins, 1987). Often an older adult will seek treatment with a primary care physician rather than with a psychologist. This phenomenon is seen at a greater frequency in rural areas as compared with urban areas because rural areas often lack mental health professionals, causing primary care physicians to provide mental health services, which usually consists of prescribing medications for psychological disorders (Komiti, Judd, & Jackson, 2006). In addition, women, rather than men, seek mental health treatment at a greater rate, causing men to be underserved by psychologists and medical professionals (Mojtabai, Olfson, & Mechanic, 2002; Narrow et al., 2000; Olfson et al., 2002).

Self-stigma is seen in an older adult experiencing a psychotic disorder when he or she engages in self-blame for delusional disorders or schizophrenia (Sadock & Sadock, 2008). Institutional stigma is seen in the United States when institutional policy constructs a temporal barrier to treatment causing, in most cases, a delay of up to 8 years for initial treatment contact for depression and a delay of up to 5 years for drug and alcohol (see Chapter 6) initial treatment contact (Wang et al., 2005). This is critical because the number of older adults affected by substance abuse is projected to increase from 2.5 million in 1999 to 5 million in 2020 (Gfoerer, Penne, Pemberton, & Folson, 2008). It is estimated that the newly arriving older adult cohort of baby boomers will show an exponential increase in prescription drug abuse, from 1.2% in 1999 to 2.4% in 2020 (Menninger, 2002; Pennington, Butler, & Eagger, 2000; Rigler, 2000).

Racism/Poverty

Racism and poverty are dichotomous types of stigma that, more often than not, intersect. Many stigmatized older adults who are impoverished are Latinas and African American women and men (Ojeda & McGuire, 2006). Underservice by health and psychological professionals to Latina women and African American women and men occurs because of the lower socioeconomic status these older adults share and the consequent social value constraints caused by their impoverished state (Ojeda & McGuire, 2006). This is consistent with findings made by Gray-Little and Hafdahl (2000), who found that African Americans, as compared with Whites, have a higher incidence of psychological problems. Researchers (Mui & Shibusawa, 2008; Ortiz & Telles, 2012) find that, similar to African Americans, Mexican Americans and Asian Americans experience psychological problems that are often linked to their encounters with discrimination by the White majority.

Another barrier making it difficult for psychologists to provide mental health services to minority groups is the lack of cultural and language competence in many psychologists (Miranda et al., 2005). Historically, psychologists have been adapting therapeutic modalities developed for the White majority because minorities are less likely than are Whites to seek mental health services (Alegria et al., 2002; Husaini et al., 2002; Miranda & Cooper, 2004; Swartz et al., 1998). This phenomenon underscores a need for new psychotherapeutic modalities to be developed for minority older adults.

Sexual Orientation

There are many stereotypic forces from the majority heterosexual population that cause stigmatization of lesbian, gay male, bisexual, and transgender (LGBT) older adults. A typical example is the importance of being in a partnered/marital relationship to maintain positive mental and medical health. There is a dearth of research on nonheterosexual older couples, causing psychologists to extrapolate psychological interventions for such couples from research on heterosexual couples. Fortunately, there is a beginning trend to widen researchers' lenses to develop initiatives to intervene regarding the effects of homophobia on the LGBT community (Altman et al., 2012). This is extremely important to help lessen the psychological consequences that arise from LGBT older adults avoiding a partner/marriage relationship. This is important because such partnering is an excellent means to combat the psychologically damaging effects of loneliness, lack of emotional support, and lack of opportunities for sexual intimacy (see Chapter 5).

It is highly important for psychologists to develop a research agenda for studying LGBT older adults. The *theory of intersectionality* suggests that there are significant cultural, social, and psychological differences within each subcategory of LGBT older adults (Cronin & King, 2010). This is equivalent to the significant differences within each age cohort of older adults (see Chapter 1). However, most research, as reported in Chapter 1, is limited to research on heterosexual older adults. The lack of research on LGBT older adults is thought to be a product of differences in self-identification among the LGBT cohort of older adults (Cahill, 2007; Cahill & Valadez, 2013), and the lack of institutional funding of research on older LGBT adults (Van Voorhis & Wagner, 2001).

REFERENCES

Alegria, M., Canino, G., Rios, R., Vera, M., Calderon, J., Rusch, D., & Ortega, A. N. (2002). Inequalities in use of specialty mental health services among Latinos, African Americans, and non-Latino Whites. *Psychiatric Services*, 53(12), 1547–1555.

Altman, D., Aggleton, P., Williams, M., Kong, T., Reddy, V., Harrad, D., & Parker, R. (2012). Men who have sex with men: Stigma and discrimination. *The Lancet*, 380(9839), 439–445.

Anti-aging Task Force. (2006). *Ageism in America*. New York, NY: International Longevity Center.

Barber, S. J., & Mather, M. (2013). Stereotype threat can enhance, as well as impair, older adults' memory. *Psychological Science, 24,* 2522–2529.

Barber, S. J., & Mather, M. (2014). Stereotype threat in older adults: When and why does it occur, and who is most affected? In P. Verhaeghen & C. Hertzog (Eds.), *The Oxford handbook of emotion, social cognition, and everyday problem solving during adulthood* (pp. 302–320). Oxford, England: Oxford University Press.

Bayer, J. K., & Peay, M. Y. (1997). Predicting intentions to seek help from professional mental health services. *Australian New Zealand Journal of Psychiatry, 31,* 504–513.

Becker, E. (1973). *The denial of death.* New York, NY: Free Press.

Begle, A. M., Strachan, M., Cisler, J. M., Arnstadter, A. B., Hernandez, M. A., & Acierno, R. (2011). Elder mistreatment and emotional symptoms among older adults in a largely rural population: The South Carolina Elder Mistreatment Study. *Journal of Interpersonal Violence, 26*(11), 2321–2332.

Bockting, W. O., Robinson, B. E., & Rosser, B. R. S. (1998). Transgender HIV prevention: A qualitative needs assessment. *AIDS Care, 10*(4), 505–525.

Bodner, E., & Lazar, A. (2009). On the origins of ageism among older and younger adults: A review. *International Psychogeriatrics, 21,* 1–12.

Bucholz, K. K., & Robins, L. N. (1987). Who talks to a doctor about existing depressive illness? *Journal of Affective Disorders, 12,* 241–250.

Burgess, A. W., Dowdel, E. B., & Prentky, R. A. (2000). Sexual abuse of nursing home residents. *Journal of Psychosocial Nursing & Mental Health Services, 38*(6), 8–10.

Burgess, A. W., & Morgenbesser, L. I. (2005). Sexual violence and seniors. *Brief Treatment and Crisis Intervention, 5*(2), 193.

Burke, B. L. (2011). What can motivational interviewing do for you? *Cognitive and Behavioral Practice, 18,* 78–81.

Burke, B. L., Martens, A., & Fauchner, E. H. (2010). Two decades of terror management theory: A meta-analysis of mortality salience research. *Personality and Social Psychology Review, 14,* 155–195.

Butler, R. N. (1969). Ageism: Another form of bigotry. *The Gerontologist, 9,* 243–246.

Butler, R. N. (1975). *Why survive? Being old in America.* New York, NY: Harper & Row.

Butler, R. N. (1995). Ageism. In G. Maddox (Ed.), *The encyclopedia of aging* (pp. 38–39). New York, NY: Springer Publishing Company.

Cahill, S. (2007). The coming GLBT senior boom. *The Gay & Lesbian Review Worldwide, 14*(1), 19–25.

Cahill, S. P., & Valadez, R. M. S. W. (2013). Growing older with HIV/AIDS: New public health challenges. *American Journal of Public Health, 103*(3), E7–E15.

Calasanti, T., & Kiecolt, K. J. (2007). Diversity among late-life couples. *Generations, 31*(3), 10–17.

Callahan, D. (1987). *Setting limits: Medical goals in an aging society.* New York, NY: Simon & Schuster.

Campbell, A. I. (2003). *How policies make citizens: Senior political activism and the American welfare state.* Princeton, NJ: Princeton University Press.

Cavelti, M., Kvrgic, S., Beck, E.-M., Rusch, N., & Vauth, R. (2012). Self-stigma and its relationship with insight, demoralization, and clinical outcome among people with schizophrenia spectrum disorders. *Comprehensive Psychiatry, 53*(5), 468–479. doi:10.1016/j.comppsych.2011.08.001

Cheng, S.-T., & Heller, K. (2009). Global aging: Challenges for community psychology. *American Journal of Community Psychology, 44,* 161–173.

Corrigan, P. W. (2007). How clinical diagnosis might exacerbate the stigma of mental illness. *Social Work, 52*(1), 31–39.

Corrigan, P. W., Watson, A. C., & Barr, L. (2006). The self-stigma of mental illness: Implications for self-esteem and self-efficacy. *Journal of Social and Clinical Psychology, 25*(8), 875–884.

Cronin, A., & King, A. (2010). Power, inequality and identification: Exploring diversity and intersectionality amongst older LGB adults. *Sociology, 44*(5), 876–892.

Cuddy, A. J. C., & Fiske, S. T. (2002). Doddering, but clear: Process, content, and function in stereotyping of older persons. In T. D. Nelson (Ed.), *Stereotyping and prejudice against older persons* (pp. 3–26). Cambridge, MA: MIT Press.

Darkwa, O. K., & Mazibuko, F. N. M. (2002). Population aging and its impact on elderly welfare in Africa. *International Journal of Aging and Human Development, 54,* 107–123.

Daveson, B. A., Bausewein, C., Murtagh, F. E. M., Calanzani, N., Higginson, I. J., Harding, R., . . . Gomes, B. (2013). To be involved or not to be involved: A survey of public preferences for self-involvement in decision-making involving mental capacity (competency) within Europe. *Palliative Medicine, 27*(5), 418–427. doi:10.1177/0269216312471883

Davies, A. S., Greene, G., Macbridge-Stewart, S., & Sheperd, M. (2009). The health, social care and housing needs of lesbian, gay, bisexual, and transgender older people: A review of the literature. *Health Social Care Community, 17*(6), 647–658.

DiGiacomo, M., Davidson, P. M., Byles, J., & Nolan, M. (2013). An integrative and social-cultural perspective of health, wealth, and adjustment to widowhood. *Health Care for Women International, 34*(12), 1067–1083.

Dixon, J., Levine, M., Reicher, S., & Durrheim, K. (2012). Beyond prejudice: Are negative evaluations the problem and is getting us to like one another more the solution? *Behavioral and Brain Sciences, 35*(6), 411–425. doi:10.1017/S0140525X11002214

Doka, K. J. (2002). *Disenfranchised grief: New directions, challenges, and strategies for practice.* Champaign, IL: Research Press.

Dong, X., & Simon, M. (2013). Association between reported elder abuse and rates of admission to skilled nursing facilities: Findings from a longitudinal population-based cohort study. *Gerontology, 59*(5), 464–472.

Ebihara, S., Freeman, S., Ebihara, T., & Kohzuki, M. (2010). Missing centenarians in Japan: A new ageism. *The Lancet, 376*(9754), 1739.

Eich, T. S., Murayama, K., Castel, A. D., & Knowlton, B. J. (2014). The dynamic effects of age-related stereotype threat on explicit and implicit memory performance in older adults. *Social Cognition, 32*(6), 559–570. doi:101521soco2014326559

Freud, S. (1953). On psychotherapy. In J. Strachey (Ed. & Trans.), *The standard edition of the complete psychological works of Sigmund Freud* (Vol. 6, pp. 249–263). London, England: Hogarth Press. (Original work published 1900)

Gfoerer, J. C., Penne, M. A., Pemberton, M. R., & Folson, J. R. E. (2008). The aging baby boom cohort and future prevalence of substance abuse. In S. P. Korper & C. L. Council (Eds.), *Substance use by older adults: Estimates of future impact on the treatment system* (DHHS Publication No. SMA 03-3763, OAS Analytic Series A-21; pp. 71–94). Rockville, MD: Substance Abuse and Mental Health Services Administration.

Giles, H., & Gasiorek, J. (2011). Intergenerational communication practices. In K. W. Schaie & S. L. Willis (Eds.), *Handbook of the psychology of aging* (7th ed., pp. 233–247). San Diego, CA: Elsevier.

Giles, H., McCann, R. M., Ota, H., & Noels, K. A. (2002). Challenging intergenerational stereotypes: Across Eastern and Western cultures. In M. S. Kaplan, N. Z. Henkin, & A. T. Kusano (Eds.), *Linking lifetimes:*

A global view of intergenerational exchange (pp. 13–28). Honolulu, HI: University Press of America.

Glick, P., & Fiske, S. T. (2001). An ambivalent alliance: Hostile and benevolent sexism as complementary justifications for gender inequality. *American Psychologist, 56*, 109–118.

Goffman, E. (1963). *Stigma: Notes on the management of spoiled identity.* Garden City, NY: Prentice Hall.

Gray-Little, B., & Hafdahl, A. R. (2000). Factors influencing racial comparisons of self-esteem: A quantitative review. *Psychological Bulletin, 126*, 26–54.

Greenberg, J., & Arndt, J. (2011). Terror management theory. In P. Kruglanski, A. M. Van Lange, & E. T. Higgins (Eds.), *Handbook of theories of social psychology* (Vol. 1, pp. 339–415). New York, NY: Sage.

Greenberg, J., Pyszczynski, T., Solomon, S., Rosenblatt, A., Veeder, M., Kirkland, S., & Lyon, D. (1990). Evidence for terror management theory II: The effects of mortality salience on reactions to those who threaten or bolster the cultural worldview. *Journal of Personality and Social Psychology, 58*, 308–318.

Greenberg, J., Solomon, S., & Pyszczynski, T. (1997). Terror management theory of self-esteem and cultural worldviews: Empirical assessments and conceptual refinements. In M. P. Zanna (Ed.), *Advances in experimental social psychology* (Vol. 29, pp. 61–139). San Diego, CA: Academic Press.

Haggstrom, E., Mamhidir, A. G., & Kihlgren, A. (2010). Caregivers' strong commitment to their relationship with older people. *International Journal of Nursing Practice, 16*(2), 99–105.

Hain, D. J., & Sandy, D. (2013). Partners in care: Patient empowerment through shared decision-making. *Nephrology Nursing Journal, 40*(2), 153–157.

Hess, T. M., Hinson, J. T., & Hodges, E. A. (2009). Moderators of and mechanisms underlying stereotype threat effects on older adults' memory performance. *Experimental Aging Research, 35*, 153–177.

Hummert, M. L., & Ryan, E. B. (2001). Patronizing. In W. P. Robinson & H. Giles (Eds.), *The new handbook of language and social psychology* (pp. 253–269). Chichester, England: Wiley.

Husaini, B. A., Sherkat, D. E., Levine, R., Bragg, R., Holzer, C., Anderson, K., . . . Moten, C. (2002). Race, gender, and health care service utilization and costs among Medicare elderly with psychiatric diagnoses. *Journal of Aging and Health, 14*(1), 79–95.

Kakani, P. (2011). *Runaway Medicare and Medicaid spending*. Retrieved from http://harvardpolitics.com/arusa/runaway-medicare-and-medicaid-spending/

Kalish, R. (1979). The new ageism and the failure models: A polemic. *The Gerontologist, 19*, 398–402.

Kemper, S., Otrhick, M., Gerhing, H., Gubarchuk, J., & Billington, C. (1998). The effects of practicing speech accommodations to older adults. *Applied Psycholinguistics, 19*, 175–192.

Kenagy, G. P. (2005). Transgender health: Findings from two needs assessment studies in Philadelphia. *Health & Social Work, 30*(1), 19–26.

Kite, M. E., & Wagner, L. S. (2002). Attitudes toward older adults. In T. D. Nelson (Ed.), *Ageism: Stereotyping and prejudice against older persons* (pp. 129–161). Cambridge, MA: MIT Press.

Komiti, A., Judd, F., & Jackson, H. (2006). The influence of stigma and attitudes on seeking help from a GP for mental health problems. *Social Psychiatry and Psychiatric Epidemiology, 41*(9), 738–745.

Kübler-Ross, E. (1975). *Death: The final stage of growth*. New York, NY: Simon & Schuster.

Lachman, M. E. (2000). Promoting a sense of control over memory aging. In L. Backman, R. D. Hill, & A. Stigsdotter-Neely (Eds.), *Cognitive rehabilitation in old age* (pp. 106–120). New York, NY: Oxford University Press.

Lambert, G. J., & Bieliaukas, L. A. (1993). Distinguishing between depression and dementia in the elderly: A review of neuropsychological findings. *Archives of Clinical Neurology, 8*, 149–170.

Lee, B., Hatzenbuehler, M. L., Phelan, J. C., & Link, B. G. (2013). The role of stigma in health disparities. *American Journal of Public Health, 103*(8), E4–E5.

Lee, K. M., Volans, P. J., & Gregory, N. (2003). Attitudes towards psychotherapy with older adults among trainee clinical psychologists. *Aging & Mental Health, 7*, 133–141.

Lee, S., Lee, M. T., Chiu, M. Y., & Kleinman, A. (2005). Experience of social stigma by people with schizophrenia in Hong Kong. *British Journal of Psychiatry, 186*, 153–157.

Li, S. (2004). "Symbiotic niceness": Constructing a therapeutic relationship in psychosocial palliative care. *Social Science & Medicine, 58*, 2571–2583.

Martens, A., Goldenberg, J. L., & Greenberg, J. (2005). A terror management perspective on ageism. *Journal of Social Issues, 61*, 223–239.

Menninger, J. A. (2002). Assessment and treatment of alcoholism and substance-related disorders in the elderly. *Bulletin of the Menninger Clinic, 66*, 166–184.

Miller, C. A. (2009). *Nursing for wellness in older adults*. Philadelphia, PA: Lippincott Williams & Wilkins.

Miranda, J., Bernal, G., Lau, A., Kohn, L., Hwang, W. C., & LaFromboise, T. (2005). State of the science on psychosocial interventions for ethnic minorities. *Annual Review of Psychology, 1*, 113–142.

Miranda, J., & Cooper, L. A. (2004). Disparities in care for depression among primary care patients. *Journal of General Internal Medicine, 19*, 120–126.

Moffit, R. E., & Senger, A. (2013). *Medicare's rising costs—and the urgent need for reform*. Retrieved from http://www.heritage.org/research/reports/2013/03/medicares-rising-costsand-the-urgent-need-for-reform

Mojtabai, R., Olfson, M., & Mechanic, D. (2002). Perceived need and help-seeking in adults with mood, anxiety, or substance use disorders. *Archives of General Psychiatry, 59*, 77–84.

Mui, A. C., & Shibusawa, T. (2008). *Asian American elders in the 21st century: Key indicators of psychological well-being*. New York, NY: Columbia University Press.

Narrow, W. E., Regier, D. A., Norquist, G., Rae, D. S., Kennedy, C., & Arons, B. (2000). Mental health service use by Americans with severe mental illness. *Social Psychiatry and Psychiatric Epidemiology, 35*, 147–155.

National Institute of Mental Health. (2007). *Older adults: Depression and suicide facts*. Retrieved from http://www.nimh.nih.gov/health/publications/older-adults-depression-and-suicide-facts-fact-sheet/index.shtml

Ojeda, V. D., & McGuire, T. G. (2006). Gender and racial/ethnic differences in use of outpatient mental health and substance use services by depressed adults. *Psychiatric Quarterly, 77*(3), 211–222.

Olfson, M., Marcus, S. C., Druss, B. G., Elinson, L., Tanielian, T., & Pincus, H. A. (2002). National trends in the outpatient treatment of depression. *JAMA, 287*(2), 203–209.

Ortiz, V., & Telles, E. (2012). Racial identity and racial treatment of Mexican Americans. *Race and Social Problems, 4*(1), 41–56.

Ostman, M., & Kjellin, L. (2002). Stigma by association: Psychological factors in relatives of people with mental illness. *British Journal of Psychiatry, 181*, 494–498.

Palmore, E. B. (2001). The ageism survey: First findings. *The Gerontologist*, *41*, 572–575.

Palmore, E. B., Branch, L., & Harris, D. (Eds.). (2005). *Encyclopedia of ageism*. Binghamton, NY: Haworth Press.

Pennington, H., Butler, R., & Eagger, S. (2000). The assessment of patients with alcohol disorders by an old age psychiatric service. *Aging & Mental Health*, *4*, 182–185.

Peterson, P. G. (1999). *Gray dawn: How the coming age wave will transform America and the world*. New York, NY: Times Books.

Pompili, M., Mancinelli, I., & Tararelli, R. (2003). Stigma as a cause of suicide. *British Journal of Psychiatry*, *183*, 173–174.

Rigler, S. K. (2000). Alcoholism in the elderly. *American Family Physician*, *61*, 1710–1716.

Rowe, J. W., & Kahn, R. L. (1998). *Successful aging*. New York, NY: Dell.

Rupp, D., Vodanovich, S., & Crede, M. (2005). The multidimensional nature of ageism: Construct validity and group differences. *Journal of Social Psychology*, *145*, 335–362.

Ruscher, J. B. (2001). *Prejudiced communication: A social psychological perspective*. New York, NY: Guilford Press.

Ryff, C. D., Keyes, C. L. M., & Hughes, D. L. (2003). Status inequalities, perceived discrimination, and eudaimonic well-being: Do the challenges of minority life hone purpose and growth? *Journal of Health and Social Behavior*, *44*(3), 275.

Sadock, B. J., & Sadock, V. A. (2008). *Kaplan & Sadock's concise textbook of clinical psychiatry* (3rd ed.). Philadelphia, PA: Wolters Kluwer/Lippincott Williams & Wilkins.

Satorius, N., Gaebel, W., Cleveland, H. R., Stuart, H., Akiyama, T., Arboleda-Florez, J., . . . Tasman, A. (2010). WPA guidance on how to combat stigmatization of psychiatry and psychiatrists. *World Psychiatry*, *9*, 131–144.

Schmeichel, B. J., Gailliot, M. T., Filardo, E., McGregor, I., Gitter, S., & Baumeister, R. F. (2009). Terror management theory and self-esteem revisited: The roles of implicit and explicit self-esteem in mortality salience effects. *Journal of Personality and Social Psychology*, *96*, 1077–1087.

Shrivastava, A., Bureau, Y., Rewari, N., & Johnston, M. (2013). Clinical risk of stigma and discrimination of mental illnesses: Need for objective assessment and quantification. *Indian Journal of Psychiatry*, *55*(2), 178–182. doi:10.4103/0019-5545.111459

Stahl, S., & Metzger, A. (2012). College students' ageist behavior: The role of aging knowledge and perceived vulnerability to disease. *Gerontology & Geriatrics, 2,* 175–180.

Swartz, M. S., Wagner, H. R., Swanson, J. W., Burns, L. K., George, L. K., & Padgett, D. K. (1998). Comparing use of public and private mental health services: The enduring barriers of race and age. *Community Mental Health Journal, 34*(2), 133–144.

Tatara, T. (2001). Characteristics of victims and perpetrators. In T. Tatara (Ed.), *Elder abuse.* Tokyo, Japan: Chuohoki Shuppan.

Van Voorhis, R., & Wagner, M. (2001). Coverage of gay and lesbian subject matter in social work journals. *Journal of Social Work Education, 37,* 147–159.

Wang, P. S., Berglund, P., Olfson, M., Pincus, H. A., Wells, K. B., & Kessler, R. C. (2005). Failure and delay in initial treatment contact after first onset of mental disorders in the National Comorbidity Survey Replication. *Archives of General Psychiatry, 62,* 603–613.

Weiss, M. G., & Ramakrishna, J. (2006). Stigma interventions and research for international health. *The Lancet, 367,* 536–538.

Williams, A., & Nussbaum, J. F. (2001). *Intergenerational communication across the lifespan.* Mahwah, NJ: Lawrence Erlbaum.

Williams, D. R., & Mohammed, S. A. (2009). Discrimination and racial disparities in health: Evidence and needed research. *Journal of Behavioral Medicine, 32,* 20–47.

Winkielman, P., & Berridge, K. C. (2004). Unconscious emotion. *Current Directions in Psychological Science, 13,* 120–123.

Youdin, R. (2014). *Clinical gerontological social work practice.* New York, NY: Springer Publishing Company.

Psychological Problems That Older Adults Experience

The DSM categories for mental illness are the only
disease categories in all of medicine that do not take
etiology or cause into account. In psychiatry, we have disease
categories based only on symptoms. That would never occur
in cancer or cardiology or immunology, where you always
diagnose on the basis of both the symptoms and the cause.
Jerome Kagan (quoted in Winerman, 2012)

TWO MODELS FOR VIEWING AN OLDER ADULT WITH PSYCHOLOGICAL PROBLEMS: AN INHERENT CONFLICT FOR A PSYCHOLOGIST

The prevalence rate of psychological problems in older adults is 25%, which includes all psychopathological categories (Gatz & Smyer, 2001). Psychological problems associated with the various dementias are discussed in Chapter 4. Sadock and Sadock indicate that older adults are at risk for psychological disorders when faced with "loss of long-term social roles, loss of autonomy, financial pressures, death of close friends and relatives, cognitive problems, and isolation" (2008, p. 695) (Vignette 3.1).

VIGNETTE 3.1   The Case of Maria

(*Note:* Names and other identifying information have been changed to preserve confidentiality.)

Maria is an 83-year-old widow who lives in a small, one-bedroom apartment in Somerville, Massachusetts. She recently moved to this apartment after selling her house, which she had lived in with her husband throughout the 62 years they were married. Her husband died a year ago after suffering a massive heart attack. Maria did not want to leave the town she had lived in with her husband, causing her to reject offers from her two children to move to where they were living so that they would be able to take care of her. Her older daughter lives in Brooklyn, New York, and her younger daughter lives in Washington, DC.

About 6 months ago, Maria experienced her first panic attack. She was at a local supermarket and suddenly felt as if she was going to die. Her heart started to pound "out of control," she began sweating profusely, she felt as if her arms and legs were "shaking out of control," and she felt that she was having difficulty breathing. When this happened she did not want to ask for help out of embarrassment. She leaned against her shopping cart until these feelings passed, and then went immediately home.

(continued)

VIGNETTE 3.1 (*continued*)

Approximately every 2 weeks she experienced another panic attack, each occurring when she was out of her apartment. She decided that it would be best if she did not travel far from her apartment to do errands, even if it meant going to a bodega to buy food rather than a supermarket, which would be less expensive. She no longer was willing to go to her hair salon on the other side of town and began avoiding traveling to visit friends who lived a distance from her, because she felt it was unsafe to travel.

As time went by, Maria only felt a sense of serenity and safety when she was in her apartment. Not having enough food available, Maria began losing weight. Even though she was hungry most of the time, she was too afraid to venture out to buy the amount and types of food she needed and wanted. When friends would call to see her, she made excuses and did her best to avoid any social interaction.

One of Maria's friends telephoned her daughter in New York and told her daughter that she was concerned about Maria. Her daughter called Maria, and Maria denied that there was any problem. Maria's daughter became suspicious, and the next day she made a trip, unannounced, to Maria's apartment. When she was arrived she became alarmed at Maria's appearance. Maria was emaciated, pale, and acting very nervous. Maria kept denying that anything was wrong, but her daughter persisted in questioning her. After several discussions, Maria admitted to what has happened to her during the past several weeks.

Maria's daughter took Maria to Maria's internist to get an opinion about her condition. After examining Maria, her physician indicated that there was nothing medically wrong with Maria, but felt that the recent death of her husband may have instigated some psychological problem. He referred Maria to a psychologist who specialized in working with older adults so that Maria could be assessed and get the help that she desperately needed.

When faced with assessing an older adult for the possibility that the older adult is experiencing a psychological problem, a psychologist experiences a dilemma. That dilemma is which theoretical model of psychopathology to choose when determining a diagnosis and subsequent treatment. Does the psychologist choose the *medical model* based on the current version of the *Diagnostic and Statistical Manual of Mental Disorders* (5th ed.; *DSM-5*; American Psychiatric Association [APA], 2013) that views psychological problems as a disease, or the *person-in-environment model* that focuses on biopsychosocial etiologies of psychological problems? Further complicating this dilemma for a psychologist are the conflicting views of the *DSM-5*, the current manual used by psychologists for diagnosing the psychological problems their patients are experiencing. The APA and the American Psychological Association support the use of the *DSM-5* as a valid system for determining psychopathology. An opposing view is presented by the National Institute of Mental Health (NIMH), which views the *DSM-5* as an *unscientific and subjective system* (Lane, 2013).

Neither view is entirely relevant for a psychologist attempting to assess and diagnose psychological problems in older adults. The *DSM-5* is based primarily on research with children, adolescents, and young/middle-aged adults, which causes a psychologist to extrapolate concepts taught in most psychotherapy classes that discuss the diagnosis and treatment of children and young/middle-aged adults to older adults (Lewis, Hems, Bosanquet, & Overend, 2013). The person-in-environment model (described later in this chapter) does not provide linkage to *DSM-5* diagnoses that are needed for insurance, Medicare, and Medicaid reimbursement. In addition, the medical model, using the *DSM-5*, associates the various psychopathologies with specific psychiatric medications. The person-in-environment model does not provide such associations.

However, it must also be said that the combination of acute administration of psychiatric medications (medical model) and psychotherapy (person-in-environment model) repeatedly has been shown to be more effective than either modality alone in cases where psychological problems cause extreme dysfunction in social/vocational/academic functioning in children, adolescents, and young/middle-aged adults (Lewis et al., 2013; Sinaikin, 2010). In the case of older adults, Sadock and Sadock indicate that "the major goals of the pharmacological treatment of older persons are to improve the quality of life, maintain persons in the community, and delay or avoid their placement in nursing homes" (2008, p. 697). Therefore, positive use of psychopharmaceutical interventions in many cases prevents institutionalization of older adults, allowing for aging in place (Youdin, 2014). Negative use of psychopharmaceuticals creates many risk factors for older adults. These include dangerous side effects when psychopharmaceuticals are combined with medications used for treating chronic medical problems in older adults (*polypharmacy*), the use of antipsychotic medications to chemically restrain older adults who may be difficult to provide care for, and the risk for addiction in older adults (see Chapter 6) who are prescribed benzodiazepines for anxiety-related symptoms (Stafford et al., 2009). Therefore, because there is a limited utility in using psychopharmacological treatment for older adults, when assessing the risk/benefit ratio of such treatment, this ratio is skewed toward risk (Azermai, Bourgeois, Somers, & Petrovic, 2013).

Viewing An Older Adult Using the Medical Model

The medical model of psychopathology currently guides psychiatrists and many psychologists who are treating older adults experiencing psychological problems. Use of this model causes contradictions and distortions for the treating clinician and limits the effectiveness of treatment for older adults experiencing psychological problems. There are three areas of concern that illustrate these contradictions and distortions.

The first area of concern is the fact that only two classes of psychiatric diagnoses meet the characteristics of a disease. A disease is thought to be a phenomenon caused by an underlying biological lesion (Healy, 2002). Psychiatric diagnoses are considered diseases, but not because of a known biological cause; they are assumed to be diseases because their symptoms are similar across different cultures and social contexts, and symptoms are reduced or eliminated when treated with specific classes of medications (Horowitz, 2002). Two of the most widely accepted diagnoses fitting this definition are *schizophrenia* and *bipolar disorder*, both of which are treated with medications such as Risperdal (risperidone) and Eskalith and Lithobid (lithium).

Unfortunately, the biological theory explaining these two classes of diagnoses is inappropriately extended to all psychiatric diagnoses listed in the *DSM-5*. This represents an ongoing trend in psychiatry that reduces psychological problems to biological entities analogous to medical diseases such as cardiovascular disease, diabetes, or other disorders. Once diagnosed as a chronic psychological disease, a patient will need a lifetime of pharmacological maintenance under the assumption that if not maintained on a particular medication there is a high probability of relapse.

The second area of concern is how the current use of the *DSM-5* continues a tradition among psychiatry, managed-care companies, and insurance companies that puts pressure on psychiatrists, psychologists, hospitals, and psychiatric rehabilitation facilities to treat in the most cost-effective and short-term manner (Conrad, 2007; Harris, 2011). Therefore, psychopharmaceutical interventions are preferred over traditional talk therapies, strict limits are placed on reimbursement for the number of psychotherapy sessions in a given calendar year, and the ability to administer psychiatric medications has been extended to primary care physicians who have little or no training in psychiatry. This severely limits a psychologist's ability to treat an older adult with psychotherapeutic interventions that psychologists are trained to administer. The phenomenon of psychiatric medications being preferred over psychotherapy coincided with the development of the third edition of the *DSM*, the *DSM-III* (APA, 1980; discussed later in this chapter); psychiatrists moved their method of practice from *psychoanalysis* to *pharmacotherapy* due to the fact that traditional psychoanalysis (5 days per week for 5 years, except the month of August for the psychiatrists' vacations) was no longer reimbursable by most insurance policies (Mojabai & Olfson, 2008).

The third area of concern is the relationship that has occurred between psychiatry and pharmaceutical marketing forces. Sinaikin (2010) feels that this trend causes people, and with respect to this book, older adults, to have their psychological problems reduced to *decontextualized clusters of symptoms* that are correlated with the preestablished diagnostic categories of the *DSM-5*. Conrad (2007) indicates that the common tagline

"'*Ask your doctor if [Viagra, Paxil, Zoloft, etc.] is right for you'* reflects the new relationship between pharmaceutical manufacturers, consumers and physicians" (p. 157). This alarming trend manipulates people to self-diagnose a psychological problem, link it to a psychiatric diagnosis, and then pressure a physician to prescribe an advertised psychiatric medication. A direct consequence of this relationship between psychiatry and the pharmaceutical industry is having psychiatrists participate in marketing psychiatric medications as key *opinion leaders* while simultaneously accepting financial subsidies from the pharmaceutical industry (Elliot, 2010).

The Diagnostic and Statistical Manuals—A Brief History

The history of the *DSM*, published by the APA, begins in 1952 (APA, 2015). The first edition was called the *DSM-I*. Interestingly, this version insinuated that psychiatric problems were the reactions of one's personality to biopsychosocial stressors, which is the main premise of the person-in-environment model, discussed later in the chapter. This was followed by the *DSM-II* (APA, 1968), which was essentially the same as the *DSM-I*, but eliminated the construct of psychiatric problems caused by a reaction to biopsychosocial stressors, and advocated for the need for more comprehensive descriptions of psychiatric disorders. Both of these versions were influenced by psychoanalytic theories.

The *DSM-III* was introduced by the APA in 1980, and its authors claimed a broad consensus on diagnostic issues and categories among psychiatric professionals (Bayer & Spitzer, 1985). Despite this broad consensus, Frances (2013) indicates that psychiatric diagnoses are based on subjective judgments, not on demonstrable biological findings. Another criticism of this broad consensus is indicated by Goffman (as cited in Manning, 1980), who feels that psychiatry is composed of *tinkers*, or the invention of psychiatric syndromes to justify medical interventions under the guise of scientific identification of diseases (p. 267). The *DSM-III* was reviewed for inconsistencies and updated in 1987 to the *DSM-III-R* (APA, 1987). This version became more precise in its descriptions of psychiatric diagnoses.

A major feature of the *DSM-III* and *DSM-III-R* was the introduction of a *five-axial diagnostic system*. The five-axial system was developed to increase the precision of the process of diagnosing psychiatric disorders. The five-axial system guided the psychologist to view a patient from a comprehensive description of the symptomatology of a diagnosis or diagnoses, divided between primary psychiatric diagnoses (Axis I); personality disorders, developmental disorders, and mental retardation (Axis II); medical diagnoses and treatments that might be contributory to the psychiatric diagnosis or diagnoses being considered (Axis III); environmental factors that are affecting the patient (Axis IV); and a level of global assessment of functioning (GAF; Axis V; Halter, Rolin-Kenny, & Dzurec, 2013).

In 1994, the next edition, the *DSM-IV*, replaced the *DSM-III-R*. Despite the fact that the APA (1994) claimed that "Whatever the original cause, it must be considered a manifestation of a behavioral, psychological, or biological dysfunction in the individual" (p. 3), the emphasis of the diagnostic categories continued to promote psychiatric diagnoses as disease entities to be treated primarily by biological interventions. These biological interventions include pharmacotherapy, electroconvulsive treatment (Spector & Orrell, 2010), and capsulotomy, the successor to frontal lobotomy (Ruck et al., 2008). The *DSM-IV-TR* (4th ed., text rev.; APA, 2000) left the *DSM-IV* virtually unchanged but provided more extensive descriptions of the diagnostic categories. In addition, the five-axial system remained unchanged from its introduction in the *DSM-III*.

This trend of reducing psychological diagnoses to a biological etiology continues today, and it causes psychotherapy to be a less prominent choice of intervention, with the increased emphasis on treating patients with psychopharmacotherapy (Olfson & Marcus, 2010). For example, the *DSM-IV* produced a phenomenon of children being overdiagnosed with emotional and behavioral problems (Batstra et al., 2012) and resulted in the subsequent rampant use of psychostimulants such as Ritalin and Adderall. In addition, when psychologists do not emphasize psychotherapy, it puts older adults in a *one-down position* in which a psychiatrist or

TABLE 3.1 History of the Number of Diagnoses in Each
Edition of the *Diagnostic and Statistical Manual of Mental Disorders (DSM)*

DSM Version	Year Introduced	Number of Psychiatric Diagnoses
DSM-I	1952	106
DSM-II	1968	182
DSM-III	1980	265
DSM-III-R	1987	292
DSM-IV	1994	297
DSM-IV-TR	2000	297
DSM-5	2013	312

family physician assumes a dominant position in treatment decisions, causing a greater incidence of the use of psychiatric medications (Vilhelmsson, Svensson, & Meeuwisse, 2013).

The *DSM-5* was introduced in 2013 and continues the tradition of identifying multiple psychiatric diagnoses (Table 3.1)
that in turn are linked to various pharmacological compounds
as the primary means of treatment. This revision eliminated the
five-axial system first introduced by the *DSM-III*. The five-axial
system was eliminated because it was considered to have no scientific basis (Halter et al., 2013).

The *DSM-5* continues the *DSM* tradition of medicalization
of psychological problems (Frances, 2013), and thus puts older
adults at risk for inappropriate exposure to psychiatric medications in lieu of much-needed support and psychotherapy from
psychologists trained in geropsychology. In addition, with the
multitude of psychiatric diagnoses (Table 3.1), it is predicted that
greater numbers of people diagnosed with psychiatric conditions
will support and increase the stigmatization (see Chapter 2) of
people experiencing psychological problems (Halter et al., 2013).

Viewing an Older Adult Using the Person-in-Environment Model

As noted in the discussion of the various versions of the
DSM, viewing an older adult through a *DSM-5* lens causes a

psychologist to attribute an older adult's psychological problem to a biological etiology. If a psychologist makes this assumption, he or she places an older adult in a position diametrically opposed to other older adults with no diagnosis of psychopathology (Doll, 2008; Keyes, 2007). This inaccurate etiological view of an older adult with psychological problems caused by a biological disease precludes any possibility that he or she has the capacity of *self-restoration* and *self-upgrade* (Carr, 2008).

Self-restoration and self-upgrade are concepts explained by the *differentiated and integrated person-in-environment theory*, which explains that instead of reacting passively to environmental stressors (*passive accommodation*), an older adult engages in active problem solving with a psychologist, who may work individually with an older adult or integrate therapy with a spouse/partner, relatives, or caregiver to facilitate the older adult's problem solving (Hebblethwaite, 2013; Wapner & Demick, 2005).

The *person-in-environment theory*, developed out of *Lawton's ecological model* (Lawton & Nahemow, 1973; Nahemow, 2000), is also foundational to environmental gerontological psychology (Wahl & Weisman, 2003; see Chapter 8). The *person-in-environment model* views an older adult as interfacing with many environmental stressors—biological, psychological, and social—and the degree to which he or she is able to cope positively (*resilience*) with these converging environmental influences, or the degree of *reduction in resilience*, is reflected by symptoms that the *DSM-5* refers to as psychopathology. Consequently, a psychologist's restriction of his or her focus to a negative pathological view of an older adult may lead to a poorer clinical outcome because this view leaves absent positive aspects of an older adult that may be mobilized to facilitate treatment and improve treatment outcomes (Tedeschi & Kilmer, 2005).

Therefore, in addition to assessing negative stressors that converge on an older adult and his or her degree of resilience to such stressors, a psychologist needs to assess the strengths in an older adult's environment, and the strengths within the older adult, supporting resilience. This is an orientation developed from a subdivision of psychology called *positive psychology*.

Positive psychology was first described by Seligman and Csikszentmihalyi (2000) and later by Saleeby (2009), who further developed positive psychology in the field of social work. Therefore, the ultimate person-in-environment assessment examines the negative stressors in an older adult's environment, the strengths in the older adult's environment, and the degree of resilience within the older adult (Snyder, Ritschel, Rand, & Berg, 2006). This balanced approach has been researched and developed for children (Rashid & Ostermann, 2009), but needs to be extended to the assessment and treatment of older adults by psychologists.

The degree of resilience an older adult has when dealing with the complex and converging biopsychosocial environmental stressors can be understood through the *dialectical approach to personality development* described by Levinson (1986). The dialectical approach describes an older adult's ability to sense and understand the ever-changing environmental influences and his or her ability to cope with these influences (resilience), or his or her inability to cope with one or more of these environmental influences (reduction in resilience). The person-in-environment theory extends this dialectical approach to understanding that an older adult is interacting with many subsystems, with each forming multiple feedback loops, thus requiring complex processing by the older adult. The degree to which the older adult can process these feedback loops in a positive manner is the degree of resilience inherent in the older adult at any given time.

A final aspect of the person-in-environment theory is a psychologist's incorporation of the *theory of mindfulness*. Kabat-Zinn (1982, 1994) was one of the first theorists to integrate mindfulness with the basic concepts of the person-in-environment theory. When practicing mindfulness, a psychologist teaches an older adult to attend, as a purposeful behavior, and without judgment, to the present moment he or she is experiencing. This enables an older adult to examine aspects of his or her self and their interaction with the environment, thus facilitating choice of the most effective problem-solving strategies.

Mindfulness techniques include meditation, guided imagery, yoga, and an understanding of the relationship between a change in thinking (*reframing and cognitive restructuring*) and the resulting *positive neuroplasticity* (Sipe & Eisendrath, 2012). Positive neuroplasticity occurs when interneuronal connections are established in the brain by introducing novel stimuli. This interconnectivity between neurons creates more complex cognitive pathways that give an older adult an increased cognitive reserve. An older adult can increase his or her cognitive reserve by introducing the implementation of mindfulness relaxation techniques and cognitive restructuring.

Rosen and Erickson (1991) indicate that the optimal phenomenology of the therapeutic relationship is one in which there is a state of *positive rapport* between psychologist and patient. This is consistent with Geller, Greenberg, and Watson (2010), who feel that when a psychologist is able to bring a positive sense of self into the relationship with a patient on four levels—*physical, emotional, cognitive,* and *spiritual*—successful therapy occurs. Therefore, mindfulness techniques have the capability to enhance the well-being of the older adult patient, as well as the treating psychologist (Hölzel et al., 2011), increasing the positive rapport between the psychologist and the older adult. In addition, mindfulness practices by the psychologist help him or her to increase empathy for patients due to the development of a greater ability to experience and communicate a shared experience of the patient's suffering. Such communication of common factors in the therapeutic relationship facilitates a sense of safety in the older adult patient, causing the patient to communicate both body sensations and psychological feelings (Davis & Hayes, 2011; Hauser & Hays, 2011) to better understand his or her psychological problem, and, from such understanding, to develop problem-solving strategies.

PSYCHOLOGICAL PROBLEMS THAT OLDER ADULTS EXPERIENCE

The following subsections provide descriptions of the most common classes of psychological problems a psychologist will confront when treating an older adult patient. This discussion is restricted to classes of psychological problems rather than direct references to the *DSM-5* because the NIMH considers the *DSM-5* to be an *unscientific and subjective system* (Lane, 2013); in addition, this system is criticized as lacking evidence-based research on older adults and featuring age-biased categories that do not address older adults (Van Alphen, Sadavoy, Derksen, & Rosowsky, 2012; Van Alphen et al., 2015) . To rectify these problems, psychologists need to contribute to evidence-based research that focuses on the unique aspects of psychological problems that older adults experience. This continued evidence-based initiative is necessary because most of the information available on the various types of psychological disorders is based on studies of younger and middle-aged adults (Lewis et al., 2013).

Anxiety Disorders

Specific phobias are the most common anxieties that older adults experience, with prevalence rates in older adults up to 25.6% (Bryant, Jackson, & Ames, 2008; Sadock & Sadock, 2008). A specific phobia is an irrational fear of an object (e.g., an elevator) or a situation (e.g., a thunderstorm). Specific phobias in older adults may be co-occurring with major depression; therefore, psychologists need to rule out major depression when assessing an older adult who is experiencing a specific phobia (Chou, 2009). Likewise, most anxiety disorders in older adults often coincide with other depressive disorders (Beattle & Pachana, 2010; Gale et al., 2011). Thus, a psychologist assessing an older adult for an anxiety problem must also rule out a co-occurring depressive disorder.

There are instances in which an older adult may be misdiagnosed with an anxiety disorder. This phenomenon may occur when an older adult is suffering from sensory impairments or medical conditions. Symptoms of these impairments or conditions may mimic the symptoms of anxiety (Costa et al., 2007; Kaminer, Seedat, Potocnik, & Stein, 2002). Another problem confounding the diagnosis of an anxiety disorder, with reference to this chapter's earlier discussion of the history of the *DSM*, is that assessment information and symptom constellations developed for younger populations are not always relevant for older adults, which may cause a psychologist to overlook an anxiety disorder that an older adult is experiencing. Therefore, there is a need for the continued development of assessment instruments specifically constructed for older adults (Dennis, Boddingron, & Funnell, 2007). A comprehensive assessment procedure for older adults that is currently in use by psychologists and social workers is described by Youdin (2014, pp. 22–36).

Older adults are more likely than younger adults to experience anxiety about their health (*health anxiety*) than are younger persons (Boston & Merrick, 2010) because older adults frequently experience multiple medical problems, some acute, and most chronic. Older adults who have a high degree of frailty have a higher probability of experiencing health anxiety when compared with older adults with a low degree of frailty (Bourgault-Fagnou & Hadjistavropoulos, 2009). Health anxiety is not a traditionally assessed diagnosis, according to the medical model and the *DSM-5* (discussed earlier). However, according to the person-in-environment model (discussed earlier), the biological status of an older adult (acute or chronic medical illness) is one of the environmental stressors that may reduce an older adult's resilience. The lowering of resilience may produce symptoms characteristic of health anxiety. These symptoms include excessive worrying about medical problems, the construction of fearful outcome projections for the medical diagnosis, a constant focus on and search for information about the medical condition, and compulsive questioning of the treating physician about the prognosis of the medical condition. Health anxiety must be differentiated from hypochondria, which is a condition similar to health anxiety with the exception that the worrying and focus are on medical conditions that do not exist.

When a psychologist is treating an older adult for a dementia disorder (see Chapter 4) and subsequently has contact with whoever is providing caregiving to the older adult patient, the psychologist should be alert to whether the caregiver is a first-degree relative who may be experiencing *dementia anxiety*. Dementia anxiety is an anxiety experienced by a caregiver who is a first-degree relative of an older adult patient; the caregiver dreads and feels anxious about developing dementia, especially Alzheimer's disease, at some time in his or her lifetime (Roberts & Connell, 2000). Nearly one quarter of first-degree relatives providing care for an older adult with dementia report clinically significant anxiety (Mahoney, Regan, Katona, & Livingston, 2005). This is in contrast to caregivers of older adults who are not experiencing dementia. These caregivers do not show significant levels of caregiver anxiety (Kim & Schultz, 2008).

Mood Disorders

Major depression has a lower prevalence in older adults than in younger and middle-aged adults, but the consequences of major depression are equally serious in older adults (Blazer, 2003). Researchers predict that the number of older adults with a history of depression across the life span will continue to increase until 2050 (Heo, Murphy, Fontaine, Bruce, & Alexopoulos, 2008). Depressive symptoms in older adults have a prevalence rate of 15% (Sadock & Sadock, 2008). Future increased rates of depression in older adults may be distorted due to the removal of the exclusion for normal bereavement from a major depression diagnosis in the *DSM-5* version. This removal of the bereavement exclusion may cause an increase in major depression diagnoses because a psychologist following *DSM-5* guidelines can no longer separate a normal grief reaction from major depression (Lamb, Pies, & Zisook, 2010). Making inappropriate diagnoses of major depression in older adults will cause unnecessary inappropriate uses of antidepressant medications and electroconvulsive treatment, both, in effect, being examples of elder abuse (see Chapter 7). In previous versions of the *DSM*, it was recognized that a person can experience normal bereavement and that it is fundamentally different from major depression (Lamb et al., 2010).

With reference to the person-in-environment model, the occurrence of depression in older adults is influenced by socioeconomic status. Communities that have a disparity in socioeconomic status show higher rates of depression in older adults when compared with communities where older adults feel relatively equal in economic status (Romero, Ortiz, Finley, Wayne, & Lindeman, 2005; Takkinen et al., 2004). Consequences of depression include the exacerbation of medical conditions, physical impairments, and dementia, and, at times, death.

As noted in the earlier discussion of anxiety disorders, depressive disorders in older adults often coincide with anxiety (Gale et al., 2011). A psychologist assessing an older adult for a depressive disorder must also rule out a co-occurring anxiety disorder. In addition, a psychologist treating an older adult experiencing dementia must be alerted to assess whether a caregiver who is a first-degree relative is experiencing a depressive disorder from the distress of caring for a relative with dementia, especially if the older adult is suffering from Alzheimer's disease (Mahoney et al., 2005; Chapter 4).

Insomnia often precedes depressive disorders in older adults (Perlis et al., 2006), with an increased level of insomnia positively correlated with an increased level of depression (Manber & Chambers, 2009). Sadler, McLaren, and Jenkins (2013) feel that the facilitators of the connection between insomnia and subsequent depression are an older adult's dysfunctional beliefs about sleep (e.g., attributing events during the evening when awakened, such as needing to go the bathroom, or focusing on environmental causes for lack of sleep, such as light in the environment or sounds in the environment, as inaccurate indicators of time not asleep) and the feelings of hopelessness these beliefs create.

The majority of older adults with a bipolar diagnosis have an onset of bipolar disorder before the age of 30 (Depp & Lebowitz, 2007). Bipolar disorder in older adults is often misdiagnosed as schizophrenia, with misdiagnosis rates for minority older adults twice that of White older adults (Luggen, 2005). Bipolar disorder in older adults represents approximately 10% of admissions to psychiatric hospitals (Sherrod, Quinlan-Colwell, Lattimore, Shattell, & Kennedy-Malone, 2010). As a function of the increased longevity of older adults, bipolar diagnoses and severe psychotic and depressive diagnoses are expected to increase the prevalence of these disorders by two to three times the current rates over the next 30 years (Depp & Lebowitz, 2007). In addition, older adults with a bipolar diagnosis are at a high risk for suicide (Sherrod et al., 2010).

Older Adult Suicide

Older adults who attempt or complete suicide are more likely than younger people to have a plan and intent (Administration on Aging & Substance Abuse and Mental Health Services Administration, 2012), and are more unlikely to tell a psychologist unless directly asked specifically about *suicidal ideation, plan, intent,* and *means.* There is a gender difference in the rate of suicide. Older adult men die by suicide at a rate five times higher than the rate in older adult women (Centers for Disease Control and Prevention, 2015).

From a person-in-environment perspective, there are several risk factors (Van Orden & Conwell, 2011) that may lower an older adult's resilience and cause depression that, if severe enough, moves an older adult to high risk for a suicide attempt or suicide completion. Examples of these risk factors include polypharmacy side effects, chronic medical illnesses, poverty, death of a loved one, increased frailty, increasing incidence of subsyndromal depressive disorders, and major depression. The risk of suicide attempt or suicide completion is exponentially higher in older adults who are socially isolated (Fassberg et al., 2012).

Personality Disorders

The *DSM-5* is criticized for lacking sufficient information specific to older adults for a psychologist to assess whether an older adult has a personality disorder (Van Alphen, Bolwerk et al., 2012). Examples of the criteria suggested to determine a personality disorder appear to be age biased. These include assessing disturbance in vocational and academic functioning and interpersonal disturbances. Interpersonal disturbances is a broad category that does not exclude circumstances that might cause an older adult to have disruptions in his or her interpersonal relationships due to medical illness, disability, moving into an institutional setting, or experiencing cognitive changes and/or dementia, all of which are not appropriate indicators for a personality disorder (Segal, Coolidge, & Rosowsky, 2006; Van Alphen, Sadavoy, et al., 2012). Personality disorders, in theory, are an ongoing psychopathological process throughout the continuum of adult development (Youdin, 2014). However, many psychologists are uninformed of the changes in manifestations of personality disorders that occur in late life (Van Alphen, Rossi, Segal, & Rosowsky, 2013). This contributes to the underdiagnosis of personality disorders in older adults, or a misdiagnosis of a personality disorder (Van Alphen et al., 2015).

Psychotic Disorders

Older adults experience psychotic symptoms that are the same as those that younger and middle-aged adults experience. Symptoms may be subclinical (i.e., not fitting requirements for any recognized psychotic disorder). Ostling and Skoog (2002) studied 85-year-old adults who had psychotic symptoms but did not have co-occurring dementia (see Chapter 4). These authors found that 6.9% experienced hallucinations, 5.5% experienced delusions, and 6.9% experienced paranoid hallucinations. Because of the paucity of evidence-based research on psychotic disorders in older adults, the etiology of these symptoms is unclear. These symptoms may occur as a side effect of polypharmacy, co-occur with dementia, or occur with schizophrenic spectrum disorder (late onset), delusional disorders, major depression, bipolar disorders, substance-induced psychosis, or delirium.

Sadock and Sadock (2008) claim that late-onset schizophrenia is rare in older adults. There is a question as to whether older adults experience late-onset schizophrenia or what is seen as a *schizophrenic spectrum disorder*, which is now the favored diagnostic interpretation (Vahia et al., 2010). However, when schizophrenic spectrum disorder does occur, it is more prevalent in older adult women than in older adult men. The intensity of symptoms in older adults experiencing a schizophrenic episode is attenuated as compared with the same symptoms as experienced by children and younger adults. Interestingly, there is one reported case of a centenarian (see Chapter 1) being diagnosed with schizophrenia (Cervantes, Rabins, & Slavney, 2006). Risk factors for a schizophrenic spectrum diagnosis include paranoid and/or schizoid personality traits, being an older adult woman, social isolation, and being a recent immigrant with an overwhelming feeling of being an outsider (Mitter et al., 2005). Like schizophrenic spectrum disorder, any of the delusional disorder subtypes may occur at any time in late life (Sadock & Sadock, 2008), usually in older adults who had a prior history of being diagnosed with a personality disorder.

Later chapters describe psychotic symptoms in dementias (Chapter 4) and substance-induced psychotic symptoms (Chapter 6).

REFERENCES

Administration on Aging & Substance Abuse and Mental Health Services Administration. (2012). *Older Americans behavioral health. Issue Brief 4: Preventing suicide in older adults.* Retrieved from http://www.aoa .gov/AoA_Programs/HPW/Behavioral/docs2/Issue%20Brief%204% 20Preventing%20Suicide.pdf

American Psychiatric Association. (1952). *Diagnostic and statistical manual of mental disorders* (1st ed.). Washington, DC: Author.

American Psychiatric Association. (1968). *Diagnostic and statistical manual of mental disorders* (2nd ed.). Washington, DC: Author.

American Psychiatric Association. (1980). *Diagnostic and statistical manual of mental disorders* (3rd ed.). Washington, DC: Author.

American Psychiatric Association. (1987). *Diagnostic and statistical manual of mental disorders* (3rd ed., text rev.). Washington, DC: Author.

American Psychiatric Association. (1994). *Diagnostic and statistical manual of mental disorders* (4th ed.). Washington, DC: Author.

American Psychiatric Association. (2000). *Diagnostic and statistical manual of mental disorders* (4th ed., text rev.). Washington, DC: Author.

American Psychiatric Association. (2013). *Diagnostic and statistical manual of mental disorders* (5th ed.). Washington, DC: Author.

American Psychiatric Association. (2015). *DSM: History of the manual.* Retrieved from http://www.psychiatry.org/practice/dsm/dsm-history-of-the-manual

Azermai, M., Bourgeois, J., Somers, A., & Petrovic, M. (2013). Inappropriate use of psychotropic drugs in older individuals: Implications for practice. *Aging Health, 9*(3), 255–264. doi:10.2217/ahe.13.17

Batstra, L., Hadders-Algra, M., Nieweg, E., Van Tol, D., Pigl, S. J., & Frances, A. (2012). Childhood emotional and behavioral problems: Reducing overdiagnosis without risking undertreatment. *Developmental Medicine and Child Neurology, 54,* 492–494.

Bayer, R., & Spitzer, R. L. (1985). Neurosis, psychodynamics, and *DSM-III*: A history of the controversy. *Archives of General Psychiatry, 42*(2), 187–196.

Beattle, E. R. A., & Pachana, N. A. (2010). Double jeopardy: Co-morbid anxiety and depression in late life. *Research in Gerontological Nursing, 3,* 209–220.

Blazer, D. G. (2003). Depression in late life: Review and commentary. *Journal of Gerontology A: Biological Sciences and Medical Sciences, 58A,* 249–265.

Boston, A. F., & Merrick, P. L. (2010). Health anxiety among older people: An exploratory study of health anxiety and safety behaviors in a cohort of older adults in New Zealand. *International Psychogeriatrics, 22,* 549–558.

Bourgault-Fagnou, M. D., & Hadjistavropoulos, H. D. (2009). Understanding health anxiety among community dwelling seniors with varying degrees of frailty. *Aging and Mental Health, 13,* 226–237.

Bryant, C., Jackson, H., & Ames, D. (2008). The prevalence of anxiety in older adults: Methodological issues and a review of the literature. *Journal of Affective Disorders, 109,* 233–250.

Carr, A. (2008). *Positive psychology: The science of happiness and human strengths* (X. Xheng, Trans.). Beijing, China: China Light Industry Press.

Centers for Disease Control and Prevention. (2015). *Welcome to WISQARS™ [Web-based Injury Statistics Query and Reporting System].* Atlanta, GA: National Center for Injury Prevention and Control, Centers for Disease Control and Prevention. Retrieved from http://www.cdc.gov/injury/wisqars/

Cervantes, A. N., Rabins, P. V., & Slavney, P. R. (2006). Onset of schizophrenia at age 100. *Psychosomatics, 47,* 356–359.

Chou, K. L. (2009). Specific phobia in older adults: Evidence from the National Epidemiologic Survey on Alcohol and Related Conditions. *American Journal of Geriatric Psychiatry, 17,* 376–386.

Conrad, P. (2007). *The medicalization of society: On the transformation of human conditions into treatable disorders.* Baltimore, MD: Johns Hopkins University Press.

Costa, E., Barreto, S. M., Uchoa, E., Firmo, J. O. A., Lima-Costa, M. F., & Prince, M. (2007). Prevalence of *International Classification of Diseases,* 10th revision: Common mental disorders in the elderly in a Brazilian community—The Bambui Health Aging Study. *American Journal of Geriatric Psychiatry, 15,* 17–27.

Davis, D. M., & Hayes, J. A. (2011). What are the benefits of mindfulness? A practice review of psychotherapy-related research. *Psychotherapy, 48,* 198–208.

Dennis, R. E., Boddingron, S. J. A., & Funnell, N. J. (2007). Self-report measures of anxiety: Are they suitable for older adults? *Aging and Mental Health, 11,* 668–677.

Depp, C. A., & Lebowitz, B. D. (2007). Psychiatry (Edgemont). *Innovations in Clinical Neuroscience, 4*(6), 22–32.

Doll, B. (2008). The dual-factor model of mental health in youth. *School Psychology Review, 37,* 69–73.

Elliot, C. (2010). The secret lives of big pharma's "thought leaders." *The Chronicle of Higher Education.* Retrieved from http://chronicle.com/article/The-Secret-Lives-of-Big/124335/

Fassberg, M. M., van Orden, K. A., Duberstein, P., Erlangsen, A., Lapierre, S., Bodner, E., . . . Waern, M. (2012). A systematic review of social factors and suicidal behavior in older adulthood. *International Journal of Environmental Research and Public Health, 9*(3), 722–745.

Frances, A. (2013). The new crisis of confidence in psychiatric diagnosis. *Annals of Internal Medicine, 159*(10), 720–721.

Gale, C. R., Sayer, A. A., Cooper, C., Dennison, E. M., Starr, J. M., Whalley, L. J., . . . Deary, I. J. (2011). Factors associated with symptoms of anxiety and depression in five cohorts of community-based older people: The HALCyon (Healthy Ageing Across the Life Course) Programme. *Psychological Medicine, 41*(10), 2057–2073.

Gatz, M., & Smyer, M. A. (2001). Mental health and aging at the outset of the 21st century. In J. E. Birren & K. W. Schaie (Eds.), *Handbook of the psychology of aging* (5th ed.). San Diego, CA: Academic Press.

Geller, S. M., Greenberg, L. S., & Watson, J. C. (2010). Therapist and client perceptions of therapeutic presence: The development of a measure. *Psychotherapy Research, 20,* 599–610.

Halter, M. J., Rolin-Kenny, D., & Dzurec, L. C. (2013). An overview of the *DSM-5:* Changes, controversy, and implications for psychiatric nursing. *Journal of Psychosocial Nursing & Mental Health Services*, *51*(4), 30–39. doi:10.3928/02793695-20130226-02

Harris, G. (2011). Talk doesn't pay, so psychiatry turns instead to drug therapy. *The New York Times*. Retrieved from http://www.nytimes .com/2011/03/06/health/policy/06doctors.html?_r=1&scp=1&sq= tal%20doesnt%20pay,%20so%20psychiatry%20turn%20to%20 drug%20therapy&st=cse

Hauser, M., & Hays, D. G. (2011). The slaying of a beautiful hypothesis: The efficacy of counseling and the therapeutic process. *Journal of Humanistic Counseling, Education and Development*, *49*, 32–44.

Healy, D. (2002). *The creation of psychopharmacology*. Cambridge, MA: Harvard University Press.

Hebblethwaite, S. (2013). "I think that it could work but...": Tensions between the theory and practice of person-centred and relationship-centred care. *Therapeutic Recreation Journal*, *47*(1), 13–34.

Heo, M., Murphy, C. F., Fontaine, K. R., Bruce, M. L., & Alexopoulos, G. S. (2008). Population projection of US adults with lifetime experience of depressive disorder by age and sex from year 2005 to 2050. *Geriatric Psychiatry*, *23*, 1266–1270.

Hölzel, B. K., Lazar, S. W., Gard, T., Schumann-Oliver, Z., Vago, D. R., & Ott, U. (2011). How does mindfulness meditation work? Proposing mechanisms of action from a conceptual and neural perspective. *Perspectives on Psychological Science*, *6*, 537–559.

Horowitz, A. (2002). *Creating mental illness*. Chicago, IL: University of Chicago Press.

Kabat-Zinn, J. (1982). An outpatient program in behavioral medicine for chronic pain patients based on the practice of mindfulness meditation: Theoretical considerations and preliminary results. *General Hospital Psychiatry*, *4*, 33–47.

Kabat-Zinn, J. (1994). *Wherever you go there you are: Mindfulness meditation in everyday life*. New York, NY: Hyperion.

Kaminer, D., Seedat, S., Potocnik, F., & Stein, D. (2002). Anxiety disorders in the aged. In D. J. Stein & E. Hollander (Eds.), *Textbook of anxiety disorders* (pp. 429–440). Washington, DC: American Psychiatric Press.

Keyes, C. L. M. (2007). Promoting and protecting mental health as flourishing. A complementary strategy for improving national mental health. *American Psychologist*, *62*, 95–108.

Kim, Y., & Schultz, R. (2008). Family caregivers' strains: Comparative analysis of cancer caregiving with dementia, diabetes, and frail elderly caregiving. *Journal of Aging and Health*, *20*, 483–503.

Lamb, K., Pies, R., & Zisook, S. (2010). The bereavement exclusion for the diagnosis of major depression: To be, or not to be. *Psychiatry, 7*, 19–25.

Lane, C. (2013). The NIMH withdraws support for *DSM-5*. *Psychology Today.* Retrieved from https://www.psychologytoday.com/blog/side-effects/201305/the-nimh-withdraws-support-dsm-5

Lawton, M. P., & Nahemow, L. (1973). Ecology and the aging process. In C. Eisdorfer & M. P. Lawton (Eds.), *The psychology of adult development and aging* (pp. 619–674). Washington, DC: American Psychological Association.

Levinson, D. J. (1986). A conception of adult development. *American Psychologist, 41*, 3–13.

Lewis, H. J., Hems, D. J., Bosanquet, K. N., & Overend, K. J. (2013). Is enough being done to treat depression in the elderly? *Aging Health, 9*(3), 243–245. doi:10.2217/ahe.13.9

Luggen, A. S. (2005). Bipolar disorder: An uncommon illness? Recognizing and caring for the elderly person with bipolar disorder. *Geriatric Nursing, 26*, 326–329.

Mahoney, R., Regan, C., Katona, C., & Livingston, G. (2005). Anxiety and depression in family caregivers of people with Alzheimer's disease: The LASER-AD study. *American Journal of Geriatric Psychiatry, 13*, 795–801.

Manber, R., & Chambers, A. S. (2009). Insomnia and depression: A multifaceted interplay. *Current Psychiatry Reports, 11*, 437–442.

Manning, P. K. (1980). Goffman's framing order: Style as structure. In J. Ditton (Ed.), *The view from Goffman* (p. 267). New York, NY: St. Martin's Press.

Mitter, P., Reeves, S., Romero-Rubiales, F., Bell, P., Stewart, R., & Howard, R. (2005). Migrant status, age, gender and social isolation in very late-onset schizophrenia-like psychosis. *International Journal of Geriatric Psychiatry, 20*, 1046–1051.

Mojabai, R., & Olfson, M. (2008). National trends in psychotherapy by office-based psychiatrists. *Archives of General Psychiatry, 65*(8), 962–970.

Nahemow, L. (2000). The ecology theory of aging: Powell Lawton's legacy. In R. Rubenstein, M. Moss, & M. Kleban (Eds.), *The many dimensions of aging* (pp. 22–40). New York, NY: Springer Publishing Company.

Olfson, M., & Marcus, S. C. P. (2010). National trends in outpatient psychotherapy. *American Journal of Psychiatry, 167*(12), 1456–1463.

Ostling, S., & Skoog, I. (2002). Psychotic symptoms and paranoid ideation in a nondemented population-based sample of the very old. *Archives of General Psychiatry, 59*, 53–59.

Perlis, M. L., Smith, L. J., Lyness, J. M., Matteson, S. R., Pigeon, W. R., Jungquist, C. R., & Tu, X. (2006). Insomnia as a risk factor for onset of depression in the elderly. *Behavioral Sleep Medicine, 4*, 104–113.

Rashid, T., & Ostermann, R. F. (2009). Strength-based assessment in clinical practice. *Journal of Clinical Psychology, 65*, 488–498.

Roberts, J. S., & Connell, C. M. (2000). Illness representations among first-degree relatives of people with Alzheimer's disease. *Alzheimer Disease and Associated Disorders, 14*, 129–136.

Romero, L. J., Ortiz, I. E., Finley, M. R., Wayne, S., & Lindeman, R. D. (2005). Prevalence of depressive symptoms in New Mexico Hispanic and non-Hispanic White elderly. *Ethnicity and Disease, 15*, 691–697.

Rosen, S., & Erickson, M. H. (1991). *My voice will go with you: The teaching tales of Milton H. Erickson, M.D.* New York, NY: W. W. Norton.

Ruck, C., Karlsson, A., Steele, D., Edman, G., Meyerson, B. A., Kaj, E., . . . Svanborg, P. (2008). Capsulotomy for obsessive-compulsive disorder: Long-term follow-up of 25 patients. *Archives of General Psychiatry, 65*(8), 914–922.

Sadler, P., McLaren, S., & Jenkins, M. (2013). A psychological pathway from insomnia to depression among older adults. *International Psychogeriatrics, 25*(8), 1375–1383.

Sadock, B. J., & Sadock, V. A. (2008). *Kaplan & Saddock's concise textbook of clinical psychiatry* (3rd ed.). Philadelphia, PA: Wolters Kluwer/ Lippincott Williams & Wilkins.

Saleeby, D. (2009). *The strengths perspective in social work practice.* Boston, MA: Allyn & Bacon.

Segal, D. L., Coolidge, F. L., & Rosowsky, E. (2006). *Personality disorders and older adults: Diagnosis, assessment and treatment.* Hoboken, NJ: John Wiley.

Seligman, M. E. P., & Csikszentmihalyi, M. (2000). Positive psychology: An introduction. *American Psychologist, 55*, 5–14.

Sherrod, T., Quinlan-Colwell, A., Lattimore, T. B., Shattell, M. M., & Kennedy-Malone, L. (2010). Older adults with bipolar disorder: Guidelines for primary care providers. *Journal of Gerontological Nursing, 36*(5), 20–27.

Sinaikin, P. (2010). *Psychiatryland.* New York, NY: iUniverse.

Sipe, W. E. B., & Eisendrath, S. J. (2012). Mindfulness-based cognitive therapy: Theory and practice. *Canadian Journal of Psychiatry, 57*(2), 63–69.

Snyder, C. R., Ritschel, L. A., Rand, K. L., & Berg, C. (2006). Balancing psychological assessments: Including strengths and hope in client reports. *Journal of Clinical Psychology, 62,* 33–46.

Spector, A., & Orrell, M. (2010). Using a biopsychosocial model of dementia as a tool to guide clinical practice. *International Psychogeriatrics, 22*(6), 957–965. doi:10.1017/S1041610210000840

Stafford, A. C., Tenni, P. C., Peterson, G. M., Jackson, S. L., Hejlesen, A., Villesen, C., & Ramussen, M. (2009). Drug-related problems identified in medication reviews by Australian pharmacists. *Pharmacy World and Science, 31*(2), 216–233.

Takkinen, S., Gold, C., Pederson, N. L., Malmberg, B., Nilsson, S., & Rovine, M. (2004). Gender differences in depression: A study of older unlike-sex twins. *Aging and Mental Health, 8*(3), 187–195.

Tedeschi, R. G., & Kilmer, R. P. (2005). Assessing strengths, resilience, and growth to guide clinical interventions. *Professional Psychology: Research and Practice, 36,* 230–237.

Vahia, I. V., Palmer, B. W., Depp, C., Fellows, I., Golshan, S., & Kraemer, H. C. (2010). Is late-onset schizophrenia a subtype of schizophrenia? *Acta Psychiatrica Scandinavica, 122,* 414–426.

Van Alphen, S. P. J., Bolwerk, N., Videler, A. C., Tummers, H. A., van Royen, R. J. J., Barendse, H. P. J., . . . Rosowsky, E. (2012). Age-related aspects and clinical implementations of diagnosis and treatment of personality disorders in older adults. *Clinical Gerontologist, 1,* 27–41.

Van Alphen, S. P. J., Rossi, G., Segal, D. L., & Rosowsky, E. (2013). Issues regarding the proposed *DSM-5* personality disorders in geriatric psychology and psychiatry. *International Psychogeriatrics, 25*(1), 1–5. doi:10.1017/S1041610212001597

Van Alphen, S. P. J., Sadavoy, J., Derksen, J. J. L., & Rosowsky, E. (2012). Features and challenges of personality disorders in late life. *Aging and Mental Health, 16,* 805–810.

Van Alphen, S. P. J., van Dijk, S. D. M., Videler, A. C., Rossi, G., Diercks, E., Bouckaert, R., & Oude Voshaar, R. C. (2015). Personality disorders in older adults: Emerging research issues. *Current Psychiatry Reports, 17,* 538–545.

Van Orden, K., & Conwell, Y. (2011). Suicides in late life. *Current Psychiatry Reports, 13*(3), 234–241.

Vilhelmsson, A., Svensson, T., & Meeuwisse, A. (2013). A pill for the ill? Patients' reports of their experience of the medical encounter in the treatment of depression. *PLoS One, 8*(6), 1–8. doi:10.1371/journal.pone.0066338

Wahl, H., & Weisman, G. D. (2003). Environmental gerontology at the beginning of the new millennium: Reflections on its historical, empirical, and theoretical development. *The Gerontologist, 43*, 616–627.

Wapner, S., & Demick, J. (2005). Critical person-in-environment transitions across the lifespan. In J. Valsiner (Ed.), *Heinz Werner and developmental science* (pp. 285–305). New York, NY: Kluwer Academic/Plenum.

Winerman, L. (2012, October). The ghost in the lab. *Monitor on Psychology*. Retrieved March 15, 2015, from http://www.apa.org/monitor/2012/10/ghost.aspx

Youdin, R. (2014). *Clinical gerontological social work practice*. New York, NY: Springer Publishing Company.

Normal Cognitive Decline, Mild Cognitive Impairment, and Dementia

*Imagine a foreign country assaulting our nation and killing
500,000 Americans. We would commit hundreds of billions of
dollars to vanquish the enemy. Yet 500,000 Americans die of
Alzheimer's annually, and we continue to allocate only 1.5 percent
of the budget of the National Institutes of Health to
Alzheimer's research.*
Stanley B. Prusiner, MD (2014, p. 255)

THE PSYCHOLOGIST'S ROLE IN TREATING AN OLDER ADULT WITH DEMENTIA

A psychologist's first task when assessing an older adult for dementia is to discriminate between *normal cognitive decline, mild cognitive impairment,* and *dementia.* Normal cognitive decline occurs when one ages, but is significantly different from mild cognitive impairment and the dementias described later in this chapter. Normal cognitive decline is evidenced in many cognitive domains (McGuire, Ford, & Ajani, 2006). These include executive functioning, language difficulty, memory (Lachman, 2000), psychomotor ability (difficulty with movements), language, and speed of processing. These are normal changes in cognitive functioning that have minor effects on instrumental activities of daily living (IADLs). Examples of IADLs include an older adult's ability to drive safely, manage his or her finances, manage multiple medication schedules, or remember important appointments with health care providers. Even though these mild impairments are distressing to the older adult, they do not cause significant loss of autonomy, or require the need for supervision in the home environment (Frank et al., 2006).

If a psychologist finds during an assessment that an older adult is experiencing normal cognitive decline, the older adult must in addition be assessed for any increased level of distress that he or she may be experiencing (Vignette 4.1). This distress can be an indication that the older adult is fearing that he or she may be experiencing the beginning stages of a dementia, especially *Alzheimer's disease* (Lachman, 2000). The anxiety reaction the older adult may experience is evidenced by symptoms of disturbance in interpersonal functioning, sleep disturbance, or exacerbation of a preexisting anxiety disorder (see Chapter 3). Consequently, this fear of dementia may be heightened by the stereotype that often stigmatizes older adults (see Chapter 2) with mild memory lapses, falsely implying that they are demented (Barber & Mather, 2013; Hess, Hinson, & Hodges, 2009). Many older adults who focus on changes in their memory (between 25% and 75%, depending on the study) report that their memory has worsened as compared with when they were younger (Hanninen, Hallikinen, & Tuomainen, 2002; Jonker, Geerlings, & Schmand, 2000). Of these, 8% do progress to developing dementia (Lindsay, Sykes, McDowell, Verreault, & Laurin, 2004).

VIGNETTE 4.1 The Case of Bertha

(*Note:* Names and other identifying information have been changed to preserve confidentiality.)

Bertha is a 91-year-old widow living in a residential care facility in Los Angeles, California. Bertha has been a widow for the past 21 years. In the years immediately after her husband died, Bertha maintained an active social life and was able to continue working as an accountant for a national property development company. At age 80, Bertha retired and moved to a residential care community, one of the properties owned by her former employer. Bertha decided to move to this facility because, as she did with everything else in life, she always made plans that were conservative and with anticipation of future events. The facility she moved to seemed ideal to Bertha. She would live in her own apartment, and if necessary, she would stay in the same community and move to the company's assisted living facility, which was an extension to the building her apartment was located in. And if the worst happened, the company had a separate facility that specialized in care for Alzheimer's disease patients.

Approximately 2 years ago, Bertha's son came to visit her and noticed something out of the ordinary. On the dining room table, Bertha had stacks and stacks of bills neatly piled. Her son looked through the bills and noticed that some were 4 or 5 months old. He asked Bertha why she had all these bills piled on the dining room table. Bertha told him that the bills were very overwhelming and that she had a friend help her organize them. Her son asked if they were all paid, and Bertha said that she had not gotten to them yet. Her son became concerned, because Bertha, being an accountant, always exerted due diligence with financial matters and always paid her bills on time, never letting any bills accrue interest or penalties.

(continued)

Her son asked her if she would mind if he took over paying bills for her so that she would not be so troubled by all the bills piled on the table. Bertha replied that his help would not be necessary and that she would attend to them that week.

Her son returned to Bertha's apartment 1 month later and was shocked to see that the stack of bills was piled higher and that several collection notices were also in evidence. Her son called his brother and told him what he discovered at their mother's apartment. They arranged to meet with each other the next day.

At the meeting, they discussed having Bertha evaluated for any sign of dementia. They knew nothing about dementia, but because of her age, the obvious stereotype of dementia in older people concerned them. They called Bertha's family physician to express their concerns and ask for her advice. Bertha's physician said that she would be delighted to meet with Bertha and do an initial screening to see if there was truly something to worry about.

At the appointment with the family physician, Bertha was asked several questions, and at the end of the meeting, the physician indicated that Bertha appeared to have some cognitive problems. Her short-term memory had some disturbance, she appeared confused about her financial affairs, and, at times, she seemed to be unaware and nonparticipatory in the subsequent conversation between the physician, Bertha, and her sons. Her family physician recommended that her sons take her to a neuropsychologist for testing to determine the extent and type of her cognitive difficulties. In addition, she made a referral to a neurologist who would assess Bertha for any pathology that may be occurring in her brain that would be another reason for her symptoms. The physician indicated that the neuropsychologist and neurologist often work together to complete a comprehensive and accurate assessment when an older adult begins to show cognitive disturbances.

If an older adult is diagnosed with mild cognitive impairment or one of the many dementias (both described later in this chapter), a psychologist must take into consideration when formulating a treatment plan that a spouse/partner, relative, and/or caregiver are necessary adjuncts to the proposed treatment plan. A spouse/partner, relative, and/or caregiver may be in need of psychoeducation about mild cognitive impairment or dementia, and more often than not may be experiencing anxiety or a depressive reaction to the distress of caring for an older adult with dementia. The anxiety may be an exacerbation of a preexisting anxiety disorder, or may be *dementia anxiety*. Dementia anxiety is an anxiety most often experienced by a first-degree relative, in which this relative dreads and feels anxious about developing dementia, especially Alzheimer's disease, at some time in his or her lifetime (Roberts & Connell, 2000). A first-degree relative may also be experiencing a depressive disorder from the distress of caring for a relative with dementia, especially if the older adult is suffering from Alzheimer's disease (Mahoney, Regan, Katona, & Livingston, 2005; see Chapter 3).

NEUROPSYCHOLOGICAL CONCEPTS FOR UNDERSTANDING COGNITIVE DEFICITS IN MILD COGNITIVE IMPAIRMENT AND DEMENTIA

It must be understood by a psychologist that an older adult diagnosed with mild cognitive impairment may progress to a diagnosis of Alzheimer's disease. Similar to an older adult with mild cognitive impairment, an older adult diagnosed with any of the dementias will experience a progressive decline in functioning, which is incurable and most often fatal unless the older adult dies from another co-occurring disease or normal causes. Therefore, a good part of a psychologist's role in treating an older adult with mild cognitive impairment or a dementia is that of psychoeducation. The diagnosed older adult and his or her spouse/partner, relative, and/or caregiver are in need of understanding the pathological process the older adult is experiencing. This increase in understanding facilitates the treatment of the older adult with dementia and a reduction of consequent anxiety or depressive reactions in all participants in the treatment plan. Therefore, a psychologist must increase his or her understanding of the following neuropsychological aspects that underlie mild cognitive impairment and the various dementias.

Neuroplasticity

Neuroplasticity is a phenomenon whereby the brain has the capacity to change as a product of interpersonal (Badenoch, 2008; Siegal, 2006) interaction, in response to novel stimuli and activities (Fields, 2009), or as a result of high levels of education (Barnes & Yaffe, 2011). This is commonly known as the *use-it-or-lose-it phenomenon* (Ball, Vance, Edwards, & Wadley, 2004), or in more scientific terms, *positive neuroplasticity* and *negative neuroplasticity*. Positive neuroplasticity occurs when interneuronal connections are established. This interconnectivity between neurons creates more complex cognitive pathways that give an older adult an increased cognitive reserve. An older adult can increase his or her cognitive reserve by introducing novel stimuli such as brain-teaser puzzles, learning a new foreign language, or engaging in a task using a nondominant hand (e.g., combing one's hair with the other hand). In addition, this phenomenon of increasing cognitive reserves may occur in older adults experiencing early stages of Alzheimer's disease (see following discussion) or mild cognitive impairment (see following discussion) when the older adult engages in a challenging educational activity (Roe et al., 2008; Ye et al., 2013) or cognitive training (Belleville, 2008). Teaching an older adult how to increase positive neuroplasticity is a useful intervention that will improve functioning in an older adult experiencing mild cognitive impairment, and will delay the progression of cognitive deterioration in an older adult experiencing dementia.

Conversely, negative neuroplasticity occurs when there is a disruption in the connectivity between neurons, causing a diminishment of cognitive reserve in an older adult. This breakdown in connectivity occurs when the older adult is in a nonstimulating and/or non-novel environment, or when a biological process is causing atrophy in the brain. Such biological processes can result from stroke, tumors, plaque formation, and prions (proteins associated with brain damage causing dementia; Prusiner, 2014). When the environment is less complex, or biological disease is present, a consequential diminishment of neuroplasticity will occur, significantly lessening the cognitive reserve available to the older adult. This results in mild cognitive impairment, or any of the dementias described later in the chapter. Therefore, it is important for a psychologist to begin psychoeducation immediately after diagnosing an older adult with mild cognitive impairment, or dementia, in order to reverse as much as possible the progression of negative neuroplasticity by introducing techniques to augment and enhance positive neuroplasticity.

A dramatic example of the difference between positive neuroplasticity and negative neuroplasticity is found in a study of London taxi and bus drivers (Maguire, Woollett, & Spiers, 2006). In this study, the authors compared the imaging of the brains of taxi drivers who were given the task of driving to novel destinations with the brain imaging of bus drivers who routinely spent their time driving to fixed destinations (non-novel) in London. The taxi drivers, who were trained to memorize destinations throughout London over a 4-year period, consequently drove passengers to destinations at the passengers' request, making each trip a novel experience. After examining MRI scans of the brains of London taxi drivers and bus drivers, these researchers found that novel stimuli enhanced the cognitive reserves of London taxi drivers. The taxi drivers showed an increased volume of neurons in the hippocampus of their midbrains as compared with the bus drivers, who drove routine, predictable (non-novel) routes and did not show a corresponding increase in the hippocampus of their midbrains. The hippocampus (Figure 4.1) is the site in the midbrain in which memory is formed and consolidated.

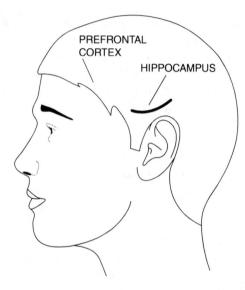

FIGURE 4.1 The location of the hippocampus in the midbrain.
Adapted from Youdin (2014).

Memory and Memory Impairments

In order to understand what type of memory is impaired, a psychologist must discriminate between *crystallized intelligence* and *fluid intelligence* (Kay, 2005). Crystallized intelligence is the representation of knowledge accumulated and stored as memory. These memories include past interpersonal relationships and associated feelings, information accrued from education, and various life experiences such as hobbies, extravocational activities, travels and vacations, and so forth. Older adults have a large storage of crystallized memories due to their longevity.

Fluid intelligence is a dynamic intelligence that indicates one's level of cognitive functioning rather than what has been learned and experienced in the past and subsequently stored. Dysfunction in any aspect of fluid intelligence may be the first indication of a dementia process (Elias & Saucier, 2006; Kay, 2005), or may be a normal occurrence in the normal aging process (Park,

O'Connell, & Thomson, 2003). Deficits in fluid intelligence are a red flag signaling further assessment by the treating psychologist.

Fluid intelligence includes *executive functioning, language, memory, psychomotor ability,* and *speed of processing.* Executive functioning (Elias & Saucier, 2006) refers to the ability of an older adult to plan and organize, rational reasoning, and the ability to problem solve. Language encompasses visual and auditory processing and the relationship of such processing to fluid as well as crystallized intelligences (Abrams, Farrell, & Margolin, 2010; Vance, Robertson, McGuinness, & Fazeli, 2010). In addition, language includes vocabulary and the ability to detect misspellings (Abrams et al., 2010). In memory, aspects of fluid intelligence are reflected in an older adult's ability to recall previously learned information and/or personal experiences (Fleischman, Wilson, Gabrieli, Bienias, & Bennett, 2004). Psychomotor ability refers to an older adult's ability to maintain his or her gait (ability to walk correctly, and speed of walking), perform gross motor movements (moving arms and legs and positioning them properly), and perform fine motor movements, as measured in reaction time and mirror tracing tests (Elias & Saucier, 2006). Speed of processing is the older adult's ability to automatically perform overlearned cognitive tasks, or easy novel tasks, with relative ease (Inzitari et al., 2007; Rodrigue, Kennedy, & Raz, 2005). This type of processing requires an older adult to process information with great speed devoid of intentional thinking and consideration. Therefore, the assessment of fluid memory is a multidimensional assessment process performed by a psychologist, usually in conjunction with a treating neurologist.

Deficits in Olfactory Functioning

Assessment of deficits in olfactory functioning are potentially useful for a psychologist who is attempting to differentiate between cognitive disturbances of normal aging and mild cognitive impairment that may progress to Alzheimer's disease. Most older adults with olfactory deficits have little or no awareness of such deficits (Djordjevic, Jones-Gotsman, De Sousa, & Cherkow,

2007). However, because the olfactory sensory system (sense of smell) is intimately connected to the gustatory sensory system (sense of taste), older adults with olfactory deficits may complain that their foods do not taste right or the same as they are used to, or may start using excessive amounts of salt or spices to enhance the taste of their foods. Such complaints may alert the treating psychologist, spouse/partner, relative, and/or caregiver that olfactory functioning is impaired in the older adult.

Deficits in olfactory functioning in an older adult are thought to herald the onset of mild cognitive impairment, and are a possible predictor of Alzheimer's disease (Djordjevic et al., 2007; Eibenstein et al., 2005; Luzzi et al., 2007). Because olfactory deficits limit an older adult from detecting odors, an older adult may be at risk due to not recognizing a gas leak in his or her home, eating spoiled food, or not being able to smell smoke from a fire in the house.

MILD COGNITIVE IMPAIRMENT AND THE MOST COMMON DEMENTIAS TREATED BY A PSYCHOLOGIST

Mild cognitive impairment and the most common dementias seen by a psychologist are described here. All of these diagnoses are complicated to make and have multidimensional symptoms. As noted earlier, the dementias are incurable and in most cases are the primary cause of death for older adults who suffer from dementia. The psychologist's role in treating an older adult is also multidimensional. He or she needs to provide psychoeducation, interventions to enhance positive neuroplasticity, treatment for secondary anxiety or depressive problems, and psychotherapeutic care for the spouse/partner, relative, and/or caregiver of an older adult experiencing mild cognitive impairment or dementia. In addition, a psychologist may be called upon to provide care to survivors of an older adult who dies after being treated for mild cognitive impairment or dementia (see Chapter 9).

Mild Cognitive Impairment

Historically, *mild cognitive impairment* (MCI; Krahn et al., 2006) is considered a *bridge diagnosis* that occurs between the functioning of a normal older adult and an older adult experiencing one of the dementia diagnoses (Petersen et al., 1999; Tröster, 2008). The diagnosis of MCI (Krahn et al., 2006) is a dichotomous diagnosis made in two distinctly different cognitive domains—*single-domain* and *multiple-domain MCI* (Petersen, 2004). Single-domain MCI is indicated when an older adult's memory is impaired without impairment in the other aspects of fluid intelligence—executive functioning, language, psychomotor ability, and speed of processing. Multiple-domain MCI is indicated when one or more of the aspects of fluid intelligence are dysfunctional along with a dysfunction in memory (Saunders & Summers, 2010, 2011). MCI is considered to be a *preclinical stage* of dementia (Lyketsos et al., 2002; Mega et al., 2000).

Single- and multiple-domain MCIs are further classified into four subtypes by other authors (Albert et al., 2011; Winbald et al., 2004) as follows: *single-domain amnestic MCI* (a-MCI), in which there is a presence of memory disturbance; *multiple-domain amnestic MCI* (a-MCI+), in which there is a presence of memory disturbance along with a disturbance in executive functioning, language, memory, psychomotor ability, and/or speed of processing; *single-domain nonamnestic MCI* (na-MCI); in which there is dysfunction in one domain but not in memory; and *multiple-domain nonamnestic-MCI* (na-MCI+), in which there are multiple-domain dysfunctions but no dysfunction in memory.

In addition to determining whether an older adult is presenting with single- or multiple-domain MCI subtypes, a psychologist must also ascertain whether the older adult has a co-occurring depressive disorder, anxiety, and/or apathy (Apostolova & Cummings, 2008; Geda et al., 2008; Lyketsos et al., 2002; see Chapter 3). Any of these diagnoses often precedes a diagnosis of a single- or multiple-domain MCI subtype. Conversely, a psychologist assessing an older adult with any of these psychological diagnoses must ascertain whether the older adult is experiencing any dysfunction in executive functioning, language, memory, psychomotor ability, and speed of processing (Spira, Rebok, Stone, Kramer, & Yaffe, 2012; Tung, Chen, & Takahashi, 2013) in order to diagnose a co-occurring MCI, whether of the single- or multiple-domain subtype. These co-occurring diagnoses are also considered risk factors for progression from MCI to Alzheimer's disease (Mondrego & Ferrandez, 2004; Teng, Lu, & Cummings, 2007). Ramakers et al. (2013) dispute this finding and feel that these co-occurring psychological diagnoses are not predictors for progression to Alzheimer's disease (see following discussion of Alzheimer's disease). Jungwirth, Zehetmayer, Hinterberger, Tragl, and Fischer (2012) feel that MCI may predispose an older adult to *vascular dementia* (see following discussion of vascular dementia). Further research is needed to clarify whether MCI is truly a bridge diagnosis to the dementias.

Vascular Dementia

Vascular dementia (VaD) is the second-most-common type of dementia throughout the world (Bandyopadhyay et al., 2014). VaD can result from multiple strokes or any injury to the small or large vessels in the brain. VaD may occur suddenly and progress over time, or may subside periodically during an older adult's lifetime. VaD is often preceded by a-MCI (Petersen et al., 2001; Winbald et al., 2004) or na-MCI (Petersen, 2004). VaD may predispose an older adult to Alzheimer's disease (Jagust, 2001; see following discussion of Alzheimer's disease).

When an older adult suffers multiple small strokes (*punctate strokes*) with no behavioral or psychological symptoms, VaD is diagnostically considered as *vascular cognitive impairment* (VCI). VCI causes cognitive dysfunction in executive functioning, language, memory, psychomotor ability, and speed of processing, the same symptomatology as seen in MCI (described earlier). In addition, VaD can cause psychological symptoms, which are categorized as *behavioral and psychological symptoms of dementia* (BPSDs; Gupta et al., 2013). BPSDs in VaD include agitation, aggression, apathy, and depressive symptoms.

Risk factors for VaD include *atrial fibrillation* (an abnormal heart rhythm that causes the heart to beat rapidly, with irregular beats) and *metabolic syndrome* (Raffaitin et al., 2009). Metabolic syndrome comprises five symptoms: hypertension, abdominal obesity, high triglycerides, low levels of high-density-lipoprotein (HDL) cholesterol, and elevated fasting glycemia (diabetes). In addition, another risk factor for VaD is elevated blood cholesterol levels.

Frontotemporal Dementia (Pick's Disease/ Complex)

Frontotemporal dementia (FTD) was previously termed *Pick's disease* or *Pick's complex* (Hodges, 2001; Kertesz, 2003). FTD is often preceded by na-MCI (Petersen, 2004). Older adults with this disorder have an abnormal amount of *Pick bodies* and *Pick cells* inside of the nerve cells in the frontal and temporal lobes of the brain (Figure 4.2). These cells contain an abnormal amount of a protein called *tau*. This is thought to be the cause of FTD. When studied at autopsy, FTD has a prevalence rate of 3% to 10% in patients previously diagnosed with dementia (Kertesz, 2005). FTD is often confused with Alzheimer's disease (see following discussion of Alzheimer's disease) by clinicians (Snowden et al., 2001). Despite this confusion, clinical reports indicate an FTD prevalence of approximately 20% of older adults diagnosed with dementia (Varma et al., 1999).

FTD has combined behavioral (Boxer & Miller, 2005; Chan et al., 2009; Hodges, 2001; Thompson, Patterson, & Hodges, 2003) and cognitive symptoms (Hodges, Martinos, Woollams, Patterson, & Adlam, 2008; Hodges & Patterson, 2007; Knibb & Hodges, 2005; Snowden, Thompson, & Neary, 2004). They include *apathy* (lack of feeling, emotions, or interest; Kumfor & Piguet, 2012), *loss of insight, perseveration* (repetition of a word, phrase, or gesture), *personal neglect, logopenia* (difficulty understanding complex instructions, frequent pauses when speaking, inability to repeat sentences or string of words), *anomia* (inability to name objects), and *semantic aphasia* (difficulty generating or recognizing

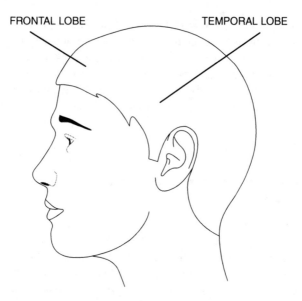

FIGURE 4.2 The frontal and temporal lobes of the brain.
Adapted from Youdin (2014).

familiar words). Other researchers consider FTD to be a heterogeneous diagnosis with two sub diagnoses (Valverde, Jimenez-Escrig,
Gobernado, & Barón, 2009). FTD has a behavior variant (bv-FTD)
with symptoms of *loss of insight*, *personality changes*, and *disturbances
in social cognition* (lack of concern about social norms, impaired
emotional judgment, and gluttony), and a language variant called
primary progressive aphasia (McKeith et al., 2005), with symptoms
of *logopenia*, *anomia*, and *semantic aphasia*.

Dementia With Lewy Bodies

Dementia with Lewy bodies (DLB) was originally described as
Lewy body disease in 1980 (Kosaka, Matsushita, Oyanagi, &
Mehraein, 1980). Lewy bodies are spherical structures that
are found in neurons in the brain and were first described in
1912 by F. H. Lewy (Lewy, 1912). DLB and VaD are the second most common dementias aside from Alzheimer's disease,

and DLB is often preceded by na-MCI or a-MCI (Chiba et al., 2012; Molano et al., 2010; Petersen, 2004; Winbald et al., 2004). In addition, older adults with DLB often experience *prodromal symptoms* (symptoms preceding a diagnosis) of *REM sleep behavior disorder, constipation, orthostatic hypotension* (dizziness on standing), *visual hallucinations,* and *sensory motor dysfunction* (movement problems). DLB is seen as a spectrum disorder with *Alzheimer's disease* and *Parkinson's disease dementia.*

Three prominent psychopathological symptoms (Ballard et al., 2001) differentiate DLB from Alzheimer's disease. Visual hallucinations are more frequent with DLB, occurring in more than 50% of cases, and delusions in DLB are more evident than in Alzheimer's disease, found in up to 75% of cases. In addition, unlike in Alzheimer's disease, delusions in DLB are not as persistent. In some older adults with DLB the visual hallucinations may be coupled with a belief by the older adult that he or she has been replaced by an identical imposter (Josephs, 2007; Thaipisuttikul, Lobach, Zweig, Gurnani, & Galvin, 2013). This phenomenon is called *Capgras syndrome.* Unlike in Alzheimer's disease, the use of antipsychotic medications for delusions and visual hallucinations is contraindicated for DLB because this would produce profound *extrapyramidal symptoms,* such as continuous spasms and muscle contractions, motor restlessness, muscle rigidity, tremor, and irregular jerky movements (Ballard et al., 2001). Conversely, when an older adult is diagnosed with Alzheimer's disease, antipsychotic medications are administered. Finally, depression is more frequent in DLB (approximately 30% of cases) but, as with delusions, is not as persistent in DLB as it is in Alzheimer's disease.

Lewy Body Dementia and Parkinson's Disease Dementia

When dementia occurs with *Parkinson's disease* (PD), dementia symptoms that occur simultaneously with the onset of PD or within 1 year of the diagnosis of PD are attributed to DLB. About 70% of older adults suffering from DLB have PD (Graeber & Müller, 2003). Dementia symptoms that occur after 1 year of the onset of PD are considered *Parkinson's disease dementia* (PDD;

Emre et al., 2007). A psychologist often makes diagnostic errors as to the type of dementia occurring with PD because in many cases it is difficult to pinpoint the onset of PD. DLB is differentiated from PDD (McKeith et al., 2005) by *visual hallucinations* and *cognitive symptoms* that are more predominant in DLB. There are greater disturbances in executive functioning in DLB than in PDD, whereas in PDD there are greater auditory attention deficits (Aarsland, Londos, & Ballard, 2009; Singleton & Gwinn-Hardy, 2004).

Alzheimer's Disease

In 1911, Alois Alzheimer presented a clinical case at a medical conference in Tübingen, Germany, of an older adult experiencing memory problems, behavioral dysfunctions, and neuropathological findings of *plaques* and *neurological tangles* that today is diagnosed as *Alzheimer's disease*. After the Alzheimer's case presentation, noted psychiatrist Emil Kraepelin, who was a pioneer in attributing mental dysfunction to a biological basis, named the syndrome described by Alois Alzheimer as Alzheimer's disease (Möller & Graeber, 1998). It is estimated that by the year 2040 there will be approximately 81 million older adults suffering from Alzheimer's disease due to the increased longevity older adults are now experiencing, increasing the opportunity for chronic debilitating Alzheimer's disease to manifest in older adults worldwide (Ferri et al., 2005). Alzheimer's disease ranks third in causes of death in the United States, and the threat of being diagnosed with Alzheimer's disease is an anticipatory anxiety (Laditka et al., 2011) experienced by many older adults (Clark & Karlawish, 2003).

Alzheimer's disease is a chronic, debilitating disease process that begins with inclusions of abnormal proteins (*tau* and *amyloid plaques*) in neurons in the brain, although this stage of the illness does not demonstrate any cognitive impairment in the older adult. This is followed by subtle changes in cognition and memory (see earlier discussion of MCI), and then more obvious cognitive decline and memory impairment that leads to significant dementia and death in end-stage Alzheimer's disease

(Albert et al., 2011; Dubois et al., 2010; Jack et al., 2011; Petersen et al., 2001; Winbald et al., 2004).

The progression just described can be broken down into seven stages of Alzheimer's disease (Beers, Porter, Jones, Kaplan, & Berkwits, 2011; Youdin, 2014). This description of the seven stages of Alzheimer's disease is useful for a psychologist to know when assessing an older adult for dementia, and/or counseling an older adult's spouse/partner, relative, or caregiver who is seeking information and advice on the care of an older adult experiencing Alzheimer's disease. These stages (adapted from Youdin, 2014) are as follows:

Stage 1: The older adult at this stage does not show any discernable memory problem on assessment. However, on a neuronal level, structural changes may occur as early as 20 years prior to recognition by a psychologist, which usually occurs in Stage 3. In addition, mild disturbances in executive functioning, language, psychomotor ability, and speed of processing may occur.

Stage 2: During this stage, an older adult may begin experiencing forgetfulness with names of acquaintances, and may lose or misplace personal objects such as car or house keys, a wallet, eyeglasses, or other items regularly used by the older adult. This type of forgetfulness is recognized by the older adult, but is not obvious to others who are in frequent contact with the older adult or the older adult's psychologist.

Stage 3: In contrast to Stage 2, people who are in frequent contact with the older adult in Stage 3 might notice problems in the older adult's memory that occur in a home setting or workplace. Errors in naming people close to the older adult become obvious. The struggle of the older adult to remember new names of acquaintances or fellow workers becomes more frequent and obvious to others. This stage shows a more obvious deterioration in executive functioning, language, memory, psychomotor ability, and speed of processing, in addition to memory problems.

Concentration difficulties occur, which begin to impair social and/or occupational functioning. Disorganization in the older adult increases, as evidenced by a greater frequency of losing objects, and problems in the older adult's ability to organize daily activities at home and/or in a vocational setting. Concentration difficulties begin to be evidenced in an older adult's ability to read, and the individual often has difficulty in following a story or passage because of an increasing inability to retain information from passages read.

Stage 4: In this stage, an older adult has increasing difficulty in remembering recent events or recently learned information. A mental status exam reveals a marked inability to perform calculations or remember digital spans. An older adult will have difficulty in abstract thinking, which is manifested as having difficulties in managing finances, forgetting to pay bills, having difficulty planning social events with others, and displaying marked impairment in vocational settings. On examination, an older adult will have difficulty remembering aspects of his or her personal history. These reduced cognitive abilities often cause an older adult to socially withdraw, which is often misdiagnosed as depression or social anxiety.

Stage 5: At this stage, a continued deterioration in executive functioning, language, memory, psychomotor ability, and speed of processing occurs. Memory impairment is marked, evidenced by severe deficits in daily functioning. Family members are often needed to assist in the activities of daily living (ADLs) of the older adult, or to retain outside help for this assistance. Assistance with ADLs includes dressing (choosing proper combinations of clothing), housecleaning, meal preparation, and financial organization. On assessment, the older adult will often be disoriented in regard to person, time, or place. The older adult will make errors or be unable to respond to questions of general knowledge. Greater deficits are seen in performing calculations, remembering three objects, and recalling digital spans. Impairment in knowledge of personal details becomes more extensive, generalizing from recalling his or her name to errors and omissions of personal historical events.

Stage 6: Most, if not all, recent events are difficult for the individual at this stage to remember. However, distant events may still be recalled, because crystallized memory is relatively intact. Help with ADLs is needed. These include eating, bathing, and bathroom activities. In many older adults at this stage, delusional thinking is evidenced along with paranoid thought processes. These pathological thought processes might lead to violent behavior. In addition, it is not uncommon for the older adult to be disoriented in two or more spheres (person, place, or time).

Stage 7: This final stage finds the older adult bedridden, unable to feed himself or herself, and incontinent. In addition, the older adult is unable to communicate except in very primitive ways, such as hand signaling or verbal grunts, rather than clear verbal commands.

SECONDARY CONSEQUENCES OF THE DEMENTIAS

Driving Retirement

A psychologist is often called upon by a spouse/partner, relative, or caregiver to determine if and when driving must be prevented with an older adult who has dementia (Breen, Breen, Moore, Breen, & O'Neil, 2007). Unfortunately, there is no definite marker that would indicate driver retirement (Eby & Molnar, 2012). Having a diagnosis of dementia does not automatically mean retirement from driving. However, some of the symptomatology of the dementias become risk factors for dangerous driving and require vigilance by a spouse/partner, relative, or caregiver to provide feedback to the psychologist, who may then determine the threshold where driving by the older adult with dementia must stop. Symptoms of concern include cognitive decline, dysfunction in fluid memory, problems with visuospatial and sensory motor awareness, attention difficulties, and problems with executive functioning (Aksan et al., 2012). At some point during the first 3 years after the diagnosis of dementia, the decision of driving cessation usually occurs (Aksan et al., 2012).

Inappropriate Sexual Behaviors

Psychologists who work in continuing care residential settings or nursing homes, or with spouses/partners, relatives, or caregivers of an older adult experiencing dementia, often have to deal with the inappropriate sexual behaviors (ISBs) exhibited by an older adult experiencing a dementia. ISBs are defined as sexual behaviors that interfere with functioning and occur at inappropriate times with nonconsenting people (Alkhalil, Tanvir, Alkhalil, & Lowenthal, 2004). ISBs include inappropriate unwanted fondling, exposure of the genitals, public masturbation, removal of one's clothes in a public place, delusions of marital infidelity, and the display of pornographic material in public (Alagiakrishnan et al., 2005; Tsatali, Tsolaki, Christodoulou, & Papaliagkas, 2011; Youdin, 2014). Older adults in nursing homes or continuing care residential settings may exhibit ISBs by entering the bed of a fellow resident without being invited or making unwanted sexual advances to staff members, residents, or visitors (Higgins, Barker, & Begley, 2005). ISBs are more common in men and older adults in the moderate to severe stages of dementia (Alagiakrishnan et al., 2005).

DEMENTIA IN IMPRISONED OLDER ADULTS

Forensic geropsychology, a subfield of geropsychology, offers opportunities for psychologists who are interested in working in correctional settings. Imprisoned adults over the age of 50 constitute the fastest-growing cohort of the prisoner population, which corresponds to the overall increase in the population of older adults outside of prison in the United States (Beckett, Peternelj-Taylor, &

Johnson, 2003; Reimer, 2008). This creates an opportunity for psychologists interested in a career in forensic geropsychology to study the needs of this population of older adults.

For those older adults experiencing dementia, Fazel, McMillan, and O'Donnell (2002) indicate that incarceration of these older adults is inappropriate because the prison facilities are not equipped to handle the needs of older adults suffering from dementia. There are limited resources available to these older adults because prisons are designed for a younger and more violent population (Crawley & Sparks, 2005; Crawley, Wallace, Loeffelholz, & Sales, 2005). Older adults have difficulty walking long distances for meals, recreation, or vocational activity. Correction officers are trained to maintain order and are not trained to assist older adults with ADLs (see Chapter 1). Older adult prisoners suffering from dementia are more likely to be abused by younger prisoners and older prisoners who are not suffering from dementia (Kerbs & Jolley, 2007).

From a policy and humanistic standpoint, older adult prisoners suffering from dementia need not be in prison. These older adults are no longer a threat to society and would be better served in a nursing home setting with the required security, or, better still, through the initiation of a compassionate release for older adult prisoners suffering from dementia (Williams, Sudore, Greifinger, & Morrison, 2011). This would enable them to have their medical and psychological needs met, and in the case of release from prison, they may return to spouses/partners and relatives who could provide the care they require (Binswanger, Krueger, & Steiner, 2009). Removing an older adult with dementia from prison is an advocacy opportunity for psychologists to facilitate proper treatment of these older adults suffering from dementia.

REFERENCES

Aarsland, D., Londos, E., & Ballard, C. (2009). Parkinson's disease dementia and dementia with Lewy bodies: Different aspects of one entity. *International Psychogeriatrics*, 21(2), 216–219. doi:10.1017/S1041610208008612

Abrams, L., Farrell, M. T., & Margolin, S. J. (2010). Older adults' detection of misspellings during reading. *Journals of Gerontology. Series B, Psychological Sciences and Social Sciences, 65,* 680–683.

Aksan, N., Anderson, S. W., Dawson, J. D., Johnson, A. M., Uc, E. Y., & Rizzo, M. (2012). Cognitive functioning predicts driver safety on road tests 1 and 2 years later. *Journal of the American Geriatrics Society, 60,* 99–105.

Alagiakrishnan, K., Lim, D., Brahim, A., Wong, A., Wood, A., Senthilselvan, A., . . . Kagan, L. (2005). Sexually inappropriate behaviour in demented elderly people. *Postgraduate Medical Journal, 81,* 463–466.

Albert, M. S., DeKosky, S., Dickson, D., Dubois, B., Feldman, H. H., Fox, N. C., . . . Phelps, C. H. (2011). The diagnosis of mild cognitive impairment due to Alzheimer's disease: Recommendations from the National Institute on Aging–Alzheimer's Association workgroups on diagnostic guidelines for Alzheimer's disease. *Alzheimer's & Dementia, 7*(3), 270–279.

Alkhalil, C., Tanvir, F., Alkhalil, B., & Lowenthal, D. T. (2004). Treatment of sexual disinhibition in dementia: Case reports and review of the literature. *American Journal of Therapeutics, 11,* 231–235.

Apostolova, L. G., & Cummings, J. L. (2008). Neuropsychiatric manifestations in mild cognitive impairment: A systematic review of the literature. *Dementia and Geriatric Cognitive Disorders, 25,* 115–126.

Badenoch, B. (2008). *Being a brain-wise therapist: A practical guide to interpersonal neurobiology.* New York, NY: W. W. Norton.

Ball, K. K., Vance, D. E., Edwards, J. D., & Wadley, V. G. (2004). Aging and the brain. In M. Rizzo & P. J. Eslinger (Eds.), *Principles and practice of behavioral neurology and neuropsychology* (pp. 795–809). Philadelphia, PA: Saunders.

Ballard, C., O'Brien, J. T., Swann, A. G., Thompson, P., Neill, D., & McKeith, I. G. (2001). The natural history of psychosis and depression in dementia with Lewy bodies and Alzheimer's disease: Persistence and new cases over 1 year of follow-up. *Journal of Clinical Psychiatry, 62,* 46–49.

Bandyopadhyay, T., Biswas, A., Roy, A., Guin, D., Gangopadhyay, G., Sarkhel, S., . . . Senapati, A. (2014). Neuropsychiatric profiles in patients with Alzheimer's disease and vascular dementia. *Annals of Indian Academy of Neurology, 17*(3), 325–330. doi:10.4103/0972-2327.138520

Barber, S. J., & Mather, M. (2013). Stereotype threat can enhance, as well as impair, older adults' memory. *Psychological Science, 24,* 2522–2529.

Barnes, D. E., & Yaffe, K. (2011). The projected effect of risk factor reduction on Alzheimer's disease prevalence. *The Lancet Neurology, 10*, 819–828.

Beckett, J., Peternelj-Taylor, C., & Johnson, R. L. (2003). Growing old in the correctional system. *Journal of Psychosocial Nursing & Mental Health Services, 41*(9), 12–18.

Beers, M., Porter, R. S., Jones, T. V., Kaplan, J. L., & Berkwits, M. (Eds.). (2011). *Merck manual of diagnosis and therapy* (18th ed.). Whitehouse Station, NJ: Merck Research Laboratories.

Belleville, S. (2008). Cognitive training for persons with mild cognitive impairment. *International Psychogeriatrics, 20*(1), 57–66.

Binswanger, I. A., Krueger, P. M., & Steiner, J. F. (2009). Prevalence of chronic medical conditions among jail and prison inmates in the USA compared with the general population. *Journal of Epidemiology and Community Health, 63*(1), 912–919.

Boxer, A. L., & Miller, B. L. (2005). Clinical features of frontotemporal dementia. *Alzheimer Disease and Associated Disorders, 19*, S3–S6.

Breen, D. A., Breen, D. P., Moore, J. W., Breen, P. A., & O'Neil, D. (2007). Driving and dementia. *British Medical Journal, 334*, 1365–1369.

Chan, D., Anderson, V., Pijenburg, Y., Whitwell, J., Barnes, J., Scahill, R., . . . Fox, N. C. (2009). The clinical profile of right temporal lobe atrophy. *Brain, 132*, 1287–1298.

Chiba, Y., Fujishiro, H., Iseki, E., Ota, K., Kasanuki, K., Hirayasu, Y., & Satoa, K. (2012). Retrospective survey of prodromal symptoms in dementia with Lewy bodies: Comparison with Alzheimer's disease. *Dementia and Geriatric Cognitive Disorders, 33*, 273–281.

Clark, C. M., & Karlawish, J. H. T. (2003). Alzheimer disease: Current concepts and emerging diagnostic and therapeutic strategies. *Annals of Internal Medicine, 138*(5), 400–410.

Crawley, E., & Sparks, R. (2005). Hidden injuries? Researching the experiences of older men in English prisons. *Howard Journal of Criminal Justice, 44*, 345–356.

Crawley, E., Wallace, R. B., Loeffelholz, P. L., & Sales, M. (2005). Institutional thoughtlessness in prisons and its impacts on the day-to-day prison lives of elderly men. *Journal of Contemporary Criminal Justice, 21*, 350–363.

Djordjevic, J., Jones-Gotsman, M., De Sousa, K., & Cherkow, H. (2007). Olfaction in patients with mild cognitive impairment and Alzheimer's disease. *Neurobiology of Aging, 29*, 693–706.

Dubois, B., Feldman, H. H., Jacova, C., Cummings, J. L., DeKosky, S., Barberger-Gateau, P., . . . Scheltens, P. (2010). Revising the definition of Alzheimer's disease: A new lexicon. *The Lancet Neurology, 9*(11), 1118–1127.

Eby, D. W., & Molnar, L. J. (2012). Cognitive impairment and driving safety. *Accident Analysis & Prevention, 49,* 261–262.

Eibenstein, A., Fioretti, A. B., Simaskou, M. N., Sucapane, P., Mearelli, S., Mina, C., . . . Fusetti, M. (2005). Olfactory screening test in mild cognitive impairment. *Neurological Sciences, 26,* 156–160.

Elias, L. J., & Saucier, D. M. (2006). *Neuropsychology: Clinical and experimental foundations.* Boston, MA: Pearson.

Emre, M., Aarsland, D., Brown, R., Burn, D. J., Duyckaerts, C., Mizuno, Y., . . . Dubois, B. (2007). Clinical diagnostic criteria for dementia associated with Parkinson's disease. *Movement Disorders, 22*(12), 1689–1707.

Fazel, S., McMillan, J., & O' Donnell, I. (2002). Dementia in prison: Ethical and legal implications. *Journal of Medical Ethics, 28*(3), 156–159.

Ferri, C. P., Prince, M., Brayne, C., Brodaty, H., Fratiglioni, L., Ganguli, M., . . . Scazufca, M. (2005). Global prevalence of dementia: A Delphi consensus study. *The Lancet, 366,* 2112–2117.

Fields, R. D. (2009). *The other brain: From dementia to schizophrenia, how new discoveries about the brain are revolutionizing medicine and science.* New York, NY: Simon & Schuster.

Fleischman, D. A., Wilson, R. S., Gabrieli, J. D. E., Bienias, J. L., & Bennett, D. A. (2004). A longitudinal study of implicit and explicit memory in old persons. *Psychology and Aging, 19,* 617–625.

Frank, L., Lloyd, A., Flynn, J. A., Kleinman, L., Matza, L. S., Margolis, M. K., . . . Bullock, R. (2006). Impact of cognitive impairment on mild dementia patients and mild cognitive impairment patients and their informants. *International Psychogeriatrics, 18,* 151–162.

Geda, Y. E., Roberts, R. O., Knopman, D. S., Petersen, R. C., Christianson, T. J., Pankratz, V. S., . . . Rocca, W. A. (2008). Prevalence of neuropsychiatric symptoms in mild cognitive impairment and normal cognitive aging. *Archives of General Psychiatry, 65,* 1193–1198.

Graeber, M. B., & Müller, U. (2003). Dementia with Lewy bodies: Disease concept and genetics. *Neurogenetics, 4*(4), 157–162. doi:10.1007/s10048-003-0155-y

Gupta, M., Dasgupta, A., Khwaja, G., Chowdhury, D., Patidar, Y., & Batra, A. (2013). The profile of behavioral and psychological symptoms in vascular cognitive impairment with and without dementia. *Annals of Indian Academy of Neurology, 16*(4), 599–602. doi:10.4103/0972-2327.120488

Hanninen, T., Hallikinen, M., & Tuomainen, S. (2002). Prevalence of mild cognitive impairment: A population-based study in elderly subjects. *Acta Neurologica Scandinavica, 106,* 148–154.

Hess, T. M., Hinson, J. T., & Hodges, E. A. (2009). Moderators of and mechanisms underlying stereotype threat effects on older adults' memory performance. *Experimental Aging Research, 35,* 153–177.

Higgins, A., Barker, P., & Begley, C. (2005). Hypersexuality and dementia: Dealing with inappropriate sexual expression. *British Journal of Nursing, 13,* 1130–1134.

Hodges, J. R. (2001). Frontotemporal dementia (Pick's disease): Clinical features and assessment. *Neurology, 56,* S6–S10.

Hodges, J. R., Martinos, M., Woollams, A. M., Patterson, K., & Adlam, A. L. (2008). Repeat and point: Differentiating semantic dementia from progressive non-fluent aphasia. *Cortex, 44,* 1265–1270.

Hodges, J. R., & Patterson, K. (2007). Semantic dementia: A unique clinicopathological syndrome. *The Lancet Neurology, 6,* 1004–1014.

Inzitari, M., Newman, A. B., Yaffe, K., Boudreau, R., de Rekeneire, N., Shorr, R., . . . Rosano, C. (2007). Gait speed predicts decline in attention and psychomotor speed in older adults: The Health, Aging and Body Composition Study. *Neuroepidemiology, 29,* 156–162.

Jack, C. J., Albert, M. S., Knopman, D. S., McKhann, G. M., Sperling, R. A., Carriool, M. C., . . . Phelps, C. H. (2011). Introduction to the recommendations from the National Institute on Aging–Alzheimer's Association workgroups on diagnostic guidelines for Alzheimer's disease. *Alzheimer's & Dementia, 7*(3), 257–262.

Jagust, W. (2001). Untangling vascular dementia. *The Lancet, 358*(9299), 2097–2098.

Jonker, C., Geerlings, M. I., & Schmand, B. (2000). Are memory complaints predictive for dementia? A review of clinical and population-based studies. *International Journal of Geriatric Psychiatry, 15,* 983–991.

Josephs, K. A. (2007). Capgras syndrome and its relationship to neurodegenerative disease. *Archives of Neurology, 64,* 1762–1766.

Jungwirth, S., Zehetmayer, S., Hinterberger, M., Tragl, K. H., & Fischer, P. (2012). The validity of amnestic MCI and non-amnestic MCI at age 75 in the prediction of Alzheimer's dementia and vascular dementia. *International Psychogeriatrics, 24*(6), 959–966. doi:10.1017/S1041610211002870

Kay, J. (2005). Crystallized intelligence versus fluid intelligence. *Psychiatry*, *68*, 9–13.

Kerbs, J. J., & Jolley, J. M. (2007). Inmate-on-inmate victimization among older male prisoners. *Crime and Delinquency*, *53*, 187–218.

Kertesz, A. (2003). Pick Complex: An integrative approach to frontotemporal dementia: Primary progressive aphasia, corticobasal degeneration, and progressive supranuclear palsy. *Neurologist*, *9*, 311–317.

Kertesz, A. (2005). Frontotemporal dementia: One disease, or many? Probably one, possibly two. *Alzheimer Disease and Associated Disorders*, *19*(Suppl. 1), S19–S24.

Knibb, J. A., & Hodges, J. R. (2005). Semantic dementia and primary progressive aphasia: A problem of categorization? *Alzheimer Disease and Associated Disorders*, *19*(Suppl. 1), S7–S14.

Kosaka, K., Matsushita, M., Oyanagi, S., & Mehraein, P. (1980). A cliniconeuropathological study of the "Lewy body disease." *Seishin Shinkeigaku Zasshi*, *82*, 292–311.

Krahn, D. D., Bartels, S. J., Coakley, E., Oslin, D. W., Chen, H., McIntyre, J., . . . Levkoff, S. E. (2006). PRISM-E: Comparison of integrated care and enhanced specialty referral models in depression outcomes. *Psychiatric Services*, *57*(7), 946–953.

Kumfor, F., & Piguet, O. (2012). Disturbance of emotion processing in frontotemporal dementia: A synthesis of cognitive and neuroimaging findings. *Neuropsychology Review*, *22*(3), 280–297. doi:10.1007/s11065-012-9201-6

Lachman, M. E. (2000). Promoting a sense of control over memory aging. In L. Backman, R. D. Hill, & A. Stigsdotter-Neely (Eds.), *Cognitive rehabilitation in old age* (pp. 106–120). New York, NY: Oxford University Press.

Laditka, J. N., Laditka, S. B., Liu, R. U. I., Price, A. E., Wu, B. E. I., Friedman, D. B., . . . Logsdon, R. G. (2011). Older adults' concerns about cognitive health: Commonalities and differences among six United States ethnic groups. *Ageing and Society*, *31*(7), 1202–1228. doi:10.1017/S0144686X10001273

Lewy, F. E. (1912). Paralysis agitans I. Pathologische Anatomie (von F. H. Lewy). In M. Lewandowsky & G. Abelsdorff (Eds.), *Handbuch der Neurologie III*. Berlin, Germany: J. Springer.

Lindsay, J., Sykes, E., McDowell, I., Verreault, R., & Laurin, D. (2004). More than the epidemiology of Alzheimer's disease: Contributions of the Canadian Study of Health and Aging. *Canadian Journal of Psychiatry*, *49*(2), 83–91.

Luzzi, S., Snowden, S. S., Neary, D., Coccia, M., Provinciali, L., & Lambon Ralph, A. M. (2007). Distinct patterns of olfactory impairment in Alzheimer's disease, semantic dementia, frontotemporal dementia and corticobasal degeneration. *Neuropsychologia, 45,* 1823–1831.

Lyketsos, C. G., Lopez, O., Jones, B., Fitzpatrick, A. L., Breitner, J., & DeKosky, S. (2002). Prevalence of neuropsychiatric symptoms in dementia and mild cognitive impairment: Results from the Cardiovascular Health Study. *JAMA, 288,* 1475–1483.

Maguire, E. A., Woollett, K., & Spiers, H. J. (2006). London taxi drivers and bus drivers: A structural MRI and neurophysiological analysis. *Hippocampus, 16,* 1091–1101.

Mahoney, R., Regan, C., Katona, C., & Livingston, G. (2005). Anxiety and depression in family caregivers of people with Alzheimer's disease: The LASER-AD study. *American Journal of Geriatric Psychiatry, 13,* 795–801.

McGuire, L. C., Ford, E. S., & Ajani, U. A. (2006). Cognitive functioning as a predictor of functional disability in later life. *American Journal of Geriatric Psychiatry, 14,* 36–42.

McKeith, I. G., Dickson, D., Lowe, J., Emre, M., O'Brien, J. T., Feldman, H. H., . . . Yamada, M. (2005). Diagnosis and management of dementia with Lewy bodies: Third report of the DLB Consortium. *Neurology, 65*(12), 1863–1872.

Mega, M. S., Lee, L., Dinov, I. D., Mishkin, F., Toga, A. W., & Cummings, J. L. (2000). Cerebral correlates of psychotic symptoms in Alzheimer's disease. *Journal of Neurology, Neurosurgery and Psychiatry, 69,* 167–171.

Molano, J., Boeve, B. F., Ferman, T., Smith, G. E., Parisi, J., Dickson, D., . . . Petersen, R. C. (2010). Mild cognitive impairment associated with limbic and neocortical Lewy body disease: A clinicopathological study. *Brain, 133,* 540–556.

Möller, H. J., & Graeber, M. B. (1998). The case described by Alois Alzheimer in 1911. Historical and conceptual perspectives based on the clinical record and neurohistological sections. *European Archives of Psychiatry and Clinical Neuroscience, 248,* 111–122.

Mondrego, P. J., & Ferrandez, J. (2004). Depression in patients with mild cognitive impairment increases the risk of developing dementia of the Alzheimer type: A prospective cohort study. *Archives of Neurology, 61,* 1290–1293.

Park, H. L., O'Connell, J. E., & Thomson, R. G. (2003). A systematic review of cognitive decline in the general elderly population. *International Journal of Geriatric Psychiatry, 18,* 1121–1134.

Petersen, R. C. (2004). Mild cognitive impairment as a diagnostic entity. *Journal of Internal Medicine, 256*, 183–194.

Petersen, R. C., Doody, R., Kurz, A., Mohs, R. C., Morris, J. C., Rabins, P. V., . . . Winbald, B. (2001). Current concepts in mild cognitive impairment. *Archives of Neurology, 58*, 1985–1992.

Petersen, R. C., Smith, G. E., Waring, S. C., Ivnik, R. J., Tangalos, E. G., & Kokmen, E. (1999). Mild cognitive impairment: Clinical characterization and outcome. *Archives of Neurology, 56*, 303–308.

Prusiner, S. B. (2014). *Madness and memory.* New Haven, CT: Yale University Press.

Raffaitin, C., Gin, H., Empana, J.-P., Helmer, C., Berr, C., Tzourio, C., . . . Barberger-Gateau, P. (2009). Metabolic syndrome and risk for incident Alzheimer's disease or vascular dementia: The Three-City Study. *Diabetes Care, 32*(1), 169–174.

Ramakers, I. H. G. B., Verhey, F. R. J., Scheltens, P., Hampel, H., Soininen, H., Aalten, P., . . . Visser, P. J. (2013). Anxiety is related to Alzheimer cerebrospinal fluid markers in subjects with mild cognitive impairment. *Psychological Medicine, 43*(5), 911–920. doi:10.1017/S0033291712001870

Reimer, G. (2008). The graying of the U.S. prisoner population. *Journal of Correctional Health Care, 14*, 202–208.

Roberts, J. S., & Connell, C. M. (2000). Illness representations among first-degree relatives of people with Alzheimer's disease. *Alzheimer Disease and Associated Disorders, 14*, 129–136.

Rodrigue, K. M., Kennedy, K. M., & Raz, N. (2005). Aging and longitudinal change in perceptual-motor skill acquisition in healthy adults. *Journals of Gerontology. Series B, Psychological Sciences and Social Sciences, 60*, P174–P181.

Roe, C. M., Mintun, M. A., D'Angelo, G., Xiong, C., Grant, E. A., & Morris, J. C. (2008). Alzheimer's disease and cognitive reserve: Variation of education effect with carbon 11-labeled Pittsburgh compound B uptake. *Archives of Neurology, 64*, 1467–1471.

Saunders, N. L. J., & Summers, M. J. (2010). Attention and working memory deficits in mild cognitive impairment. *Journal of Clinical and Experimental Neuropsychology, 32*, 350–357.

Saunders, N. L. J., & Summers, M. J. (2011). Longitudinal deficits to attention, executive and working memory in subtypes of mild cognitive impairment. *Neuropsychology, 25*, 237–248.

Siegal, D. J. (2006). An interpersonal neurobiology approach to psychotherapy: Awareness, mirror neurons, and neuroplasticity in the development of well-being. *Psychiatric Annals, 36*(4), 247–258.

Singleton, A., & Gwinn-Hardy, K. (2004). Parkinson's disease and dementia with Lewy bodies: A difference in dose? *The Lancet, 364*(9440), 1105–1107.

Snowden, J. S., Bathgate, D., Varma, B., Blackshaw, A., Gibbons, Z. C., & Neary, D. (2001). Distinct behavioral profiles in frontotemporal dementia and semantic dementia. *Journal of Neurology, Neurosurgery and Psychiatry, 70*, 323–332.

Snowden, J. S., Thompson, J. C., & Neary, D. (2004). Knowledge of famous faces and names in semantic dementia. *Brain, 127*, 860–872.

Spira, A. P. P., Rebok, G. W. P., Stone, K. L. P., Kramer, J. H. P., & Yaffe, K. (2012). Depressive symptoms in oldest-old women: Risk of mild cognitive impairment and dementia. *American Journal of Geriatric Psychiatry, 20*(12), 1006–1015.

Teng, E., Lu, P. H., & Cummings, J. L. (2007). Neuropsychiatric symptoms are associated with progression from mild cognitive impairment to Alzheimer's disease. *Dementia and Geriatric Cognitive Disorders, 24*, 253–259.

Thaipisuttikul, P., Lobach, I., Zweig, Y., Gurnani, A., & Galvin, J. E. (2013). Capgras syndrome in dementia with Lewy bodies. *International Psychogeriatrics, 25*(5), 843–849. doi:10.1017/S1041610212002189

Thompson, S. A., Patterson, K., & Hodges, J. R. (2003). Left/right asymmetry of atrophy in semantic dementia: Behavioral-cognitive implications. *Neurology, 61*, 1196–1203.

Tröster, A. I. (2008). Neuropsychological characteristics of dementia with Lewy bodies and Parkinson's disease with dementia: Differentiation, early detection, and implications for "mild cognitive impairment" and biomarkers. *Neuropsychology Review, 18*(1), 103–119. doi:10.1007/s11065-008-9055-0

Tsatali, M. S., Tsolaki, M. N., Christodoulou, T. P., & Papaliagkas, V. T. (2011). The complex nature of inappropriate sexual behaviors in patients with dementia: Can we put it into a frame? *Sexuality and Disability, 29*(2), 143–156. doi:10.1007/s11195-010-9187-z

Tung, E. E., Chen, C. Y. Y., & Takahashi, P. Y. (2013). Common curbsides and conundrums in geriatric medicine. *Mayo Clinic Proceedings, 88*(6), 630–635.

Valverde, A. H., Jimenez-Escrig, A., Gobernado, J., & Barón, M. (2009). A short neuropsychologic and cognitive evaluation of frontotemporal dementia. *Clinical Neurology and Neurosurgery, 111*(3), 251–255. doi:10.1016/j.clineuro.2008.10.012

Vance, D. E., Robertson, A. J., McGuinness, T., & Fazeli, P. L. (2010). How neuroplasticity and cognitive reserve protect cognitive functioning. *Journal of Psychosocial Nursing & Mental Health Services, 48*(4), 23–30.

Varma, A. R., Snowden, J. S., Lloyd, J. J., Talbot, P., Mann, D., & Neary, D. (1999). Evaluation of the NINCDS-ADRDA criteria in the differentiation of Alzheimer's disease and frontotemporal dementia. *Journal of Neurology, Neurosurgery and Psychiatry, 66*(2), 184–188.

Williams, B. A., Sudore, R. I., Greifinger, R. B., & Morrison, R. S. (2011). Balancing punishment and compassion for seriously ill prisoners. *Annals of Internal Medicine, 155*(2), 122–126.

Winbald, B., Palmer, K., Kivipelto, M., Jelic, V., Fratiglioni, L., Wahlund, L.-O., . . . Petersen, R. C. (2004). Mild cognitive impairment—beyond controversies, towards a consensus: Report of the International Working Group on Mild Cognitive Impairment. *Journal of Internal Medicine, 256*, 240–246.

Ye, B. S., Seo, S. W., Cho, H., Kim, S. Y., Lee, J.-S., Kim, E.-J., . . . Na, D. L. (2013). Effects of education on the progression of early- versus late-stage mild cognitive impairment. *International Psychogeriatrics, 25*(4), 597–606. doi:10.1017/S1041610212002001

Youdin, R. (2014). *Clinical gerontological social work practice.* New York, NY: Springer Publishing Company.

5

Older Adults and Their Sexual Lives

My daughter says it's disgusting. No one wants to think about
their grandparents having sex.

Erica Jong (Bussel, 2011)

Psychologists need to be alert to the phenomenon of avoiding discussing sexuality with older adult patients because they embrace the idea (see Chapter 2) (Hinchiliff & Gott, 2011) that older adults are asexual, or because they lack the knowledge of older adult sexuality (Gott, Hinchiliff, & Galena, 2004; Hillman, 2011; Lindau, Leitsch, Lundgerg, & Jerome, 2006). Bouman and Arcelus (2001) suggest that more training is needed in older adult sexuality for mental health professionals, who most often neglect taking comprehensive sexual histories of older adults during assessment sessions. This neglect in understanding older adults and their sexual lives is an example of ageism in mental health workers. Fournier called this avoidance the *cringe factor*

(Fournier, 2000). The cringe factor represents the idea that sexual activity is for the young, and that older adults engaging in sexual activity is either disgusting or does not occur (Hillman, 2011).

In addition, many older adults do not seek help with sexual problems they are experiencing because of *self-stigma* (see Chapter 2), which causes them to internalize distorted beliefs about older adult sexuality. In addition, they may lack knowledge about their sexual functioning, or have a reticence about talking with health care professionals about their sexual issues (Taylor & Gosney, 2011). Therefore, psychologists need to incorporate psychoeducation about older adult sexuality when counseling an older adult about normal and problematic sexual functioning (Shaw, 2012; Taylor & Gosney, 2011).

In contrast to the distorted concepts about older adult sexuality that many health care professionals, including psychologists, hold, when older adults are questioned about their sexuality they report that they find sexual activity enjoyable and a source of pleasure, and a significant positive aspect of their lives (Beckman, Waern, Gustafson, & Skoog, 2008; Bouman, 2008; Rosen & Bachman, 2008). Sexuality is alive and well throughout all cohorts (see Chapter 1) of older adults, no matter how old (Lindau & Gavrilova, 2010). May older adults who were in the past constrained by the notion that sexual activity should only occur within a marriage, or only for procreation, now find themselves questioning such constraint. Being in a time of life where they are no longer able to procreate, or may not be in a marriage but have a sexual partner, causes in many older adults a new sense of sexual liberation. Consequently, older adults today enjoy sexual activity within and without marriage (Fisher, 2010). Even though 85% of older adults over the age of 50 report a decrease in frequency of sexual activity, of the same group, 65% report that sexual activity is more fulfilling (Saga, 2011). This is additional evidence supporting the need for psychologists to address sexual issues with older adults and to validate older adults' interest and participation in active sexual activity (Lochlainn & Kenny, 2013).

HEALTH BENEFITS AND SEXUALITY

With the changing demographics of older people, especially with the aging of the baby-boom generation (see Chapter 1), older adults are living longer, tend to be healthier than previous cohorts, and consequently are reporting frequent and satisfying sexual lives (Fisher, 2010; Lindau & Gavrilova, 2010). Psychologists can be a key force in supporting and promoting sexual activity in older adults and educating older adults on the positive health benefits derived from sexual activity. These benefits include decreased pain sensitivity, lower levels of or no depression, a more positive view of intimate relationships, and consequent increased self-esteem (Addis et al., 2006; Araujo, Mohr, & McKinlay, 2004; Davis, 2012; Heiman et al., 2011).

Fisher (2010) indicates that this *healthy trend* is not evident in all older adults. Many older adults struggling with psychosocial stressors find a decrease in their sexual activity and consequently do not gain the advantage from the positive health benefits just discussed. A major psychosocial stressor is poverty and/or financial worries. According to the person-in-environment theory (see Chapter 3), when an older adult does not have financial worries or psychological stress converging on him or her, resilience levels remain higher, and consequently fewer symptoms of distress are evidenced, enabling these older adults to have a more satisfactory sexual life (Lindau & Gavrilova, 2010) than those with financial worries and high stress levels. Other reasons for diminished sexual activity in older adults occur when an older adult becomes disabled, has functional limitations, or experiences a loss of a sexual partner (Breland, 2013). Diminished sexual activity in some older adults leads to problems with depression and/or anxiety (see Chapter 3).

Other psychosocial variables that determine the degree of sexual activity and intimacy in older adults include biology, health status, mental health status, self-stigma, partnership/no partnership, cultural attitudes, and sexual orientation (Bach, Mortimer, VandeWeerd, & Corvin, 2013; DeLamater, 2012; Hillman, 2011; Hinchiliff & Gott, 2011; Lindau & Gavrilova, 2010; Montemurro & Gillen, 2013; Syme, 2014; Waite & Das, 2010).

HETEROSEXUAL PARTNERED OLDER ADULTS

Being in heterosexual marriages or partner relationships becomes a significant predictor of sexual interest and activity due to the ongoing ability for each person to benefit from social and emotional exchanges between them (DeLamater, 2012). Partnered older adult sexual activity remains the same between partners (relative to each partner) until at least age 74 (with 62.8% of women and 74.7% of men participating in sexual activity), and then a significant decline in sexual activity begins between the ages of 75 and 84 (with 41.4% of women and 54.2% of men participating in sexual activity) (Waite, Laumann, Das, & Schumm, 2009). The most frequent sexual behaviors that partnered couples engage in include caressing, foreplay, hugging, kissing, masturbation, and vaginal intercourse (Schick et al., 2010).

When disability or medical problems intervene, DeLamater (2012) suggests that any or all of these sexual behaviors enjoyed by older adults may transition to the use of assistive devices, sexual enhancement medications, and increased verbal communications of affection. This finding appears to be a bit naïve. When disability or medical problems interfere with an older adult's ability to maintain the sexual activity that he or she was used to, a psychologist is often needed to address how the older adult can transition to sexual activity that is other than the norm he or she would choose. In addition to supportive counseling and psychoeducation, a psychologist must recognize that this change in sexual activity is, in addition, confounded by an older adult focusing on how his or her sexual activity is no longer the same as when younger. Therefore, when an older adult is suffering from medical problems or disability, he or she finds engaging in sexual activity more difficult, despite the fact that he or she still maintains a drive to achieve sexual fulfillment (Breland, 2013). A psychologist can help the older adult construct a new purpose for his or her sexuality, building on the strength of, and motivating factor of, the sexual drive that is still intact.

Older adult men are more likely than women to continue to have the benefits of a partnered relationship due to the increased longevity of older adult women and the increased mortality of older adult men, making more women available to men than men to women (Waite & Das, 2010). In addition, these authors indicate that older adult men will tend to marry or partner with younger women, further reducing opportunities for older adult women to couple with men. This is an example of patriarchal control over women that transcends all adult developmental stages. Therefore, there is a need for psychologists to help older adult women to overcome obstacles that impede their sexual activity by intervening with emancipatory psychoeducational interventions (Baldissera, Bueno, & Hoga, 2012).

OLDER ADULT WOMEN

Older adult women who report high levels of sexual satisfaction also claim to have a strong sense of well-being and subsequent health benefits (better health, experiencing fewer medical problems) (Addis et al., 2006; Davison, Bell, LaChina, Holden, & Davis, 2009). When there is a decline in sexual activity, the cause is usually after loss of a partner (Bouman, 2008; Breland, 2013; Tressel et al., 2007). Other causes of sexual activity decline in older adult women include being a victim of sexual abuse or domestic violence, abandonment by a sexual partner, presence of an eating disorder, and presence of a negative sense of self (Wiegel, Scepkowski, & Barlow, 2006). A negative sense of self in older adult women can be attributed to the sociocultural pressures of an emphasis on beauty and youth (Montemurro & Gillen, 2013) by the media and younger adults, and the choice of older adult men to choose younger women as sexual partners over the availability of older adult women in their respective cohorts (Waite & Das, 2010).

The four most common concerns held by older adult women about their sexuality are inability to reach orgasm, lack of desire to engage in sexual activity, problems with vaginal lubrication, and experiencing pain while engaging in sexual intercourse (DeLamater, 2012). These symptoms are caused by menopause, atrophy of the vaginal wall, narrowing of the vaginal canal, and decreased vaginal lubrication.

Heterosexual women who remarry in later life report higher levels of sexual activity that transition to higher levels of emotional intimacy as compared to prior married life when they were younger (Clarke, 2006). The higher levels of emotional intimacy help overcome compromises to their sexual relationships with spouses when disability or medical conditions limit the amount or types of sexual activity the couple experience. Common medical conditions affecting older adult women's sexual activity include cardiovascular disease, cancer, degenerative and rheumatoid arthritis, diabetes, kidney disease, spinal cord injury, stroke, and urinary incontinence (Bach et al., 2013; DeLamater, 2012).

As a consequence of older adult women being socialized to be passive to a male partner, and because of the fact that most older adult men were not socialized to be a romantic partner, to invest time in foreplay, and to know how to stimulate a woman to orgasm, many older adult women report a lessening of interest in sexual activity (Baldissera et al., 2012; Basson, 2000). Therefore, there is a need for psychologists to initiate psychoeducational programs to help correct these errors in patriarchal sexual morays.

OLDER ADULT MEN

Men in general tend to maintain sexual interest and sexual activity throughout their adult developmental stages (see Chapter 1), from 35 years of age to the old-old adult developmental stage (Avis, 2000; Laumann, Paik, & Rosen, 1999). Sexual interest remains high throughout these developmental stages, but sexual activity declines in most men as they age. Kalra, Subramanyam, and Pinto (2011) found that 58% of older adults above 60 years of age reported being sexually active, as compared with older adults below the age of 60 with a 72% prevalence of sexual activity. Within these statistics, sexual activity decline is greater in women than in men. This is in part due to the lack of availability of older adult men due to the greater numbers of older adult women, and the tendency discussed earlier for older adult men to choose younger women when they lose a sexual partner.

Most older adult men attribute the decline in their sexual activity to experiencing erectile dysfunction (Tressel et al., 2007). Older adult men experiencing erectile dysfunction have a prevalence rate of 52% to 64%, irrespective of sexual desire (Smith, Mulhall, Deveci, Monaghan, & Reid, 2007). Another concern of older adult men is premature climax (Bacon, Mittleman, Kawachi, & Giovannucci, 2003; Lindau et al., 2007). Erectile dysfunction and premature ejaculation are caused by decline in testosterone and longer refractory periods (amount of time needed to achieve a new erection after ejaculation), which in turn cause a decrease in frequency of erections (Rosen, Wing, Schneider, & Gendrano, 2005).

With the current availability of oral medications for erectile dysfunction, men tend to readily present for treatment with their primary care physicians or urologists (Bacon et al., 2003). Because of pharmaceutical advertising, older adult men are put under extensive pressure to use oral medications to enhance their abilities to have and maintain erections (Conrad, 2005). This phenomenon is an outgrowth of the medicalization of sexuality and causes older adult men to be engaged in *virility surveillance*. Virility surveillance is represented by older adult men self-monitoring their sexual functioning, comparing it with their experiences from when they were young, and then determining that any deviation from their younger experiences is considered a sign of disordered sexual functioning (Marshall, 2010). In addition, the medicalization of sexuality is similar to the *medicalization of psychiatry*, discussed in Chapter 3, whereby older adults undergo a similar process of pharmaceutical advertising coercing older adults to self-diagnose psychological problems and pressure their treating physicians to prescribe psychiatric medications.

The medical status of older adult men is more predictive of their level of sexual activity than is true for women (Araujo et al., 2004; Lindau & Gavrilova, 2010). Older adult men tend to react more negatively to medical problems than older adult women, causing a greater diminishment of sexual activity in older adult men as compared with older adult women. Older adult men's health problems include cardiovascular disease, cancer, degenerative and rheumatoid arthritis, diabetes, kidney disease, spinal cord injury, stroke, and urinary incontinence (Bach et al., 2013; DeLamater, 2012). Unfortunately, these medical problems contribute to a prevalence of one third of older adult men being treated with oral medications for erectile dysfunction that does not respond to treatment (Corona et al., 2010; Hatzimouratidis & Hatzichristou, 2005). This dispels the myth promoted by pharmaceutical companies that medication will make older men perform like younger men and illustrates a negative consequence of pharmaceutical companies pressuring older adult men to ask their physicians to prescribe sexual enhancement oral medications that offer a miraculous cure for erectile dysfunction. The problem of erectile dysfunction is better addressed with counseling by a psychologist, who can determine the best course of treatment for older adult men with erectile dysfunction, be it with psychotherapy, psychoeducation, oral medications, or a combination of these interventions.

Another problem that affects older adult men is whether to use a condom or not to use a condom. This dilemma is related to misinformation about sexual risks in late life (that they exist only with younger people), anxiety related to condom use (fear of not feeling sensations and consequently an inability to maintain an erection), or a misconception that condoms are only used to prevent pregnancy (Hillman, 2011). Not using a condom becomes a risk factor for contracting, or spreading, HIV (see discussion later in this chapter) and other sexually transmitted diseases, such as herpes, chlamydia, and human papilloma virus (HPV).

SPECIAL CONSIDERATIONS FOR LGBT OLDER ADULTS

Lesbian, gay, bisexual, and transgender (LGBT) older adults are discriminated against by most researchers and clinicians who, while maintaining a heterosexual bias along with the ageist assumptions discussed earlier, have neglected to produce research and clinical reports addressing issues of sexuality unique to LGBT older adults. This is because older LGBT adults are considered to be an *invisible* population (Department of Health, 2001). Therefore, most sexual activity that is other than traditional heterosexual intercourse is not referenced as being normal, or is simply not addressed (Marshall, 2011). One possible solution to this problem is for researchers to use an inclusive lens that studies all variations of sexual activity, from hugging to various aspects of foreplay and types of intercourse to subsequent feelings of highly satisfying emotional intimacy, whether through men–women interaction, men–men interaction, or women–women interaction (Taylor & Gosney, 2011; Waite et al., 2009). This would bring about a phenomenon whereby there would be less discrimination against the LGBT community.

LGBT older adults, in the current cohorts, are fewer in number than younger cohorts when *coming out* about their sexual orientation (Hinchiliff & Gott, 2011). By limiting exposure and outward ownership of their sexual orientation, these older adults consequently limit the scope of their social environment that would enable finding suitable sexual partners, and partners for intimate relationships. In addition, many LGBT older adults (approximately 14%) report that they do not come forward as being an older gay male, older lesbian, older bisexual, or older transgender adult to their health care providers (Heaphy, Yip, & Thompson, 2003), which puts them at considerable risk for having an undiagnosed sexually transmitted disease, or transmitting such to others. This situation is further complicated by the fact that many health care providers report never encountering LGBT older adults or asking older adults about their sexual orientation (Age Concern, 2006).

As with heterosexual older adult males, as discussed earlier, older gay male adults also experience erectile dysfunction. However, these older adults are further distressed by erectile dysfunction because this is experienced as unacceptable to their lifestyle (Adams, 2003). The distress they experience arouses a conflict that underlies gay male culture—the loss of youthful sexual prowess and the subsequent limitation to the multiple sexual encounters and sexual vigor that were experienced as a young adult.

DEMENTIA AND SEXUALITY

Dementia (see Chapter 4) complicates the situation for older adults when one or both sexual partners are experiencing dementia (Vignette 5.1). The perplexing question is whether an older adult experiencing dementia has the ability to make his or her own sexual decisions and give consent for sexual activity (Hillman, 2011).

VIGNETTE 5.1   The Case of an Older Adult Man Engaging in Sexual Activity With His Wife Who Was Experiencing Dementia

In this case, which occurred in Iowa, the husband was found not guilty of sexually abusing his wife who suffered from Alzheimer's disease (Belluck, 2015). In this case, the wife of an older adult man was suffering from Alzheimer's disease and was residing in a nursing home. At times, he would engage in sexual activity in his wife's room, which she shared with a roommate. Sexual activity only occurred with a drawn curtain. At other times, sexual activity occurred when this man took his wife out of the nursing home for a home visit and church attendance.

He was arrested after his wife died, based on a complaint from his wife's roommate, who indicated that she frequently heard noises that represented sexual activity coming from the vicinity of her roommate's bed. She indicated that she did not see any sexual activity because a curtain was always drawn. In addition, the husband's semen was identified in stains on the wife's bed.

(continued)

VIGNETTE 5.1 (*continued*)

At trial, the jury found this man not guilty of sexually abusing his wife. Testimony indicated that they had a mutually loving relationship. Rape kit evidence showed that there were no signs of rape (no signs or injury, or proof of intercourse). This man indicated that he consistently followed nursing home protocol, which indicated to *limit sexual activity* with his wife, which he interpreted as *limiting intercourse*.

Di Napoli, Breland, and Allen (2013) found that 67.5% of female residents of nursing homes who were experiencing dementia were sexually active with older adult male residents who were not experiencing dementia. In comparison, 53.6% of older adult males experiencing dementia reported sexual contact with older adult females also experiencing dementia. Most staff members are uncomfortable with this type of sexual activity because they are influenced by the preconception that older adults do not engage in sexual activity as do young and middle-aged adults (Katz, 2013). This is thought to be a defense mechanism called *intrinsic unwatchability* (Williams, Ylanne, & Wadleigh, 2007). Fortunately, when exposed to psychoeducational programs initiated by psychologists, most nursing home staff members appreciate being given the necessary information and intervention techniques to help residents in their care to engage in appropriate consensual sexual activity with fellow residents (Di Napoli et al., 2013).

There is also a need for training programs for caregivers of older adults experiencing dementia. Psychologists need to develop psychoeducational caregiver programs that teach caregivers how to manage older adult patients who act out sexual behaviors (see Chapter 4). In addition, this type of training needs to be coordinated with nursing home staff members who serve the same adults (Bauer, McAuliffe, Nay, & Chenco, 2013; Beebe & Mills, 2013). Once trained, many staff members are more permissive with these residents and, surprisingly, have less negative views of same-sex couples (see earlier discussion on LGBT older adults). For those staff members who are not responsive to this training, additional interventions by a psychologist become necessary if they are allowed to maintain their employment.

HIV AND OLDER ADULTS

Approximately 16.5% of sexually active older adults have a diagnosis of HIV infection. In addition, 5% of older adults over the age of 60 die as a consequence of HIV infection (Prejean et al., 2011). Prejean et al. feel that the incidence of HIV infections in older adults will increase exponentially in the coming years. The older adults in this category do not fit the stigmatized assumption of being gay males. HIV-infected older adults are heterosexual older adult men and older adult women, gay males, lesbians, and transgendered older adults (Onen, Shacham, Stamm, & Overton, 2010).

Older adults infected with HIV report that they are divorced or have recently lost a sexual partner, that they do not have accurate knowledge of how HIV is transmitted, and that one sexual partner does not use a condom or uses a condom on a random basis (Savasta, 2004; Schick et al., 2010). Older adult women, being unconcerned about becoming pregnant, may facilitate an attitude that condom use by a sexual partner is unnecessary, increasing the risk for them to be exposed to an HIV infection, or they may be pressured by an older adult male partner that condom use is unnecessary due to the lack of a threat of pregnancy (Lindau et al., 2006, 2007). When an older adult male becomes a widower, there is an increased risk for the transmission of HIV and/or other sexually transmitted diseases, such as herpes, chlamydia, and HPV, within the first 6 months of his wife's death (Smith & Christakis, 2009) due to the phenomenon of having multiple sexual partners and not using a condom (Vignette 5.2).

VIGNETTE 5.2   The Case of Marvin—"Having the Best Time of My Life"

(*Note:* Names and other identifying information have been changed to preserve confidentiality.)

Marvin is an 86-year-old retired factory owner living in a retirement community in Boca Raton, Florida. Marvin's wife died a year ago, after 52 years of marriage. During their marriage, Marvin remained faithful to his wife. He would often say, "I didn't like those of my friends who fooled around. It's terrible what they did to their wives; I would never do that to Barbara." Marvin does admit that despite staying monogamous in his marital relationship, he found sexual activity with Barbara unexciting and at times boring. However, because of his commitment to his marriage, Marvin looked past the lack of excitement and enjoyment in his sexual life and channeled most of his energy into his business. He was able to take a small family business he inherited from his father and turn it into a multimillion-dollar international manufacturing business. To his closest friends he would confide, "Money is more exciting than sex with Barbara."

After Barbara died, Marvin found himself in a community in which men were greatly outnumbered by women. The community Marvin lived in was restricted to older adults 55 years and older. The mean age of residents in this community was 81 years of age. This is because most of the residents were original residents, never having moved. Therefore, younger older adults tended not to buy into a community of *old people*.

To Marvin's surprise, many of the women who resided in his community became flirtatious with Marvin, stimulating an interest in women, other than his deceased wife, for the first time since Marvin could remember. All of a sudden, out of nowhere, Marvin began to fantasize about several women in his community. The fantasies became so intense that Marvin decided it was time to date. Initially, Marvin carefully chose his first date, based on criteria he felt would indicate a potential mate to replace Barbara. Marvin did not like living alone and felt that he would welcome having another partner in life.

(continued)

VIGNETTE 5.2 (*continued*)

Marvin met Linda and was somewhat shocked when, on their first date, after dinner, Linda suggested that they "fool around." Marvin was taken aback and anxious about engaging in sexual activity so immediately. However, he felt that he would look like *less of a man* if he refused her offer. That evening they engaged in sexual activity, which Marvin experienced as "exciting as money." The next morning Linda told Marvin that he was the talk of the town. With very few men still alive in the community, Linda joked, "If you have a penis, and are still breathing, you are hot." She then told Marvin that he was lucky. He was in good shape for his age, he was rich and smart, and, of course, very handsome. "You can have any woman here whenever you want," she said. When Marvin responded to Linda that he was interested in a committed relationship, Linda said, "Forget about it—the women here want to have fun and, besides, how much longer do you think you will live?"

Marvin took Linda's lead and began serial dating in the community. He became very active and social, and enjoyed frequent sexual encounters with many women in his community. To anyone who would listen, he would always start his stories with "I am having the time of my life." Unfortunately, after a year of multiple sexual partners, Marvin noticed a cluster of sores on his penis. He went to his family physician, who diagnosed HPV. Marvin said to this physician, "I thought only young people get this." His physician explained how HPV is a sexually transmitted disease, and that with the promiscuous sexual activity that is occurring in his community, it is not surprising that he had contracted this infection. He advised Marvin about using a condom to prevent infecting others and cautioned him to notify his sexual partners of his infection so that their physicians may examine them.

This deeply disturbed Marvin for several reasons. He was embarrassed and humiliated to have to admit to others that he had a sexually transmitted disease. In addition, throughout his sexual lifetime, he would never use a condom because he felt that he could not feel anything and that would cause him anxiety that resulted in not being able to maintain an erection. Marvin concluded that this was the end of his sexual life, no more women, and now being stuck with these recurring sores. Within 3 months of ceasing dating, Marvin became more and more isolated, and progressively more depressed.

(continued)

> **VIGNETTE 5.2** (*continued*)
>
> Marvin sought the help of a psychologist, primarily for his depression, but with a secondary agenda of feeling better again and figuring out how he could overcome his embarrassment of having HPV so that he could resume his newly found exciting sexual activity again, albeit safe sex.

SEXUALITY AND INSTITUTIONS

Elias and Ryan (2011) found that interest in sexual activity does not decrease when an older adult is placed into institutional care; it is the opportunity to engage in sexual activity that decreases. Unfortunately, despite their continued interest in sexual activity, older adults confined to institutional settings (nursing homes and assisted living facilities) are subjected to discrimination caused by the stigma about sexuality and older adults. To counter this phenomenon, Di Napoli et al. (2013) formed focus groups with nursing home staff members to understand their attitudes and feelings about older adult patients experiencing dementia who were in their care. These authors found that staff members' attitudes toward residents engaging in sexual activity were neutral, neither negative nor positive. However, staff members presented a need for more training on how to intervene with these older adults to enable the residents to experience sexual activity in a managed way that produces positive sexual activity that is not harmful to other residents.

REFERENCES

Adams, B. (2003). Keeping it up. *The Advocate, 902*, 38–41.

Addis, I. B., Van Den Eeden, S. K., Wassel-Fyr, C. L., Vittinghoff, E., Brown, J. S., & Thom, D. H. (2006). Sexual activity and function in middle-aged and older women. *Obstetrics and Gynecology, 107*, 755–764.

Age Concern. (2006). *The whole of me. Meeting the needs of older lesbians, gay men and bisexuals in care homes and extra care housing: A resource pack for professionals.* London, England: Author.

Araujo, A. B., Mohr, B. A., & McKinlay, J. B. (2004). Changes in sexual function in middle-aged and older men: Longitudinal data from the Massachusetts Male Aging Study. *Journal of the American Geriatrics Society, 52,* 1502–1509.

Avis, N. E. (2000). Sexual function and aging in men and women: Community and population-based studies. *Journal of Gender-Specific Medicine, 3,* 37–41.

Bach, L. E., Mortimer, J. A., VandeWeerd, C., & Corvin, J. (2013). The association of physical and mental health with sexual activity in older adults in a retirement community. *Journal of Sexual Medicine, 10*(11), 2671–2680.

Bacon, C. G., Mittleman, M. A., Kawachi, I., & Giovannucci, E. (2003). Sexual function in men older than 50 years of age: Results from the Health Professionals Follow-up Study. *Annals of Internal Medicine, 139,* 161–168.

Baldissera, V. D. A., Bueno, S. M. V., & Hoga, L. A. K. (2012). Improvement of older women's sexuality through emancipatory education. *Health Care for Women International, 33*(10), 956–972.

Basson, R. (2000). The female sexual response. A different model. *Journal of Sex and Marital Therapy, 26,* 51–65.

Bauer, M., McAuliffe, L., Nay, R., & Chenco, C. (2013). Sexuality in older adults: Effect of an education intervention on attitudes and beliefs of residential aged care staff. *Educational Gerontology, 39*(2), 82–91.

Beckman, N., Waern, M., Gustafson, D., & Skoog, I. (2008). Secular trends in self-reported sexual activity and satisfaction in Swedish 70 year olds: Cross sectional survey of four populations, 1971–2001. *British Medical Journal, 337,* 279–285.

Beebe, L. H., & Mills, J. (2013). Sexuality and long-term care: Understanding and supporting the needs of older adults. *Issues in Mental Health Nursing, 34*(4), 298.

Belluck, P. (2015). *Iowa man found not guilty of sexually abusing wife with Alzheimer's.* Retrieved from http://www.nytimes.com/2015/04/23/health/iowa-man-found-not-guilty-of-sexually-abusing-wife-with-alzheimers.html?_r=0

Bouman, W. P. (2008). Sexuality in later life. In J. R. Oppenheimer & C. Dening (Eds.), *Oxford textbook of old age psychiatry* (Illustrated ed., pp. 703–723). New York, NY: Oxford University Press.

Bouman, W. P., & Arcelus, J. (2001). Are psychiatrists guilty of "ageism" when it comes to taking a sexual history? *International Journal of Geriatric Psychiatry, 16,* 27–31.

Breland, L. (2013). Lost libido or just forgotten? The legal and social influences on sexual activity in long-term care. *Law & Psychology Review, 38*, 177–192.

Bussel, R. K. (2011). Why getting older doesn't mean giving up sex. *Alternet.* Retrieved from http://www.alternet.org/story/151478/why_getting_older_doesn't_mean_giving_up_sex

Clarke, L. H. (2006). Older women and sexuality: Experiences in marital relationships across the life course. *Canadian Journal on Aging, 25*(2), 129–140.

Conrad, P. (2005). The shifting engines of medicalization. *Journal of Health and Social Behavior, 46*(1), 3–14.

Corona, G., Lee, D. M., Forti, G., O'Connor, D. B., Maggi, M., O'Neil, T. W., . . . Wu, F. C. (2010). Age-related changes in general and sexual health in middle-aged and older men: Results from the European Male Ageing Study (EMAS). *Journal of Sexual Medicine, 7*, 1362–1380.

Davis, M. (2012). Naked at our age: Talking out loud about senior sex. *American Journal of Sexuality Education, 7*(2), 176–180.

Davison, S. L., Bell, R. J., LaChina, M., Holden, S. L., & Davis, S. R. (2009). The relationship between self-reported sexual satisfaction and general well-being in women. *Journal of Sexual Medicine, 6*(10), 2690–2697.

DeLamater, J. (2012). Sexual expression in later life: A review and synthesis. *Journal of Sex Research, 49*(2–3), 125–141.

Department of Health. (2001). *The national strategy for sexual health and HIV*. London, England: Author.

Di Napoli, E. A., Breland, G. L., & Allen, R. S. (2013). Staff knowledge and perceptions of sexuality and dementia of older adults in nursing homes. *Journal of Aging & Health, 25*(7), 1087–1105.

Elias, J., & Ryan, A. (2011). A review and commentary on the factors that influence expressions of sexuality by older people in care homes. *Journal of Clinical Nursing, 20*, 1668–1676.

Fisher, L. (2010). *Sex, romance, and relationships: AARP Survey of Midlife and Older Adults* (AARP Publication No. D19234). Washington, DC: AARP.

Fournier, S. M. (2000). Social expectations for sexuality among the elderly. *Dissertation Abstracts International, 60*(12A), 4610.

Gott, M., Hinchiliff, S., & Galena, E. (2004). General practitioner attitudes to discussing sexual health issues with older people. *Social Science and Medicine, 58*, 2093–2103.

Hatzimouratidis, K., & Hatzichristou, D. G. (2005). A comparative review of the options for treatment of erectile dysfunction: Which treatment for which patient? *Drugs, 65*(12), 1621–1650.

Heaphy, B., Yip, A., & Thompson, D. (2003). *Lesbian, gay, and bisexual lives over 50: A report on the project "The Social and Policy Implications of Non-Heterosexual Ageing."* Nottingham, England: York House.

Heiman, J. R., Long, J. S., Smith, S. N., Fisher, W. A., Sand, M. S., & Rosen, R. C. (2011). Sexual satisfaction and relationship happiness in midlife and older couples in five countries. *Archives of Sexual Behavior, 40*(4), 741–753.

Hillman, J. (2011). *Sexuality and aging: Clinical perspectives.* New York, NY: Springer.

Hinchiliff, S., & Gott, M. (2011). Seeking medical help for sexual concerns in mid- and later life: A review of the literature. *Journal of Sex Research, 48*(2), 106–117.

Kalra, G., Subramanyam, A., & Pinto, C. (2011). Sexuality: Desire, activity and intimacy in the elderly. *Indian Journal of Psychiatry, 53*(4), 300–306. doi:10.4103/0019-5545.91902

Katz, A. (2013). Sexuality in nursing care facilities. *American Journal of Nursing, 113*(3), 53–56.

Laumann, E. O., Paik, A., & Rosen, R. C. (1999). Sexual dysfunction in the United States. *JAMA, 281*, 537–544.

Lindau, S. T., & Gavrilova, N. (2010). Sex, health, and years of sexually active life gained due to good health: Evidence from two U.S. population-based cross sectional surveys of ageing. *British Medical Journal, 340*, 1–11.

Lindau, S. T., Leitsch, S. A., Lundgerg, K. L., & Jerome, J. (2006). Older women's attitudes, behavior, and communication about sex and HIV: A community-based study. *Journal of Women's Health, 15*, 747–753.

Lindau, S. T., Schumm, L. P., Laumann, E. O., Levinson, W., O'Muircheartaigh, C. A., & Waite, L. J. (2007). A study of sexuality and health among older adults in the United States. *New England Journal of Medicine, 357*, 762–774.

Lochlainn, M. N., & Kenny, R. A. (2013). Sexual activity and aging. *Journal of American Medical Directors Association, 14*(8), 565–572.

Marshall, B. L. (2010). Sexual medicine, sexual bodies, and the pharmaceutical imagination. *Sociology of Health and Illness, 32*(2), 211–224.

Marshall, B. L. (2011). The graying of sexual health: A critical research agenda. *Canadian Review of Sociology, 48*(4), 390–413.

Montemurro, B., & Gillen, M. M. (2013). Wrinkles and sagging flesh: Exploring transformations in women's sexual body image. *Journal of Women and Aging, 25*(1), 3–23.

Onen, N. F., Shacham, E., Stamm, K. E., & Overton, E. T. (2010). Comparisons of sexual behaviors and STD prevalence among older and younger individuals with HIV infection. *AIDS Care, 22*(6), 711–717.

Prejean, J., Song, R., Hernandez, A., Ziebell, R., Green, T., Walker, F., . . . Hall, H. I. P. (2011). Estimated HIV incidence in the United States, 2006–2009. *PLoS One, 6*(8), e17502. Retrieved from http://www.plosone.org/article/info%3Adoi%2F10.1371%2Fjournal.pone.0017502

Rosen, R. C., & Bachman, G. A. (2008). Sexual well-being, happiness, and satisfaction in women: The case for a new paradigm. *Journal of Sex & Marital Therapy, 34*, 291–297.

Rosen, R. C., Wing, R., Schneider, S., & Gendrano, N. (2005). Epidemiology of erectile dysfunction: The role of medical comorbidities and lifestyle factors. *The Urologic Clinics of North America, 32*, 403–417.

Saga. (2011). *Sex and romance alive for the over 50s.* Retrieved from http://www.saga.co.uk/newsroom/press-releases/2011/1-9/sex-and-romance-alive-for-the-over-50s.aspx

Savasta, A. M. (2004). HIV: Associated transmission risks in older adults: An integrative review of the literature. *Journal of the Association of Nurses in AIDS Care, 15*(1), 50–59.

Schick, V., Herbenick, D., Reece, M., Sanders, S. A., Dodge, B., Middlestadt, S. E., & Fortenberry, J. D. (2010). Sexual behaviors, condom use, and sexual health of Americans over 50: Implications for sexual health promotion for older adults. *Journal of Sexual Medicine, 7*(Suppl. 5), 315–329.

Shaw, J. (2012). Approaching your highest sexual function in relationship: A reward of age and maturity. In P. J. Kleinplatz (Ed.), *New directions in sex therapy: Innovations and alternatives* (2nd ed., pp. 175–194). New York, NY: Routledge.

Smith, K. P., & Christakis, N. A. (2009). Association between widowhood and risk of diagnosis with a sexually transmitted infection in older adults. *Journal of Public Health, 99*, 2055–2062.

Smith, L. J., Mulhall, J. P., Deveci, S., Monaghan, N., & Reid, M. C. (2007). Sex after seventy: A pilot study of sexual function in older persons. *Journal of Sexual Medicine, 4*, 1247–1253.

Syme, M. L. (2014). The evolving concept of older adult sexual behavior and its benefits. *Generations, 38*(1), 35–41.

Taylor, A., & Gosney, M. A. (2011). Sexuality in older age: Essential considerations for healthcare professionals. *Age and Ageing, 40*(5), 538–543.

Tressel, L. S., Schumm, L. P., Laumann, E. O., Lewinson, W., Muircheatraigh, C. A., & Waite, L. J. (2007). A study of sexuality and health among older adults in the United States. *New England Journal of Medicine, 357,* 762–774.

Waite, L. J., & Das, A. (2010). Families, social life, and well-being at older ages. *Demography, 47*(Suppl.), S87–S109.

Waite, L. J., Laumann, E. O., Das, A., & Schumm, L. P. (2009). Sexuality: Measures of partnerships, practices, attitudes, and problems in the National Social Life, Health, and Aging Study. *Journals of Gerontology, Series B: Psychological Sciences and Social Sciences, 64*(Suppl. 1), i56–i66.

Wiegel, M., Scepkowski, I. A., & Barlow, D. H. (2006). Cognitive and affective processes in female sexual dysfunctions. In I. Goldstein, C. M. Meston, S. R. Davis, & A. M. Traish (Eds.), *Women's sexual function and dysfunction* (pp. 85–92). Abingdon, England: Taylor & Francis.

Williams, A., Ylanne, V., & Wadleigh, P. M. (2007). Selling the "elixir of life": Images of the elderly in an Olivio advertising campaign. *Journal of Aging Studies, 27,* 1–21.

Substance Abuse/ Dependence Is Not Just a Problem for Young People

*Suddenly, our familiar view of our surroundings
becomes transformed in a strange, delightful, or alarming way:
it appears to us in a new light, takes on a special meaning.
Such an experience can be as light and fleeting as a breath of air,
or it can imprint itself deeply upon our minds.*

Albert Hofmann, who discovered
lysergic acid diethylamide (LSD) (Hofmann, 2013)

ith the coming of the *gray tsunami* caused by
the aging of baby boomers, it is predicted that
by the year 2030 there will be approximately
72.1 million older adults either abusing or
misusing psychoactive substances (Agency for Healthcare Research and Quality, 2010). A reason for this large number of
older adult psychoactive substance abusers is thought to be
because the baby-boom generation has a history of greater exposure to and experience with psychoactive substance abuse/
dependence over their adult lifetimes (National Institutes of
Health, 2014), which is a significant difference from current
non–baby boomer older adult cohorts (see Chapter 1).

Cohorts prior to the baby-boom generation fit a previously predicted pattern that psychoactive substance abuse in earlier stages of
adulthood substantially declined as one ages. Current research indicates that the baby-boom generation does not follow this pattern,
and instead of lower rates of psychoactive substance abuse as one
ages, baby boomers show significantly higher rates of psychoactive
substance abuse (Blank, 2009). This baby-boom cohort, as a consequence of its current psychoactive substance abuse/dependence,
creates extreme health risks for themselves, and adds a considerable
cost and utilization burden to the health care system (Vignette 6.1).

VIGNETTE 6.1 A Benzodiazepine-Abusing Professor

(*Note:* Names and other identifying information have been changed
to preserve confidentiality.)

Gary is a 73-year-old tenured professor of computer science at a major university in Washington, DC, who has been suffering with prostatitis for the past 4 years. Six months ago, Gary complained to his
internist that his sleep was being interrupted because he had to uri-
nate several times each night. His internist, rather than deciding to re-
fer Gary to a urologist for treatment of his prostatitis, decided to treat
his sleep disturbance by prescribing 100 5-mg tablets of diazepam
(Valium) for Gary to take, one each night before sleep. His internist
told him that this would give him *100 nights of sleep*, and in 3 months

(continued)

VIGNETTE 6.1 (*continued*)

he would decide if Gary needed further treatment. Gary's internist did not warn him of diazepam's addictive potential.

Gary used this prescription for 2 weeks and found that he was sleeping better, but only for 4 to 5 hours per night. After these 2 weeks, Gary noticed that the diazepam started to not be as effective, and his sleep pattern was returning to the original disturbance. This caused Gary to make his own decision to up the dosage. He now found that taking 10 mg of diazepam returned his sleep to the 4 to 5 hours per night. However, this caused a problem for Gary. He calculated that he would finish the prescription in 43 days. This caused Gary to panic. He did not want to tell his internist that he doubled the dose because he felt that his internist would cease to prescribe diazepam to him. Gary next decided to locate two other internists in towns in contiguous states, considerable distances from where Gary lived, to see if he could obtain more diazepam. He visited each internist, and at each visit described his sleep disturbance without any reference to this prostate problem. Each internist wrote a prescription for 100 5-mg diazepam tablets, and when Gary asked for a 10-mg prescription, both internists told Gary that that the higher dosage may put Gary in danger of becoming addicted to the diazepam.

Gary was happy; he now had 200 extra diazepam tablets. He continued to take 10 mg each night until his next visit to the original internist 3 months later. At that visit, he told his original internist that the 5-mg dosage was very helpful and asked if he could continue with 5 mg/night. His internist indicated that because Gary was not abusing his prescription, he would prescribe another 100 5-mg tablets. Gary repeated the same story to the two other internists at appointments carefully selected to indicate that he was taking only 5 mg of diazepam/evening. Both of these other internists renewed his prescription of 100 5-mg tablets each.

Four months after his initial prescription, Gary was now using 40 mg of diazepam/day in various divided doses throughout the day. One evening, Gary was involved in a traffic accident in which he was charged with DUI (driving under the influence, without alcohol) because the police noticed that he was slurring his speech and was acting confused and hostile. Upon searching his automobile, the police found 250 5-mg tablets of diazepam. At trial, because this was Gary's first offense, his lawyer was able to convince the judge to mandate

VIGNETTE 6.1 (*continued*)

treatment with a psychologist in lieu of jail, and supervised probation with random urine screens for a period of 1 year.

Unbeknownst to his lawyer, internist, or wife, Gary had a prior history of abusing methaqualone (Quaaludes) in undergraduate college, and at different times during his adulthood he abused opioid pain medications at opportunities for such prescriptions when he had dental work, or after a leg injury from skiing. Each time, Gary hid the fact that he was abusing opioids from his wife and children.

A major psychological antecedent to psychoactive substance abuse in older adults is *social isolation*. Older adults experience social isolation due to the death of a spouse/partner or other family members and friends, retirement from work, disability, reduced levels of activity, and relocation. These factors increase the probability of becoming depressed, or experiencing anxiety (see Chapter 3), and seeking psychoactive substances for relief (Wilson, Knowles, Huang, & Fink, 2014). In addition, social isolation may exacerbate a preexisting psychoactive substance abuse problem. Unlike younger adults, older adults are more likely to avoid illicit substances such as cocaine, heroin, methamphetamine, psychedelics such as LSD or mescaline, and designer drugs. Historically, the psychoactive substance of choice was alcohol (Williams, Ballard, & Alessi, 2005). With the aging of the baby-boom generation, the substances of choice for older adults have expanded along with alcohol to *benzodiazepines, opioid prescription medications*, and *marijuana* (cannabis). Abuse of prescription medications by the current baby-boom generation is projected to increase from 911,000 abusers in 2006 to 2.7 million in 2020 (Colliver, Compton, Gfroerer, & Condon, 2006). All of these substances of choice fall into a gray zone of being used for medical reasons, social/recreational use, or transitioning to a clinical category of psychoactive substance abuse/dependence.

A further complication of the issue of older adult psychoactive substance abuse/dependence is the lack of clarity in the diagnosis of psychoactive substance abuse/dependence problems in older adults. As stated in Chapter 3, the 5th edition of the *Diagnostic and Statistical Manual of Mental Disorders* (*DSM-5*; American Psychiatric Association [APA], 2013), the current diagnostic manual used by psychologists, is based primarily on research with children, adolescents, and young/middle-aged adults, which causes a psychologist to use criteria for psychoactive substance abuse/dependence determinations that are inappropriate for accurately determining substance abuse/dependence in older adults. For example, the *DSM-5* guidelines are more appropriate for psychoactive substance abusers who are seeking a *high*, which is not often the case in older adults. The *DSM-5* fails to identify the phenomenon of when psychoactive medication misuse becomes an actual psychoactive substance abuse/dependence problem, as misuse does not follow the usual process of abuse and dependence seen in adolescents and younger adults. This is because an older adult who misuses psychoactive medications is not doing so in order to achieve disorientation (getting high), and is usually accidental (Blow, 2006). Therefore, many older adults who experience psychoactive substance abuse/dependence problems are often overlooked or misdiagnosed (Colliver et al., 2006; Epstein, Fischer-Elber, & Al-Otaiba, 2007; Hans, Gfroerer, Colliver, & Penne, 2009).

Another example would be an older adult with an alcohol abuse/dependence problem that is misdiagnosed by focusing on symptoms such as memory problems, confusion, depression, agitation and hostility, change in appearance, or psychomotor disturbances (problems with movement), all of which are stereotypes of old age and may lead to a diagnosis of minimal cognitive impairment, or a beginning stage of a dementia (see Chapter 4) (Blow, Oslin, & Barry, 2002; Finfgeld-Connett, 2004; Simoni-Wastila & Yang, 2006). Another example of the phenomenon of misdiagnosis of psychoactive substance abuse occurs when a psychologist diagnoses a co-occurring psychological problem of depression or anxiety and neglects to assess further for a psychoactive substance abuse/dependence problem (Vignette 6.2). This type of misdiagnosis in another contributing factor that prevents effective diagnosis and treatment of older adult psychoactive substance abusers (Rosen et al., 2013).

VIGNETTE 6.2   A Cannabis-Abusing Retired Receptionist

(*Note:* Names and other identifying information have been changed to preserve confidentiality.)

Ruth is a 82-year-old retired receptionist who has been smoking cannabis (marijuana) since she was 18 years old when she met her future husband, a jazz musician, who introduced her to "his best friend, *reefer.*" From that time to when she gave birth to her second and last child, Ruth had a fairly regular routine for smoking marijuana. She would smoke on occasion during weeknights after school and then after work as a receptionist in a hospital oncology office. On weekends, Ruth would smoke during social occasions with friends, and later with her husband. Her husband died after 10 years of marriage from an overdose of heroin.

After the birth of her second child, Ruth's pattern of marijuana smoking changed. Ruth now felt a need to smoke after breakfast each morning, and then before going to sleep. As usual, both Ruth and her husband hid their marijuana smoking from their children by taking a walk and smoking, smoking when the kids left for school, or driving to a nearby park to smoke. She claimed that this enabled her to be relaxed during the day and deal with her responsibilities at work and later at home with her family. She had a history of mild insomnia since childhood and found that smoking marijuana before bed help her have a good night's sleep.

When Ruth was 32 years old, her husband died. Ruth became a single parent and never married again. At this time, Ruth's children are married and living in other states, causing her to visit with them infrequently. As a consequence of her children moving far away from Ruth, Ruth began to isolate herself from others, experienced anxiety frequently, and found herself smoking marijuana three or four times a day, in addition to her nightly joint (marijuana cigarette) before bed. Ruth's anxiety and isolation intensified to a point where her children became concerned. Her daughter traveled to Ruth's home to arrange to join Ruth at an appointment with a psychiatrist whom Ruth's family physician recommended.

At the appointment, Ruth described her increasing anxiety, isolation, and feelings of abandonment caused by her children leaving her.

(continued)

However, Ruth did not disclose to the psychiatrist that she habitually smoked marijuana, and, as usual, her daughter had no knowledge of her cannabis use. The psychiatrist explained to Ruth and her daughter that Ruth was experiencing a mixed mood and anxiety disorder and wrote a prescription for Zoloft (sertraline HCl), an antidepressant that in addition has antianxiety effects. He also made a referral to a psychologist for psychotherapeutic treatment.

At the assessment by the psychologist, he questioned Ruth about any substance abuse history. This took Ruth by surprise because the psychiatrist did not ask such questions. She asked the psychologist why he was asking an 82-year-old about substance abuse. He said to her that some psychoactive substances might cause the symptoms she was experiencing, and that he did not believe the stereotype that older adults do not get high. She laughed at this statement and then revealed her cannabis use history. This started a process of recovery from her cannabis use, and after a period of several months of treatment and abstinence, Ruth's mood and anxiety symptoms abated and she was able to stop isolating and re-engage in socialization.

When a psychologist uses the *DSM-5* to diagnosis a substance abuse/dependence in an older adult, he or she looks for indications of recurrent psychoactive substance use that leads to impairment in work, school, or home obligations. All of these criteria are age-biased because most older adults are not employed, most older adults are not attending school, and home obligations outlined in the *DSM-5* imply neglect of children or the household. Only neglect of the household environment may apply to an older adult. In addition, substance dependence implies a change in tolerance to the psychoactive substance, which consequently causes the user to markedly increase the amount of the psychoactive substance to achieve the desired result, which in a traditional psychoactive substance abuser is an altered state, in other words, *getting high*.

This concept of tolerance (see the later section on pharmacodynamics) is not entirely appropriate to older adults because older adults undergo physiological changes in the way their bodies metabolize (see the later section on pharmacokinetics) alcohol and psychoactive medications that cause tolerance to occur at dosages far lower than would be seen in an adolescent or younger adult. In addition, many older adults experience chronic illness for which they are taking several medications (polypharmacy), and may have poor nutrition. Polypharmacy and/or poor nutrition contribute to unpredictable interactions with psychoactive medications, including alcohol, which, combined with physiological changes in metabolism, can cause longer-acting effects of psychoactive medications or substances in older adults, blurring the diagnosis of whether a psychoactive substance is being abused, misused, and/or exacerbated by interaction with other nonpsychoactive medications. This phenomenon of polypharmacy is frequently seen in the current baby-boom cohort (Votova, Blais, Penning, & Maclure, 2013).

In addition, exacerbated effects of psychoactive substances on older adults cause increased cognitive impairment with resultant social isolation that increases the probability that these older adults may not present for assessment by a psychologist (Gunter & Arndt, 2004; Menninger, 2002). Psychologists may also be under the misconception that older adults do not use psychoactive substances, or should not require an intervention because they are too old to benefit from treatment, both of which are causes for underdiagnosis (Crome & Crome, 2005). In addition, family physicians tend to prescribe benzodiazepines and opioids, motivated by empathy for their patients' psychosocial and pain problems, feeling that such prescriptions are a way to help these older adults (Siriwardena, Qureshi, Gibson, Collier, & Lathamn, 2006), rather than to explore alternative interventions in which a referral is needed to a psychologist for cognitive behavioral therapy, relaxation instruction, and self-hypnotic techniques.

Many older adults misuse prescription medications, or unintentionally combine prescription medications with alcohol, causing a process that can cause an unanticipated substance dependence, unintentional death from an overdose of such medication, or the potentiation of a psychoactive prescription medication from its interaction with alcohol (Culberson & Ziska, 2008; Satre, Sterling, Mackin, & Weisner, 2011). Misuse of prescription medications is fundamentally different from, yet just as serious as, intentional use of psychoactive medications to produce a desired high (disorientation). Misuse of psychoactive medication detection in older adults is relatively rare, with few older adults being screened for misuse, with a consequence of a low incidence of older adults misusing psychoactive substances seeking treatment. Medication misuse is often caused by older adults making errors in following the prescription directions of their physicians, not like older adults who abuse psychoactive medication with the intention to achieve disorientation (Schonfeld et al., 2010). In addition to the problem of older adults not following the prescription directions of their physicians, which are usually written on a prescription bottle, many physicians do not take the time to instruct, in person, older adults on proper use of medications, and the dangers of mixing medications or combining psychoactive medications with alcohol (Basca, 2008).

PSYCHOPHARMACOLOGICAL CONCEPTS THAT UNDERLIE SUBSTANCE ABUSE/ DEPENDENCE

In order to understand psychoactive substance abuse/dependence in older adults, a psychologist must understand the biological processes that occur when a psychoactive substance is introduced into an older adult's body, is transported in the body to the target organ (the brain), and is finally excreted from the older adult's body. These processes differ from those in younger adults due to changes that occur with aging. These changes become significant risk factors for older adults who may misuse psychoactive prescription medications, or abuse alcohol, psychoactive prescription medications, and/or cannabis. This understanding becomes an important aspect of the psychoeducation that occurs when a psychologist treats an older adult for a psychoactive substance abuse/dependence problem. In addition, this understanding is necessary when educating an older adult on how he or she may be misusing prescription medications, or inadvertently experiencing debilitating side effects from polypharmacy.

Psychopharmacology is a subfield of psychology that describes substances, whether man-made or naturally occurring, that have the potential to alter an older adult's mood, perceptions, emotional states, and behaviors. Some medications, alcohol, and cannabis are considered to be *psychoactive*. These psychoactive substances are diverse, and their effects are determined by many factors. These factors include how the psychoactive substance is administered, how the substance is absorbed into an older adult's body, how the substance affects the older adult, and how the substance is broken down and, finally, eliminated from an older adult's body. With older adults, these factors are fundamentally different than those in younger people. Therefore, a psychoactive substance's effects are determined by a complex interaction resulting from the physical properties of the substance, the physiological processes it encounters in an older adult's body, and the complex aging changes that have occurred in an older adult.

Pharmacokinetics

Pharmacokinetics is the process in which a psychoactive substance is absorbed into an older adult's body, how the psychoactive substance is distributed throughout the older adult's body, what happens when the psychoactive substance is metabolized (broken down by chemical interactions between the older adult's body and the psychoactive substance), and how the psychoactive substance is removed from the older adult's body (because it is a foreign compound that does not normally belong in the older adult's body). In other words, pharmacokinetics describes what an older adult's body does in its interaction with the psychoactive substance.

Routes of Administration

Routes of administration are the various methods by which an older adult introduces a psychoactive substance into his or her body. The route of administration determines the onset of the psychoactive effects the older adult will experience. The route will, in addition, determine the duration of the effects and the degree of the altered state that the psychoactive substance will produce. There are several routes of administration commonly used by all psychoactive substance abusers. They include inhalation, gaseous, rectal, sublingual (under the tongue), oral (swallowing by mouth), cutaneous (patch on the skin), intramuscular injection (injection into a muscle), subcutaneous injection (injection under the skin), and intravenous injection (injection into a vein).

Of these routes of administration, the oral, inhalation, sublingual, and transdermal routes are the most common routes used by an older adult to introduce a psychoactive substance into his or her body. In rare cases, an older adult with sophisticated experience with opioid (see following discussion) substances may resort to injecting such substances using the subcutaneous, intramuscular, or intravenous routes. Whatever route is chosen, each route will have unique utility for the older adult and, in addition, will have different effects depending on biological variables within the older adult.

The oral route is the most prevalent route of administration used by an older adult. Although it is the easiest and most convenient route of administration, it is not the most efficient route of administration, yet it is the safest. The psychoactive substance's action is significantly slowed, its effects are more variable, and a greater amount of the psychoactive substance is needed due to the degradation that occurs while exposed to the older adult's digestive system. It is the safest in terms of allowing a significant amount of time (in minutes) to intervene in the case of an overdose. The inhalation method can also be considered oral because if the psychoactive substance inhaled is in a powder form, it goes from the nasal cavity down the back of the throat and into the alimentary canal and the digestive system for subsequent absorption. If the psychoactive substance is in a gaseous form, the effects will be more rapid because the gas is readily absorbed in the mucous membranes of the older adult's lungs. However, the gaseous route is rarely seen in older adults. Children, adolescents, and young/middle-aged adults may inhale nitrous oxide from whipped cream canisters, amyl nitrite from ampules, or other volatile solvents such as spray paint, glues, thinners, gasoline, correction fluids, and cleaning fluids (Winger, Woods, & Hofman, 2004).

Sublingual and cutaneous routes are additional routes of administration for the absorption of a psychoactive substance. When using a transdermal patch, there is a degree of safety because the dosage is known and slowly administered by absorption through an older adult's skin. The quickest, most efficient, and most dangerous routes of administration are those in which an older adult injects the psychoactive substance. Subcutaneous injection has the slowest rate of absorption of the three injection routes. It is followed by intramuscular injection and intravenous injection. Intravenous injection is the most dangerous route of administration, as the effects of the psychoactive substance will occur within seconds, reaching the brain at maximum strength.

Absorption

Once a psychoactive substance enters the older adult's body, it becomes distributed throughout the body in varying degrees. The main distribution channels are in the water medium and plasma of the blood, both components of the circulatory system. Access to the circulatory system is either by direct intravenous injection or through absorption through the digestive system (oral route), pulmonary epithelium (linings of the lung—gaseous route), or the skin (transdermal route). The other routes (less often used or not used by older adults)—subcutaneous injection, intramuscular injection, sublingual, or rectal—require the psychoactive substance to transit through various physiological barriers before entering the circulatory system.

Metabolism

It must be emphasized that the metabolism process described here is significantly different for an older adult as compared with a young/middle-aged adult, adolescent, or child. Aging causes a significant slowdown in an older adult's ability to break down psychoactive substances and eliminate them from the body. Therefore, an older adult is at risk of experiencing psychoactive effects at significantly lower dosages, and consequently is more apt to reach lethal dosages, especially when combining a psychoactive substance with alcohol (Colliver et al., 2006; Simoni-Wastila & Yang, 2006).

Once a psychoactive substance is circulating throughout the body, a physiological process of metabolism is initiated that breaks down the substance through chemical reactions with chemicals existing in an older adult's body, to an eventual form that will be excreted from the body by the kidneys and liver. There are four metabolic processes: *oxidation, reduction, hydrolysis,* and *conjugation* (Table 6.1).

Excretion

Excretion by-products of psychoactive substances are most commonly found in the urine. In order for excretion to be initiated by the kidneys, metabolites of the original psychoactive substance must be transformed into a water-soluble form. Water-soluble psychoactive substances such as ethyl alcohol are ideal for this process of excretion. Lipid-soluble substances must undergo a chemical transformation in order to achieve a water-soluble state. Transforming a lipid-soluble psychoactive substance into a water-soluble state is a complicated chemical process that is beyond the scope of this book. Excretion by the kidneys enables the detection of an older adult who is misusing or abusing a psychoactive substance by performing a urinary drug screen. Some typical results are shown in Table 6.2.

The liver is also involved in the excretion of by-products of psychoactive substances. The liver deposits by-products into the bile, and then they are transported into the small intestine for

TABLE 6.1 The Four Metabolic Processes: Oxidation, Reduction, Hydrolysis, and Conjugation

Metabolic Process	Effect on a Psychoactive Substance	Psychoactive Substance Affected
Oxidation	Oxidation of a psychoactive substance occurs by causing an addition of an oxygen atom or the loss of a hydrogen atom from the chemical structure of the psychoactive substance.	Barbiturates and ethyl alcohol (ETOH, commonly known as alcohol)
Reduction	Reduction involves the opposite process of oxidation. A hydrogen atom is added or an oxygen atom is subtracted from the psychoactive substance. This occurs with psychoactive substances that are lipid soluble (dissolve in fat).	Benzodiazepines, opioids, and cannabis undergo reduction in order to be eliminated by the body, primarily through the kidneys.
Hydrolysis	Hydrolysis of psychoactive substances occurs when the psychoactive substance is split into fragments by the addition of water (chemically known as H_2O) into what is known as a hydroxyl group (OH^-). This chemical process occurs in the blood plasma and primarily in the liver.	Cocaine undergoes this process. In the case of an older adult, cocaine is not a frequent psychoactive substance of choice.
Conjugation	Conjugation occurs with the joining together of two compounds to produce another compound that can be eliminated from the body by the liver and the kidneys.	Alcohol, nicotine, and amphetamines (not frequently abused by older adults) undergo this process.

TABLE 6.2 Detection of Psychoactive Substances Commonly Misused or Abused by Older Adults

Psychoactive Substance	Maximum Time for Detection in Urine
Ethyl alcohol	12–48 hours
Benzodiazepines	Many days to several weeks
Opioids	2–4 days, longer if a chronic user
THC (cannabis)	Up to 30 days, longer if a chronic user

eventual excretion in the feces. Fecal excretion of psychoactive compounds also occurs when they are taken orally and fail to be absorbed in the gastrointestinal tract. An example of this is when the liver metabolizes the ethyl alcohol that is water soluble (approximately 90% or the alcohol consumed), which is then excreted into the urine. Of the remaining amount, 8% is excreted in the feces and 2% by the lungs (breath alcohol test), salivary glands, and sweat glands.

A final method of excretion occurs through the skin, saliva, hair, and pulmonary epithelium (linings of the lungs). An example of this type of excretion occurs when an older adult drinks a large quantity of alcohol, which in turn causes his or her body to use many routes of excretion to eliminate the excess alcohol and its subsequent metabolites, as described earlier.

Pharmacodynamics

Pharmacodynamics refers to the effects a psychoactive substance has on an older adult's body and the subsequent changes in an older adult's mind. Concepts underlying pharmacodynamics include synaptic interaction (how one nerve in the central nervous system communicates with another), receptor site mechanisms, and the development of tolerance, dependence, and withdrawal reactions.

Synaptic Interaction

The synapse (Figure 6.1) is where psychoactive substances change the way in which neurons communicate with each other.

143

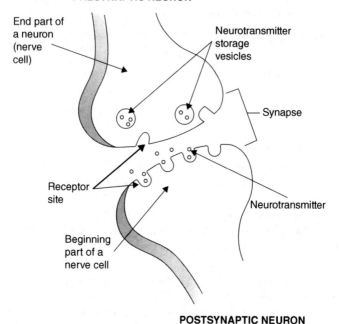

PRESYNAPTIC NEURON

End part of
a neuron
(nerve
cell)

Neurotransmitter
storage
vesicles

Synapse

Receptor
site

Neurotransmitter

Beginning
part of a
nerve cell

POSTSYNAPTIC NEURON

FIGURE 6.1 The synapse, the target of substance abuse/dependence.
Adapted from Youdin (2014).

Figure 6.1, for purpose of illustration and simplification, shows the relationship between two neurons (nerve cells in the brain, part of the central nervous system). In reality, neurons can at any given time be communicating with hundreds of neurons simultaneously. The communication occurs when the presynaptic neuron releases neurotransmitters from its storage vesicles into the synaptic cleft (the space between the neurons), which then travel to the receptor sites on the postsynaptic neuron.

The chemical transmission from one neuron to another is modulated by the introduction of psychoactive substances. Figure 6.1 shows a presynaptic neuron (the ending of a nerve) that has receptor sites, the synaptic cleft (the space between neurons), and a postsynaptic neuron (the beginning of a neuron), which also has receptor sites. In the ending of the presynaptic neuron there are storage vesicles that store neurotransmitters such as dopamine, norepinephrine, acetylcholine, and serotonin, which are excitatory neurotransmitters, and γ-aminobutyric acid (GABA), which is an inhibitory neurotransmitter. The amount of neurotransmitter diffused is modulated by psychoactive substances that are either an *agonist* (increasing) or *antagonist* (decreasing) to the presynaptic neuron receptor sites (Table 6.3), and thus increase or decrease the release of neurotransmitters. In turn, the psychoactive substance can be an agonist or antagonist to the postsynaptic neuron receptor sites, modulating the effects on the receptor sites by either increasing excitation or increasing inhibition (Table 6.4).

An agonist psychoactive substance will increase the activity of the synaptic connection. If the synaptic connection is

TABLE 6.3 Modulating Effects of Psychoactive Substances on the Release of Neurotransmitters from the Presynaptic Storage Vesicles

	Presynaptic Storage Vesicles
Agonist psychoactive substance	Increased release of neurotransmitters
Antagonist psychoactive substance	Decreased release of neurotransmitters

TABLE 6.4 The Effect of Agonist and Antagonist Psychoactive Substances on Excitatory and Inhibitory Postsynaptic Neurons in the Brain

	Excitatory Postsynaptic Neuron	Inhibitory Postsynaptic Neuron
Agonist psychoactive substance	Increases excitation	Increases inhibition
Antagonist psychoactive substance	Decreases excitation	Decreases inhibition, causing an increase in excitation

excitatory, the psychoactive agonist will increase the excitement. If the synaptic connection is inhibitory, the psychoactive agonist will increase the inhibition. The opposite occurs with a psychoactive antagonist. If the synaptic connection is excitatory, the psychoactive antagonist will make the connection less excitatory. If the synaptic connection is inhibitory, the psychoactive antagonist will make the connection less inhibitory, causing a degree of excitement.

In the section "Classes of Psychoactive Substances Misused or Abused by Older Adults," descriptions are given on how alcohol, benzodiazepines, cannabis, and opioids manipulate these neurotransmitters, with subsequent misuse and abuse/dependency problems in older adults.

Tolerance

Tolerance (Gitlow, 2001) occurs when an increased amount of a psychoactive substance is needed to achieve a desired effect (getting high, disorientation). Tolerance can also occur when one psychoactive substance causes tolerance in another psychoactive substance. This is called *cross-tolerance*. An example would be an older adult who is alcohol dependent and also becomes cross-tolerant to opioids and benzodiazepines. This can be dangerous for an older adult when opioids are needed for pain control. Because of cross-tolerance, the older adult will need a higher dosage of opioid medication to control pain. This can cause the older adult to be exposed to a dosage of an opioid medication that may cause an overdose. A final type of tolerance is called *dispositional tolerance*. Dispositional tolerance occurs when a psychoactive substance is metabolized (chemically changed within the body) in a shorter amount of time than the time needed to achieve the psychoactive effects. This too can produce a dangerous situation for an older adult, who may increase his or her dosage of a psychoactive substance in order to achieve a disorienting effect, increasing the risk for an overdose.

CLASSES OF PSYCHOACTIVE SUBSTANCES MISUSED OR ABUSED BY OLDER ADULTS

The following discussion presents descriptions of psychoactive substances that are commonly misused or abused by older adults. It is important for a psychologist to understand the psychopharmacological dynamics of each substance, how they are administered by an older adult, the symptoms of intoxication and withdrawal, and the psychosocial consequences experienced by the older adult misusing or abusing psychoactive substances. In addition to alcohol abuse/dependence, older adults have a high rate of prescription drug misuse and abuse, with benzodiazepines and opioid medications as the most often misused or abused (Culberson & Ziska, 2008; Simoni-Wastila & Yang, 2006). It must be noted that accurate statistics of psychoactive substance use by older adults are difficult to determine due to underreporting of such use by older adults and/or their health care providers. This is especially true of benzodiazepine and cannabis usage. Older adults not reporting such use are usually identified by urine drug screens when admitted to a hospital for a medical condition, or if a physician outside of an institution is alert to the possibility of an older adult using a psychoactive substance (Glintborg, Olsen, Poulsen, Linnet, & Dalhoff, 2008).

Alcohol

Psychopharmacological Dynamics

Historically, it was thought that alcohol (ethyl alcohol, or ETOH) did not have any identified receptor sites and, rather, that alcohol's main pharmacological effect was on the membranes of the neurons. The infiltration of the membranes by alcohol causes an increase in fluidity of the membranes when an older adult is involved in short-term use. Chronic alcohol use causes the neuronal membranes to thicken and become rigid, causing the multiple symptoms described in the following discussion (Sadock & Sadock, 2008). Other

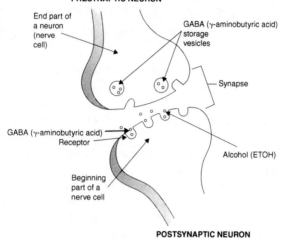

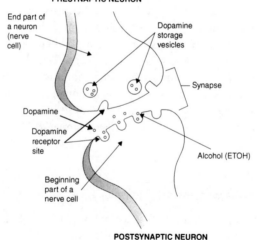

FIGURE 6.2 Alcohol (ethyl alcohol, or ETOH) postsynaptic inhibitory agonist activity on γ-aminobutyric acid (GABA) receptors in the amygdala, located in the limbic system, and postsynaptic excitatory agonist activity on dopamine receptors in the nucleus accumbens in the basal forebrain.

Adapted from Youdin (2014).

researchers have extended this theory to include alcohol's synaptic influence on neurons in the amygdala, which is located deep in the temporal lobe of the brain and is part of the limbic system. The amygdala is involved in memory, mood, fear, anxiety, and impulsivity. Alcohol is a postsynaptic agonist of GABA (Figure 6.2), causing inhibition, memory disturbance, and sedation (Gilpin & Koob, 2008; Paul, 2006). In addition, alcohol acts as a dopamine postsynaptic agonist in the nucleus accumbens (basal forebrain), causing excitability and feelings of pleasure (a biochemical reward) (Masters, 2013) (Figure 6.2).

Route of Administration

The route of administration for alcohol is the oral route.

Effects, Side Effects, and Withdrawal

Alcohol withdrawal causes many side effects. In an older adult who is alcohol dependent, withdrawal may cause death. Withdrawal symptoms occur 6 to 12 hours after ceasing ingestion of alcohol. These symptoms include intentional tremor, vomiting, excessive sweating, anxiety, and agitation. In severely dependent older adults, withdrawal symptoms may include visual, tactile, and/or auditory hallucinations. Generalized seizures may occur with these hallucinations, with the individual being disoriented to person, place, and time, as well as displaying autonomic nervous system instability (anxiety, arousal, facial flushing, pupil dilation, rapid heartbeat, and mild elevation of blood pressure) (Lüscher, 2013; Masters, 2013). In addition, excessive alcohol consumption can cause respiratory depression and aspiration of vomitus, which can cause death (Sadock & Sadock, 2008).

Biopsychosocial Consequences

Alcohol abuse in older adults causes a higher rate of medical problems, psychiatric problems, physical disabilities, and interpersonal problems, which lead to a higher frequency of emergency room visits, increased admissions to hospitals, and a higher proportion of nursing home placement for adults who abuse alcohol as compared with non–alcohol-abusing older adults (Holbert & Tueth, 2004). Medical illnesses that are co-occurring with alcohol abuse/dependence include heart disease, hypertension (high blood pressure), stroke, diabetes, and gastro-intestinal disorders. Excessive alcohol consumption can cause damage to red blood cells, resulting in megaloblastic anemia and sideroblastic anemia (Masters, 2013).

Chronic depression (see Chapter 3) in older adults increases the likelihood that they will abuse alcohol and misuse prescription medication by combining such prescribed medications with alcohol (Satre et al., 2011). Hooyman and Kiyak (2010) find that 30% of alcohol-dependent older adults have co-occurring depression (see Chapter 3), and 20% of alcohol-dependent older adults have co-occurring dementia (see Chapter 4). Older adults with depression who experience sleep disturbance and use alcohol as a sleep aid experience a paradoxical effect of their alcohol ingestion. Instead of alcohol facilitating sleep due to its inhibitory effects, it decreases REM sleep (Snyder, van Wormer, Chadha, & Jaggers) and deep physical restorative sleep (Stage 4 sleep), and causes multiple awakenings throughout an older adult's sleep (Sadock & Sadock, 2008).

Alcohol abuse in older adults can lead to traffic accidents and precipitate a decision for driver cessation (see Chapter 4). An older adult driving while impaired by alcohol may cause death or injury to himself or herself or to others. In addition, an older adult driving while impaired by alcohol may be subject to arrest and possible incarceration.

Benzodiazepines

Psychopharmacological Dynamics

Benzodiazepines are GABA agonists that increase the inhibitory GABAergic neurotransmission (Figure 6.3), which also results

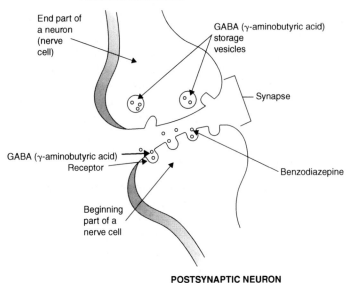

PRESYNAPTIC NEURON

End part of a neuron (nerve cell)

GABA (γ-aminobutyric acid) storage vesicles

Synapse

GABA (γ-aminobutyric acid) Receptor

Benzodiazepine

Beginning part of a nerve cell

POSTSYNAPTIC NEURON

FIGURE 6.3   Benzodiazepine agonist influence on γ-aminobutyric acid (GABA) postsynaptic receptors.

Adapted from Youdin (2014).

in the inhibition of other neurotransmitters within the brain, resulting in psychomotor retardation (slowing of movements) and depression of central nervous system activity. Clinically, benzodiazepines are anxiolytic, hypnotic/sedative, amnesic (affect memory), anticonvulsant, and antispasmodic. Therefore, benzodiazepines are useful for the treatment of anxiety disorders, muscle spasms, alcohol and amphetamine withdrawal, agitation, psychosis, and preoperative sedation (Donaghue & Lader, 2010). Clinically, benzodiazepines are divided into two classes: *short acting and long acting.* Short-acting benzodiazepines such as *lormetazepam* (not currently available in the United States) and *flunitrazepam* (Rohypnol), are used as hypnotics. Long-acting benzodiazepines, such as *diazepam* (Valium), *alprazolam* (Xanax), and *clobazam* (Onfi), are used to treat anxiety and for the treatment of muscle spasms.

Routes of Administration

The primary route of administration for benzodiazepines is the oral route. A secondary and less used route of administration is the intravenous route. This is the most dangerous route of administration for an older adult because the substance is rapidly absorbed by the body, increasing the likelihood of an overdose, and may produce a severe withdrawal syndrome, including respiratory depression, coma, and death (Littrell, 2015).

Effects, Side Effects, and Withdrawal

The effects and side effects of long-term benzodiazepine use include cognitive impairment, memory problems, impairment of motor skills (movements), and a high risk of falling. Withdrawal without medical supervision can cause a potentially fatal rise in blood pressure and seizures (Tannenbaum, Paquette, Hilmer, Holroyd-Leduc, & Carnahan, 2012; Wu, Wang, & Chang, 2009). In addition, chronic use of benzodiazepines increases the probability of traffic accidents in older adults who were not evaluated for driving cessation, the risk of arrest for driving while impaired, and the risk of hip fractures from falls (Leufkens & Vermeeren, 2009; Woolcott et al., 2009; Zint et al., 2010). Long-acting benzodiazepines increase the risk of an older adult contracting pneumonia due to their suppression of respiratory functioning (Obiora, Hubbard, Sanders, & Myles, 2013). The respiratory depression may also cause coma and eventual death. The prevalence of death from benzodiazepines is thought to be 31% worldwide (Bellerose, Lyons, Carew, Walsh, & Long, 2010).

Biopsychosocial Consequences

Benzodiazepines are the most widely prescribed psychoactive class of medications throughout the world (Donaghue & Lader, 2010), and, paradoxically, have the greatest potential for abuse and dependence (Lader, Tylee, & Donaghue, 2009). Despite their clinical effectiveness as an anxiolytic (antianxiety) medication, concerns are being raised about prescribing benzodiazepines on a chronic basis because of the abuse/dependency potential (Arbanas, & Dujam, 2009; Spanemberg et al., 2011). In addition, because of changes in metabolism, older adults are at greater risk for overdose due to a heightened sensitivity to benzodiazepines. Marienfeld, Tek, Diaz, Schottenfeld, and Chawarski (2012) found a growing trend of psychiatrists reporting reluctance to prescribe benzodiazepines to older adult patients with a past history of substance abuse. This reluctance is based on a high probability that many older adults may be manipulating the psychiatrist, or seeking to divert prescribed benzodiazepines to other substance abusers (Preville et al., 2012). If this trend to resist prescribing benzodiazepines to older adults is sustained, it would contribute to addressing the major social problem of addiction affecting older adults.

Older adults who are at high risk for benzodiazepine misuse include those who are socioeconomically disadvantaged and older adult women (Glass, Lanctôt, Hermann, Sproule, & Busto, 2005; Spanemberg et al., 2011). Those at high risk for chronic abuse/dependence are older adults who live alone, are not well educated, have a prior history of psychological problems, and have frequent health problems requiring physician consultations (Zandstra et al., 2004). Abuse of benzodiazepines causes some older adults to buy benzodiazepines from others who divert their prescribed medications to abusers when they no longer need such medications (El-Aneed et al., 2009).

Cannabis

Psychopharmacological Dynamics

The principal chemical component of cannabis is Δ 9-THC. In addition to Δ 9-THC, there are more than 400 other chemical components of cannabis, with 60 of these related to Δ 9-THC. Δ 9-THC is converted in an older adult's body to *11-hydroxy-Δ9*, which is the active metabolite in the central nervous system

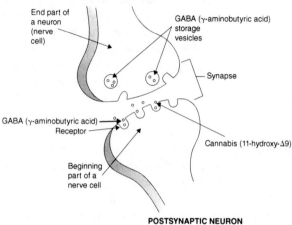

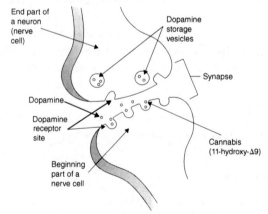

FIGURE 6.4   Cannabis is a postsynaptic agonist that affects synapses that are excitatory (monoamine neurotransmitters, primarily dopamine) and inhibitory γ-aminobutyric acid (GABA) synapses.

Adapted from Youdin (2014).

causing the many effects of cannabis. The cannabis receptors are found in the hippocampus (site for memory), basal ganglia (sends excitatory signals to the cortex and influences impulsive behavior), and cerebellum (fine motor movements and coordination). Cannabis is a postsynaptic agonist that affects synapses (Figure 6.4) that are excitatory (monoamine neurotransmitters—dopamine and norepinephrine) and inhibitory (GABA).

Routes of Administration

The primary route of administration for cannabis use is smoking (the inhalation route), which has the risk of impairing respiratory functioning as well as having impurities that may be carcinogenic. With the current trend in the United States to legalize cannabis, products are being developed to include the active ingredient of cannabis, Δ 9-THC, in food products. In addition, research is being performed internationally to identify other cannabinoids that may be beneficial for the treatment of cancer and neurological disorders, but that do not produce the disorientation caused by Δ 9-THC and its metabolite 11-hydroxy-Δ9. Both food products and pharmaceutical preparations use the oral route, eliminating the risks associated with smoking cannabis.

Effects, Side Effects, and Withdrawal

Cannabis use is associated with adverse panic reactions, anxiety attacks, and the exacerbation of mood and psychotic disorders (Coggans, Dalgarno, Johnson, & Shewan, 2004; Williamson & Evans, 2000). In addition, cannabis causes perceptual distortions, increased appetite, and sedation.

Biopsychosocial Consequences

It is estimated that by the year 2020, use of cannabis by older adults will increase by 2.9%, bringing the number of current older adult cannabis users to approximately 3.3 million older adults (Colliver et al., 2006). Blazer and Wu (2009) indicate that younger older adult cohorts (at the time of the study, ages 50–64) were more likely to use cannabis than were older adult cohorts. This is consistent with the current aging of the baby-boom cohort. Of these young-old adults (see Chapter 1), men, unmarried/no-longer-partnered older adults, and young-old adults with co-occurring depression have the highest probability of using cannabis.

Despite the problematic aspects of cannabis use, cannabis also has beneficial effects for older adults. Cannabis may be used as an adjunct for the treatment of multiple sclerosis, Parkinson's disease, and chronic pain, and for the treatment of nausea and fatigue side effects of chemotherapy (Williamson & Evans, 2000). However, a counterargument is made indicating that cannabis may facilitate the onset of mood and psychotic disorders, and exacerbate existing depression (Coggans et al., 2004; Rey & Tennant, 2002).

Opioids

Psychopharmacological Dynamics

There are two general types of opioid psychoactive substances: naturally occurring opioids and synthetic opioids. Naturally occurring opioids include opium and its derivatives morphine and codeine, and heroin, which is a chemical manipulation of morphine. Examples of synthetic opioids (pharmaceutically manufactured) are listed in Table 6.5.

Age-related changes in dopamine receptors in the midbrain nucleus accumbens (postsynaptic neuron) and dopamine release factors for the synaptic vesicles in the midbrain nucleus accumbens (presynaptic neuron) (Figure 6.5), which are associated with positive feelings of reward and normal mood, cause many older adults to experience depressed moods with subsequent perceptions of poor self-esteem and lack of self-confidence (Mazei-Robison & Nestler, 2012). The misuse and abuse of opioid psychoactive substances by older adults is a maladaptive attempt

TABLE 6.5   Examples of Synthetic Opioid Medications

Generic Name	Most Common Brand Name
Alfentanil	Alfenta
Buprenorphine	Buprenex
Butorphanol	Stadol
Fentanyl	Sublimaze, Duragesic
Hydrocodone	Vicodin
Hydromorphone	Dilaudid
Levorphanol	Levo-Dromoran
Meperidine	Demerol
Methadone	Dolophine
Nalbuphine	Nubain
Oxycodone	Percocet, Percodan, OxyContin
Oxymorphone	Numorphan
Pentazocine	Talwin
Remifentanil	Ultiva
Sufentanil	Sufenta
Tramadol	Ultram

by older adults to enhance self-confidence and self-esteem, to diminish depression, and to combat feelings associated with bereavement (Dreher, Meyer-Lindenberg, Kohn, & Berman, 2010). Older adults abusing opioids find a temporary relief of anxiety due to the inhibition of the dorsal anterior cingulated cortex. In addition, opioid receptors are found in the spinal cord (part of the central nervous system, along with the brain), and opioid use thus results in an inhibition of pain transmission to the brain (Schumacher, Basbaum, & Way, 2013).

There are three types of opioid receptors in the midbrain. The *μ-opioid receptor* regulates and mediates analgesia (blocks pain), causes respiratory depression (depresses breathing), causes constipation, and causes substance dependence. The *κ-opioid receptor* causes analgesia (blocks pain), diuresis (increased or excessive urination), and sedation. The third receptor is the *Δ-opioid receptor*, which induces analgesia (blocks pain) (Sadock & Sadock, 2008).

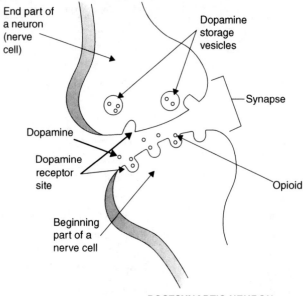

PRESYNAPTIC NEURON

End part of a neuron (nerve cell)

Dopamine storage vesicles

Synapse

Dopamine

Dopamine receptor site

Opioid

Beginning part of a nerve cell

POSTSYNAPTIC NEURON

FIGURE 6.5 The dopamine synapse, showing dopamine receptors and dopamine release factors for the synaptic vesicles in the midbrain nucleus accumbens (presynaptic neuron) and in the midbrain nucleus accumbens (postsynaptic neuron).

Adapted from Youdin (2014).

Routes of Administration

There are many routes of administration for opioids. They include the oral route (most common for opioid medications used by older adults), the inhalation route (snorting intranasally by reducing tablets into a powder), the subcutaneous route (injecting under the skin), and the transdermal route (opioid medication in a patch attached to the skin). *Fentanyl* patches, as opposed to oral or intravenous opioids and synthetic opioids, have been shown to be effective in managing pain (Zuurmond,

Davis, & Vergidis, 2002). The transdermal patch treatment shows a greater degree of safety than opioids delivered by the intravenous route, which is the most dangerous route that can be used by an older adult due to the rapid absorption, which increases the likelihood of an overdose. In addition, the intravenous route may produce severe respiratory depression, coma, and death.

Effects, Side Effects, and Withdrawal

Opioid intoxication may cause mood alteration, psychomotor retardation (slowing of movements), drowsiness, slurred speech, and impaired memory. Opioid withdrawal (Littrell, 2015; Sadock & Sadock, 2008; Winger et al., 2004) is evidenced by severe muscle cramps, bone pain, diarrhea, intestinal cramps, rhinorrhea (nasal discharge), lacrimation (tearing), and piloerection (muscle contraction that raises hair follicles). The effect of piloerection is often called *gooseflesh*, because the skin has an appearance of a plucked goose or turkey. Hence the term *cold turkey* for a person going through withdrawal.

Additional effects of opioid intoxication are yawning, increased body temperature, constricted pupils, increased blood pressure, rapid heart rate, and hypothermia (lowering of body temperature) or hyperthermia (raising of body temperature). Other severe symptoms of withdrawal occur including insomnia, restlessness, irritability, depression, tremor, muscle weakness, and nausea (in some instances vomiting). In an older adult, death may occur during withdrawal because the withdrawal syndrome may exacerbate a preexisting cardiac condition. In addition, opioid medications have an increased probability of causing dependence and co-occurring delirium in older adults (Briggs, Magnus, Lassiter, Patterson, & Smith, 2011).

Biopsychosocial Consequences

Prescribing opioids to older adults is a complicated phenomenon with high risk potential for abuse and dependence. Unfortunately, many older adults suffer with chronic pain from cancer, arthritis, postsurgical pain, or injuries, causing a need for opioid medications (Cummings & Cooper, 2011). Opioids account for the majority of prescription emergency room visits by older adults, usually because of a high frequency of falling (Colliver et al., 2006). Older adults are at risk for migrating from opioid medications prescribed by their physicians, or bought from others who divert their medications for profit, to heroin, which is less expensive and unfortunately readily available. In addition, the use of heroin, because it is illegal, puts an older adult in jeopardy with the criminal justice system.

REFERENCES

Agency for Healthcare Research and Quality. (2010). *Hospitalizations for medication and illicit drug-related conditions on the rise among Americans ages 45 and older*. Retrieved from http://archive.ahrq.gov/news/newsroom/press-releases/2010/hospmed.html

American Psychiatric Association. (2013). *Diagnostic and statistical manual of mental disorders* (5th ed.). Washington, DC: Author.

Arbanas, G. D. A., & Dujam, K. (2009). Adverse effects of benzodiazepines in psychiatric outpatients. *Psychiatria Danubina, 21*, 103–107.

Basca, B. (2008). *The elderly and prescription drug misuse and abuse*. Santa Rosa, CA: Center for Applied Research Solutions.

Bellerose, D., Lyons, S., Carew, A. M., Walsh, S., & Long, J. (2010). *Problem benzodiazepine use in Ireland: Treatment (2003 to 2008) and deaths (1998 to 2007)*. Retrieved from http://www.hrb.ie/publications/hrb-publication/publications//532/

Blank, K. (2009). *Older adults and substance use: New data highlight concerns*. Retrieved from http://media.samhsa.gov/samhsaNewsletter/Volume_17_Number_1/OlderAdults.aspx

Blazer, D. G., & Wu, L. (2009). The epidemiology of substance use and disorders among middle aged and elderly community adults: National Survey on Drug Use and Health. *American Journal of Geriatric Psychiatry, 17*, 237–245.

Blow, F. C. (2006). *Evidence-based practices for preventing substance abuse and mental health problems in older adults*. Washington, DC: SAMHSA, Older Americans Substance Abuse and Mental Health Technical Assistance Center.

Blow, F. C., Oslin, D. W., & Barry, K. L. (2002). Misuse and abuse of alcohol, illicit drugs, and psychoactive medication among older people. *Generations*, *26*, 50–54.

Briggs, W. P., Magnus, V. A., Lassiter, P., Patterson, A., & Smith, L. (2011). Substance use, misuse, and abuse among older adults: Implications for clinical mental health counselors. *Journal of Mental Health Counseling*, *33*(2), 112–127.

Coggans, N., Dalgarno, P., Johnson, L., & Shewan, D. (2004). Long-term heavy cannabis use: Implications for health education. *Drugs, Education, Prevention, and Policy*, *11*, 299–313.

Colliver, J. C., Compton, W. M., Gfroerer, J. C., & Condon, T. (2006). Projecting drug use among aging baby boomers in 2020. *Annals of Epidemiology*, *16*, 257–265.

Crome, I., & Crome, P. (2005). "At your age, what does it matter?": Myths and realities about older people who use substances. *Drugs, Education, Prevention, and Policy*, *12*, 343–347.

Culberson, J., & Ziska, M. (2008). Prescription drug misuse/abuse in the elderly. *Geriatrics*, *63*(9), 22–31.

Cummings, J. W., & Cooper, R. L. (2011). The addicted geriatric patient. In E. O. Bryson & E. A. M. Frost (Eds.), *Perioperative addiction: Clinical management of the addicted patient* (pp. 239–252). New York, NY: Springer.

Donaghue, J., & Lader, M. (2010). Usage of benzodiazepines: A review. *International Journal of Psychiatry in Clinical Practice*, *14*, 78–87.

Dreher, J. C., Meyer-Lindenberg, A., Kohn, P., & Berman, K. F. (2010). Age-related changes in midbrain dopaminergic regulation of the human reward system. *Proceedings of the National Academy of Sciences of the United States of America*, *105*, 15106–15111.

El-Aneed, A., Alaghehbandan, R., Gladney, N., Collins, K., McDonald, D., & Fischer, B. (2009). Prescription drug abuse and methods of diversion: The potential role of a pharmacy network. *Journal of Substance Use*, *14*, 75–83.

Epstein, E. E., Fischer-Elber, K., & Al-Otaiba, Z. (2007). Women, aging, and alcohol use disorders. *Journal of Women and Aging*, *19*, 31–48.

Finfgeld-Connett, D. L. (2004). Treatment of substance misuse in older women using a brief intervention model. *Journal of Gerontological Nursing*, *30*, 30–37.

Gilpin, N. W., & Koob, G. F. (2008). Neurobiology of alcohol dependence: Focus on motivational mechanisms. *Alcohol Research & Health*, *31*(3), 185–195.

Gitlow, S. (2001). *Substance use disorders: Practical guides in psychiatry*. Philadelphia, PA: Lippincott Williams & Wilkins.

Glass, J., Lanctôt, K. L., Hermann, N., Sproule, B. A., & Busto, U. E. (2005). Sedative hypnotics in older people with insomnia: Meta-analysis of risks and benefits. *British Medical Journal, 331*, 1169–1176.

Glintborg, B., Olsen, L., Poulsen, H., Linnet, K., & Dalhoff, K. (2008). Reliability of self-reported use of amphetamine, barbiturates, benzodiazepines, cannabinoids, cocaine, methadone, and opiates among acutely hospitalized elderly medical patients. *Clinical Toxicology, 46*, 239–242.

Gunter, T. D., & Arndt, S. (2004). Maximizing treatment of substance abuse in the elderly. *Behavioral Health Management, 24*, 38–41.

Hans, B., Gfroerer, J. C., Colliver, J. C., & Penne, M.A. (2009). Substance use disorder among older adults in the United States in 2020. *Addiction, 104*, 88–96.

Hofmann, A. (2013). *LSD: My problem child and insights/outlooks* (J. Ott, Trans.). Oxford, England: Beckley Foundation Press/Oxford University Press.

Holbert, K., & Tueth, M. (2004). Alcohol abuse and dependence: A clinical update on alcoholism in the older population. *Geriatrics, 59*, 38–40.

Hooyman, N. R., & Kiyak, H. A. (2010). *Social gerontology: A multidisciplinary perspective*. Boston, MA: Pearson Allyn & Bacon.

Lader, M., Tylee, A., & Donaghue, J. (2009). Withdrawing benzodiazepines in primary care. *CNS Drugs, 23*, 19–34.

Leufkens, T. R. M., & Vermeeren, A. (2009). Highway driving in the elderly the morning after bedtime use of hypnotics: A comparison between temazepam 20 mg, zopiclone 7.5 mg, and placebo. *Journal of Clinical Psychopharmacology, 29*, 432–438.

Littrell, J. (2015). *Neuroscience for psychologists and other mental health professionals: Promoting well-being and treating mental illness*. New York, NY: Springer Publishing Company.

Lüscher, C. (2013). Drugs of abuse. In B. G. Katzung, S. B. Masters, & A. Trevor (Eds.), *Basic and clinical pharmacology* (12th ed., pp. 565–580). New York, NY: McGraw-Hill.

Marienfeld, C. B., Tek, E., Diaz, E., Schottenfeld, R., & Chawarski, M. (2012). Psychiatrist decision-making towards prescribing benzodiazepines: The dilemma with substance abusers. *Psychiatric Quarterly, 83*(4), 521–529. doi:10.1007/s11126-012-9220-8

Masters, S. B. (2013). The alcohols. In B. G. Katzung, S. B. Masters, & A. Trevor (Eds.), *Basic and clinical pharmacology* (12th ed., pp. 389–402). New York, NY: McGraw-Hill.

Mazei-Robison, M. S., & Nestler, E. J. (2012). Opiate-induced molecular and cellular plasticity of ventral tegmental area and locus coeruleus catecholamine neurons. *Cold Spring Harbor Perspectives in Medicine, 2*(7), a012070.

Menninger, J. A. (2002). Assessment and treatment of alcoholism and substance-related disorders in the elderly. *Bulletin of the Menninger Clinic, 66*(2), 166–183.

National Institutes of Health. (2014). *Prescription and illicit drug abuse. NIH Senior Health: Built with you in mind.* Retrieved from http://nihseniorhealth.gov/drugabuse/illicitdrugabuse/01.html

Obiora, E., Hubbard, R., Sanders, R. D., & Myles, P. R. (2013). The impact of benzodiazepines on occurrence of pneumonia and mortality from pneumonia: A nested case-control and survival analysis in a population-based cohort. *Thorax, 68*, 163–170.

Paul, S. M. (2006). Alcohol-sensitive GABA receptors and alcohol antagonists. *Proceedings of the National Academy of Sciences of the United States of America, 103*(22), 8307–8308.

Preville, M., Bosse, C., Vasiliadis, H.-M., Voyer, P., Laurier, C., Berbiche, D., . . . Moride, Y. (2012). Correlates of potentially inappropriate prescriptions of benzodiazepines among older adults: Results from the ESA study. *Canadian Journal on Aging, 31*(3), 313–322. doi:10.1017/S0714980812000232

Rey, J. M., & Tennant, C. C. (2002). Cannabis and mental health. *British Medical Journal, 325*, 1183–1184.

Rosen, D., Engel, R. J., Hunsakeer, A. E., Engel, Y., Detlefsen, E. G., & Reynolds, C. F. (2013). Just say no: An examination of substance use disorders among older adults in gerontological and substance abuse journals. *Social Work in Public Health, 28*(3/4), 377–387.

Sadock, B. J., & Sadock, V. A. (2008). *Kaplan & Sadock's concise textbook of clinical psychiatry* (3rd ed.). Philadelphia, PA: Wolters Kluwer/Lippincott Williams & Wilkins.

Satre, D. D., Sterling, S. A., Mackin, R. S., & Weisner, C. (2011). Patterns of alcohol and drug use among depressed older adults seeking outpatient psychiatric services. *American Journal of Geriatric Psychiatry, 19*, 695–703.

Schonfeld, L., King-Kallimanis, B., Duchene, D. M., Etheridge, R. L., Herrera, J. R., Barry, K. L., & Lynn, N. (2010). Screening and brief intervention for substance misuse among older adults: The Florida BRITE Project. *American Journal of Public Health, 100*(1), 108–114.

Schumacher, M. A., Basbaum, A. L., & Way, W. L. (2013). Opioid analgesics and antagonists. In B. G. Katzung, S. B. Masters, & A. Trevor (Eds.), *Basic and clinical pharmacology* (12th ed., pp. 543–564). New York, NY: McGraw-Hill.

Simoni-Wastila, L., & Yang, H. K. (2006). Psychoactive drug abuse in older adults. *American Journal of Geriatric Pharmacotherapy, 4,* 380–394.

Siriwardena, A. N., Qureshi, Z., Gibson, S., Collier, S., & Lathamn, M. (2006). GPs' attitudes to benzodiazepine and "z-drug" prescribing: A barrier to implementation of evidence and guidance on hypnotics. *British Journal of General Practice, 56,* 964–967.

Snyder, C., van Wormer, K., Chadha, J., & Jaggers, J. W. (2009). Older adult inmates: The challenge for social work. *Social Work, 54*(2), 117–124.

Spanemberg, L., Nogueira, E. L., Belem da Silva, C. T., Dargel, A. A., Menezes, F. S., & Neto, A. C. (2011). High prevalence and prescription of benzodiazepines for elderly: Data from psychiatric consultation to patients from an emergency room of a general hospital. *General Hospital Psychiatry, 33,* 45–50.

Tannenbaum, C., Paquette, A., Hilmer, S., Holroyd-Leduc, J., & Carnahan, R. (2012). A systematic review of amnestic and non-amnestic, mild cognitive impairment induced by anticholinergic, antihistamine, GABAergic and opioid drugs. *Drugs & Aging, 29,* 639–658.

Votova, K., Blais, R. G., Penning, M. J., & Maclure, M. K. (2013). Polypharmacy meets polyherbacy: Pharmaceutical, over-the-counter, and natural health product use among Canadian adults. *Canadian Journal of Public Health, 104*(3), e222–e228.

Williams, J. M., Ballard, M. B., & Alessi, H. (2005). Aging and alcohol abuse: Increasing counselor awareness. *Adultspan, 4,* 7–18.

Williamson, E. M., & Evans, F. J. (2000). Cannabinoids in clinical practice. *Drugs, 60,* 1303–1314.

Wilson, S. R., Knowles, S. B., Huang, Q., & Fink, A. (2014). The prevalence of harmful and hazardous alcohol consumption in older U.S. adults: Data from 2005–2008 National Health and Nutrition Examination Survey (NHANES). *Journal of General Internal Medicine, 29*(2), 312–319.

Winger, G., Woods, J. H., & Hofman, F. G. (2004). *A handbook on drug and alcohol abuse: The biomedical aspects.* New York, NY: Oxford University Press.

Woolcott, J. C., Richardson, K. J., Wiens, M. O., Patel, B., Marin, J., Khan, K. M., & Marra, C. A. (2009). Meta-analysis of the impact of 9 medication classes on falls in elderly persons. *Archives of Internal Medicine, 169,* 1952–1960.

Wu, C. S., Wang, S. C., & Chang, I. (2009). The association between dementia and long-term use of benzodiazepines in the elderly: Nested case-control study using claims data. *American Journal of Geriatric Psychiatry, 17,* 614–620.

Youdin, R. (2014). *Clinical gerontological social work practice.* New York, NY: Springer Publishing Company.

Zandstra, S., van Rijswijk, E., Rijnders, C. A. T., van de Lisdonk, E., Bor, J., van Weel, C., & Zitman, F. (2004). Long-term benzodiazepine users in family practice: Differences from short-term users in mental health, coping behaviour and psychological characteristics. *Family Practice, 21,* 266–269.

Zint, K., Haefeli, W. E., Glynn, R. J., Mogun, H., Avorn, J., & Sturmer, T. (2010). Impact of drug interactions, dosage, and duration of therapy on the risk of hip fracture associated with benzodiazepine use in older adults. *Pharmacoepidemiology and Drug Safety, 14,* 280–284.

Zuurmond, W., Davis, C., & Vergidis, D. (2002). Transdermal fentanyl shows a similar safety and efficacy profile in elderly and non-elderly patients with cancer pain. *Annals of Oncology, 13*(Suppl. 5), 171.

Older Adult Abuse

Elder abuse is a multifactorial problem that may affect elderly people from different backgrounds and involve a wide variety of potential perpetrators, including caregivers, adult children, and partners.
Abolfathi Momtaz, Hamid, and Ibrahim (2013, p. 182)

oday, older adult abuse is also called *elder abuse* and *elder mistreatment*, and was originally termed *battered old person syndrome* by Butler (1975). Crystal (1986) labeled older adult abuse as the *hidden problem*. Whatever the name, the abuse is insidious and unacceptable. Older adult abuse increases an older adult's risk for morbidity (medical illness) and mortality (Dong et al., 2009). Older adult abuse is a multifactorial phenomenon that includes single or multiple acts of abuse (Abolfathi Momtaz, Hamid, & Ibrahim, 2013; von Heydrich, Schiamberg, & Chee, 2012). The abuse may be emotional, financial, physical, sexual, or self-induced. Abuse may occur within a relationship, or be caused by a stranger to the older adult. When occurring within a relationship, the abuse is a violation of an *expectation of trust*

(McCreadie, 2007). It may occur with consent from the older adult, or without consent. An example of consent would be when an older adult who suffers from dementia (see Chapter 4) and has limited executive function agrees to engage in sexual activity with a home aide, even though the older adult is too impaired to make such a decision with a complete understanding of its implications.

Vignette 7.1 illustrates how social media has become a means to financially exploit older adults, in this case an older woman.

VIGNETTE 7.1 Laura's New Love for Her New Life

(*Note:* Names and other identifying information have been changed to preserve confidentiality.)

Laura is a 79-year-old widow living in Chicago, Illinois. She has been living alone since her husband died 6 years ago. During the time since his death, she has kept herself socially isolated. Laura would often say that her husband "was the love of my life and no man would ever be able to replace him." Therefore, she had no interest in dating, and had limited social contact to a few women friends that she had for many years. Laura would only see these friends when they were not with their husbands. Laura avoided any social activity where couples were involved.

Laura's daughter recently divorced and began Internet dating. She was constantly meeting men for *coffee dates*, quickly sorting whether they were acceptable candidates for an ongoing relationship. "If not for me, then I move on to the next," she would say. One afternoon during a visit to her mother, she brought up the possibility of Laura joining an Internet dating site. She said "Because you just finished learning how to use a computer at the class in your clubhouse, why not try it out?" Laura indicated that she was not interested in dating and repeated, "No one will ever replace your father." Laura's daughter persisted over the next several months with the idea of Laura joining an Internet dating site.

(continued)

VIGNETTE 7.1 (*continued*)

Finally, after numerous attempts, Laura's daughter piqued some interest about Internet dating in Laura. Her daughter said, "Mom, why not put up a profile and see who is attractive to you; you can put your own profile on the website. They won't know who you are; you do not have to contact them. It would help you feel better about yourself knowing that you are still attractive and interesting to other men." Laura indicated that that might be an interesting thing to do, "but just as an experiment—no one could ever replace your father," she said.

That evening Laura and her daughter constructed a dating profile and uploaded it to a site for older adults interested in dating older adults. Laura was amazed to see that within minutes of uploading her profile, men started to look at her profile, some "winked" at her, and some wanted to make contact with her. Even though she got immediate positive responses, Laura indicated to her daughter, "This was fun; I guess I am still attractive, but I am not going to contact anyone."

A few months later Laura decided to go online and see if people were still interested in her. She had been thinking about how many men seemed interested in her after the time she first posted her profile. At this time, Laura began to feel that it would be nice to have some companionship with a man, even if it was just someone she could meet for coffee and lunch once in a while. When she looked online there were over 50 men who had asked for contact during the months when she did not want to go back online.

One of the men struck a chord in Laura. He was 76 years old and an engineer. Laura's husband had been an engineer, so this felt familiar to her. In addition, he indicated that he was working on a project in Saudi Arabia for the next several months. Even though he lived in a suburb of Chicago (another coincidence, Laura thought), he would not be returning to the United States for a long time. This immediately gave Laura a feeling of safety. She could get to know him through e-mail and not have to meet him in person. So, in effect, she would not have to deal with the usual things that go along with dating—*when do we kiss, when do we go to bed together, when does he meet my daughter, when do I meet his family*, and so forth.

(*continued*)

VIGNETTE 7.1 (*continued*)

The new love of Laura's life is Martin. Laura and Martin carried on an e-mail relationship for 3 months. The content of Martin's e-mails to Laura were always respectful and showed a keen interest in Laura. He wanted to know her needs and what makes her happy, he offered to help her with anything she felt conflicted about, and he was keenly interested in knowing about her family members, even welcoming discussion about Laura's deceased husband. Laura was enthralled about how loving, caring, and respectful Martin was in his e-mails. They had exchanged pictures, and Laura found Martin quite attractive, and Martin expressed the same to Laura.

The bliss of their relationship suddenly ended when Laura received an e-mail from Martin indicating that he had been arrested. He told her that he was being held in a police station and that he was given two choices. He could pay the police $50,000 and he would be released, or he would be sent to prison with no chance of a quick release. Martin explained that alcohol is forbidden in Saudi Arabia even though in the compounds where foreigners live alcohol is available (mostly homemade). Saudis who drink do so in the privacy of their own homes. Martin told Laura that he had several drinks in the compound where he lives and then stupidly decided to bring some booze to a friend's house on the outskirts of Riyadh. Usually, he would have a Saudi drive him when outside the compound. This is done because if the police stop you with a Saudi driver and you have alcohol, the police usually steal it, and most often take a small bribe. Martin said that because he was driving, he was arrested and taken to the police station.

Laura was terrified for Martin. She read numerous stories in the past about people in prison in various Arab countries and knew the awful horror Martin would face if she did not help him. So, following Martin's instructions, she wired $50,000 to him and anxiously awaited his next e-mail. Sending this large amount of money was not a problem for Laura. She had a considerable amount of money from her deceased husband's life insurance, and Martin strongly emphasized that as soon as he was released he would be able to wire her the money he borrowed.

(*continued*)

VIGNETTE 7.1 (*continued*)

Three days later Martin wrote back and told her that the $50,000 satisfied the police, but he had to now retain a lawyer to get him officially released from their custody. Because he was still in jail, he could not get access to his bank account to get more money. Laura asked him how much more he needed for the lawyer. Martin told he just a small amount, another $2,500, and he would be free. Once free, he would immediately wire her the $52,500 she helped him with, and then make arrangements to "leave this stinking country" and return to the States, and finally they could meet in person and make a life together. Laura quickly wired another $2,500 to Martin.

That was the last Laura heard from Martin. She wanted to continue trying to contact him, but other than his e-mail address she had no way of reaching Martin. Then, coincidentally, she read in the newspaper how many perpetrators are using Internet dating sites in ways similar to what she experienced to financially exploit older adult women. Laura felt devastated and foolish. So much so that she decided not to confide in anyone, especially her daughter.

Not long after finding out, Laura became progressively depressed, and was not sleeping well because she had recurring nightmares about Martin. Her depression caused her to have a noticeable weight loss, which in turn caused her daughter to question her about this change she was observing. Laura did not disclose what happened but admitted to being depressed. Laura's daughter convinced her that she needed to see a psychologist about her depression, thinking that this was a residual depression from the death of her father from which Laura never recovered.

In addition, older adult abuse may be self-inflicted without the participation of another. Self-inflicted older adult abuse is a dichotomous type of abuse in which the abuse is either *self-neglect* or *self-harm*. Examples of self-neglect include when an older adult neglects himself or herself by not bathing for long periods of time, having limited nutrition and hydration, not taking prescriptions appropriately, or not taking prescriptions at all. Self-harm is when an older adult inflicts injury on himself or herself, such as cutting his or her body without the intent to die, intentionally breaking bones, or engaging in excessive plastic surgery.

THEORETICAL MODELS OF OLDER ADULT ABUSE

Older adult abuse is a complicated and multifactorial problem. With this in mind, it is unlikely that any single causation theory is valid (Anetzberger, 2012; National Criminal Justice Reference Service, 2010). The following sections present two models that view older adult abuse from a multifactorial perspective. The *vulnerability and risk model* is an early model that uses this multifactorial lens. The *subjectivity model* describes the variability in reporting abuse, which calls into question the accuracy of older abuse statistics.

Vulnerability and Risk Model

This is an earlier dichotomous model of older adult abuse that still has significance today. This model explains older adult abuse from the perspective of variables associated with the older adult and variables associated with the caregiver or family member that precipitate abusive behaviors (Rose & Killien, 1983). These factors represent vulnerabilities that occur when an older adult is being abused and vulnerabilities that facilitate abuse behavior by a caregiver or family member. In addition, risk factors are noted for an older adult being abused, or a caregiver or family member committing abuse (Table 7.1).

Subjectivity Hypothesis Model

This model suggests that the variability in reports of older adult abuse is a product of perception that varies among individuals and situations (Ayalon, 2011). Table 7.2 shows examples of

TABLE 7.1 Vulnerability and Risk Variables Associated With Older Adult Abuse in Older Adult Victims and Caregivers and Family Members Who Abuse

VULNERABILITY	
Older Adult Abuse Victim	Caregivers or Family Members
Dementia	Caregiver distress
Difficult or aggressive behavior	Substance abuse and/or alcohol abuse
Disability	
Social isolation	Isolation
Past interpersonal relationship history	Being a foreign home-care worker
	Past interpersonal relationship history
Past family abuse	
Past and present family conflicts	Past family abuse
	Past and present family conflicts
Financial dependence	

RISK FACTORS	
Older Adult Abuse Victim	Caregivers or Family Members
Cognitive impairment	Functional status
Functional disability	History of childhood trauma
Financial dependence	Caregiver chosen by an agency rather than by the older adult
Medical illness	

different perceptions of older adult abuse and biases that mask perceptions of older adult abuse. This model is used to explain the variability in the reporting of older adult abuse.

PREVALENCE OF OLDER ADULT ABUSE

When evaluating the prevalence of older adult abuse, several categories of abuse are considered. Table 7.3 shows the prevalence rates for different types of older adult abuse described by Acierno

TABLE 7.2 Subjective Factors in Perceiving Older Adult Abuse and Factors Masking Perception of an Older Adult Being Abused

Subjective Factors in Perception of Abuse	Biases Masking Perception of Abuse by an Older Adult
Yelling may be perceived as abuse if done frequently, but may not be perceived as abuse if done on an infrequent basis.	An older adult fearing further abuse if reported
The same abusive behavior displayed toward an older adult without dementia is seen as nonabusive when displayed toward an older adult suffering from dementia.	Embarrassment experienced by an older adult who is being abused
	An older adult fearing that he or she will not be believed if reporting being abused
Foreign home-care workers are more accepting of abusive behaviors than are family members and older adult care recipients.	

TABLE 7.3 Prevalence Rates of Older Adult Abuse, Excluding Rates in Nursing Homes

Type of Older Adult Abuse	Prevalence Rate
Emotional	4.6%
Physical	1.6%
Sexual	0.6%
Financial	5.1%

et al. (2010). These rates are consistent with those found in another study (Lachs & Berman, 2011).

However, there is an exponential increase in prevalence rates of abuse when an older adult is in a nursing home. Schiamberg et al. (2012) found that the older adult abuse rate was 25% for those in nursing homes; abuse in this study consisted of forced restraint, physical abuse, and sexual abuse. Page, Conner, Prokhorov, Fang, and Post (2009) found a prevalence rate of 30%, with incidents consisting mostly of neglect, as well as sexual abuse. All of the abusers in the nursing homes studied were staff members.

PERPETRATORS OF OLDER ADULT ABUSE

Historically, perpetrators of older adult abuse were considered, in most instances, to be caregivers of frail older adults, most often a relative of the older adult. Unfortunately, when an older adult is abused, he or she is treated similar to others who were and are abused, regardless of age, by *blaming the victim* (Whittaker, 1995). Before the recent understanding of older adult abuse, an older adult who was abused by a caregiver was often blamed for the abuse, with the faulty reasoning being that if he or she was not so sick, demanding, or difficult to care for, a caregiver would not have been provoked to abuse by the older adult.

Contemporary thought is to focus on the perpetrators of abuse, and not to place responsibility and blame on the victim of abuse, the older adult. Hooyman and Kiyak (2010) found that 70% to 80% of frail older adults' caregivers are family members. They found that the abuse of the older adult was primarily neglect of the older adult, stemming from caregiver distress. This occurs when the caregiver does not provide an adequate amount of food for the older adult, does not help the older adult maintain proper hygiene, has little interaction with the older adult, or allows a hazardous environment for the older adult (see Chapter 8).

Paradoxically, being a caregiver to an older adult may cause a caregiver to experience self-abuse (Brintnall-Peterson, 2012). This type of *caregiver self-abuse* may be an exacerbation of a medical or psychological condition that the caregiver is experiencing, causing the caregiver to engage in substance abuse (see Chapter 6), or compulsive overeating (Brintnall-Peterson, 2012). In most instances, caregivers may begin caregiving to a relative with great willingness and enthusiasm. Their caregiving experience is initially perceived as purposeful and meaningful. However, as time goes by, purpose and meaning diminish and harmful effects of caregiving are experienced (Hoffman & Mendez-Luck, 2011). Therefore, in effect, there is a bilateral relationship between the abuser and the older adult. Ironically, each, in turn, suffers abuse (Lin & Giles, 2013).

However, perpetrators of older adult abuse are not limited to caregivers suffering from distress (Acierno et al., 2010; Brandl & Raymond, 2012). They also include family members, friends, health care professionals, home-care companions, institutional employees, and paid or unpaid caregivers. Brownell and Berman (2004) suggest that psychologists working with older adults who are abused need to focus on the characteristics of the abuser rather than make the error of stigmatizing the older adult (see Chapter 2), who is the victim, as being responsible for and instigating the abuse. Walsh et al. (2011) indicate that to achieve an understanding of the characteristics of an older adult abuser, a psychologist needs to take a *person-in-environment* perspective (see Chapter 3) in order to understand the biopsychosocial stressors converging on abusers that are the etiological roots for their abuse of an older adult. In addition to the bias caused by stigma, the older adult contributes to the lack of identification of the abuser by fearing retribution from the abuser, feeling embarrassed and humiliated by the abuse, or sensing that others will not believe the accusations of abuse. Unfortunately, the consequence of all of these factors is that the perpetrator is not identified (Dienemann, Glass, & Hyman, 2005; Powers et al., 2009).

RISK FACTORS FOR AN OLDER ADULT BEING ABUSED

Risk factors in older adults who are abused are shown in Table 7.4 for the abuse categories of physical abuse, financial exploitation, and neglect.

TABLE 7.4 Risk Factors in Older Adults Who Are Physically Abused, Financially Exploited, or Suffer Neglect

Type of Older Adult Abuse	Risk Factors in the Older Adult
Physical abuse	Dependence on others, confusion, dementia, psychological problems, cohabitation with the abuser, widow/widower, physically or psychologically aggressive toward the abuser, having experienced physical abuse by family members during childhood, being childless
Financial exploitation	Increased age, communication deficits, dependence on others, confusion, dementia, overburdened social support, isolation
Neglect	Increased age, communication deficits, dependence on others, medical problems, confusion, dementia, psychological problems, overburdened social support

TYPES OF OLDER ADULT ABUSE

Table 7.5 shows the multiple factors that underlie older adult abuse, and the actions taken by perpetrators when abusing older adults.

SITES WHERE OLDER ADULT ABUSE MAY OCCUR

Aging in Place

Aging in place is a way to care for older adults in their homes as an alternative to institutional care, such as nursing homes, assisted living facilities, and long-term care facilities. In addition, an

TABLE 7.5 Examples of Types of Older Adult Abuse, Perpetrator's Actions, and Environmental Factors

Type of Older Adult Abuse	Perpetrator Actions and Environmental Factors
Emotional	Lack of privacy, de-individuation by staff, disrespectful behaviors by staff, yelling, causing an older adult to experience fear, anxiety, depression
Financial	Stealing money or valuables, gaining inappropriate control over an older adult's bank account, manipulating an older adult to change his or her will to the perpetrator's benefit
Physical	Beatings, forced restraint, unexplained physical injuries on an older adult
Self-harm	Cutting oneself without the intent to die, voluntarily breaking one's bones, excessive plastic surgery
Self-neglect	Not bathing for long periods of time, poor nutrition, inadequate hydration, not taking prescriptions properly, not taking prescriptions at all, pressure sores
Sexual	Inappropriate fondling, touching, kissing, vaginal intercourse, anal intercourse, oral sex

advantage to aging in place is that it is cost-effective as compared with the cost of institutional care. Many older adults prefer to opt for aging in place because they want to stay in an environment that is familiar and, in many cases, close to family members.

However, there is a dark side to aging in place. Bringing in outside caregivers (home companions and home health aides) increases the probability of and opportunity for older adult abuse. Abuse types are the same as those that occur in institutional settings—physical, emotional, and sexual abuse; financial exploitation; and active and passive neglect. As also occurs in other settings, older adults who are aging in place are often hesitant to report being abused because of fear of further abuse as retribution by the caregiver, embarrassment about being abused, or the feeling that others will not believe that abuse occurred (Dienemann et al., 2005; Powers et al., 2009). Vignette 7.2 demonstrates an attempt to increase the precision of identifying older adult abuse victims where older adults are aging in place.

VIGNETTE 7.2   Training Apartment Service Providers to Be "Watchful Eyes" for Older Adult Residents

New York City partnered with the Harry and Jennette Weinberg Center for Elder Abuse Prevention at the Hebrew Home at Riverdale (New York City) to train doormen, concierges, porters, and other apartment building staff in the five boroughs of New York City to identify signs of older adult abuse. With this training, these building service providers become "watchful eyes" for older adults living in the apartment buildings where they work. Their training teaches them to identify whether outside service providers for older adult residents are removing valuables from the older adult residents' apartments; whether the older adult residents are showing any signs of physical abuse; and whether the older adult residents appear malnourished, seem disoriented, seem isolated, or look sickly and/or dehydrated (Winnie, 2013).

Hospitals

The hospital emergency room is a high-probability location for opportunities to detect older adult abuse. Older adults who are abused tend to use hospital health services at a greater frequency than do older adults who are not abused (Dong & Simon, 2013). The higher frequency of older adults who are abused using emergency room resources with subsequent admissions to hospitals or nursing homes adds social and economic burdens to societies worldwide (Dong, 2005).

Assisted Living Facilities and Nursing Homes

Because of the increased longevity of older adults, substantial numbers of older adults end up in some type of institutionalized residential care (Tanner & Bercaw, 2005). Unfortunately for these older adults, being placed in institutional care is also being placed in an environment that is conducive to older adult abuse. The paradox for these older adults is that older adults who are abused when aging in place have a high rate of admissions to nursing homes, where, unfortunately, being a victim of older adult abuse continues (Dong & Simon, 2013).

Types of older adult abuse that occur in institutional care are multiple. They include physical abuse, psychological/emotional abuse, sexual abuse, active and passive neglect, and financial exploitation (Dixon et al., 2010). These are all examples of violations of basic human rights, and are coupled with lack of privacy, de-individuation, and disrespectful behaviors from staff (Cohen, Halevy-Levin, Gagin, Priltuzky, & Friedman, 2010). The prevalence of such abuse in institutional care for older adults cannot be precisely measured because it is often hidden; older adults in institutional care are hesitant to report abuse, often because they fear retribution, feel embarrassed and humiliated, or fear others not believing that they were indeed abused (Ayalon, 2011; Baker & Heitkemper, 2005). As discussed later in the chapter, older adults experiencing dementia have a greater chance of being a victim of older adult abuse than do older adults not experiencing dementia. In institutional settings (Vignette 7.3), older adults experiencing dementia are the majority of the proportion of residents (Gibbs & Mosqueda, 2004).

VIGNETTE 7.3 Older Adult Abuse in Assisted Living Facilities in Florida

A newspaper reported that many residents are being abused in assisted living facilities in Miami, Florida. These abuses include a 71-year-old woman who was left in a bathtub of scalding water; a 74-year-old woman who was left in restraints that produced a blood clot that caused her death; and a 75-year-old man, an Alzheimer's disease patient, who wandered from a facility and was eventually killed by an alligator. These offenses occurred despite the fact that Florida has very strict laws pertaining to older adult abuse. These are examples of the hidden epidemic of older adult abuse (Barry, Sallah, & Miller, 2011).

Etiological factors that help explain abuse by institutional care staff members include poor salaries, small staff-to-resident ratios, high incidence of *burnout* in staff members, time pressures, and inadequate staff supervision (Hawes, 2003). Nursing aides who are new immigrants experience additional stress from the intersection of the stressors of being newcomers to a culture combined with the stressors just listed that are experienced by all institutional care staff (Patterson & Malley-Morrison, 2006). Complicating the distress of nursing aides are their low wages, few benefits, and little or no continuing education. The low wages cause financial distress within their families, and such distress carries over to their workplaces. All of these stressors lead to burnout and increase the probability that staff members of assisted living and nursing home institutions may engage in abuse of their institution's older adult residents. The burnout these staff members experience is caused by the chronic interpersonal and intrapersonal emotional stresses encountered when working in these institutions. The consequences of this burnout are emotional exhaustion, depersonalization, and a reduced sense of personal accomplishment (Jawahar, Stone, & Kisamore, 2007; Maslach, Schaufeli, & Leiter, 2001).

ABUSE OF OLDER ADULTS WITH DEMENTIA

Older adults experiencing dementia are at high risk for older adult abuse. The incidence is expected to increase exponentially along with the increase in the population of older adults, which is expected to increase from 35.6 million to 115.4 million by 2050. With this increase in the population of older adults, the prevalence of abuse of older adults experiencing dementia is predicted to reach, depending on the study, between 5.4% and 62.3% (Prince et al., 2013; Yan & Kwok, 2011). The reason for this wide range in the projected incidence is because of underreporting by hospitals, institutions, law enforcement, relatives, and caregivers. In addition, some signs of older adult abuse, such as increased dependent behaviors and/or being noncommunicative, are also symptoms associated with dementia (see Chapter 4).

ABUSE OF OLDER ADULTS WITH DISABILITIES

An older adult with a disability is at a higher risk of being abused than an older adult who does not have a disability. This is especially true for older adult women who are disabled (Brownridge, 2006; Casteel, Martin, Smith, Gurka, & Kupper, 2008; Smith, 2008). Unfortunately, the people who abuse disabled older adults are the very people they depend on. These perpetrators include health care professionals, home companions, home health aides, transportation drivers, and other service personnel (Hassouneh-Phillips & McNeff, 2004).

OLDER ADULT SELF-ABUSE

There are two types of older adult self-abuse: *self-neglect* and *self-harm*. Both types of self-abuse threaten the morbidity (medical and psychological health) of older adults and are a risk for mortality (death). There are many factors that place older adults at risk for self-neglect and self-harm.

Self-Neglect

As stated earlier, self-neglect leads to increased morbidity and higher rates of mortality for older adults as compared with older adults who do not engage in self-neglect (Burnett et al., 2012;

Dong et al., 2009). In addition, when older adults engage in self-neglect, they increase the probability that eventually they may become victims of older adult abuse. This increased probability of older adult abuse is based on a meta-analysis of older adult abuse reports to protective service agencies (Dong & Simon, 2013). In addition to being potential abuse victims, older adults engaging in self-neglect are subject to numerous medical problems, often co-occurring problems, such as medical problems co-occurring with dementia (see Chapter 4), psychological problems, and psychological problems co-occurring with medical problems (see Chapter 3). When older adults engage in self-neglect, they do not comply with medical or psychological treatments and/or are not medication compliant, which in turn increases their risk for death (Abrams, Lachs, McAvay, Keohane, & Bruce, 2002; Turner, Hochschild, Burnett, Zulfiqar, & Dyer, 2012).

Self-neglect impairs an older adult's ability to effectively engage in activities of daily living (ADLs). Failure to engage in ADLs occurs when there is a deterioration in executive functioning (see Chapter 4) that causes a diminishment or failure of an older adult to engage in goal-directed behaviors (Insel, Morrow, Brewer, & Figueredo, 2006). The consequences of this diminishment or failure in goal-directed behaviors include noncompliance with medical instructions; misusing, abusing (see Chapter 6), or not taking prescribed medications; and financial mismanagement. Older adults experiencing deterioration in executive functioning are often unaware of these changes in their cognition, resulting in a long period of time before such deterioration is identified by a friend, relative, or caregiver (Naughton, Drennan, Lyons, & Lafferty, 2013).

Deficits in ADLs lead to physical danger, financial problems, and cognitive deficits. Symptoms of problems in ADLs include poor nutrition; dehydration; poor hygiene; failure to pay bills that results in cancellation of needed services, such as utilities; failure to shut off burners on stoves; living in a dirty and/or cluttered environment; and an inability to recognize financial exploitation by others (Tierney, Snow, Moineddin, & Kiss, 2007).

Self-Harm

Self-harm is a problem usually associated with young people, and rarely thought of as occurring with older people (Youdin, 2014). The prevalence of older adults engaging in self-harm is 5% (Dong & Simon, 2013; Harwood & Jacoby, 2000; Penhale, 2010). Although it affects a relatively small percentage of older adults, self-harm is a significant predictor of the potential for a suicide attempt or suicide completion (Harwood & Jacoby, 2000). Self-harm behaviors include cutting (self-mutilation) and voluntary breaking of one's bones.

Self-harm can also be *iatrogenic* (physician enabled). With the great emphasis today on youth and a devaluing of being old, especially looking old, there is a proliferation of media propaganda and medical solutions for combating the physical representations of being old. These include hormone replacement treatments, growth hormone treatments, and plastic surgery procedures. The harms that may result from these medical interventions include a higher probability of coronary heart disease, stroke, pulmonary embolism, breast cancer, dementia, disfigurement, diabetes, and glucose intolerance (Blackman et al., 2002; Janssens & Vanderschueren, 2000; Shumaker et al., 2003).

PRISONS AND OLDER ADULT ABUSE

Crawley (2005) indicates that prison routines and rules are based on convenience to the system, and ignore the special needs of older adult inmates. This produces an institutional construction of abuse of older inmates (see Chapter 8). This abuse is in addition to the physical, emotional, and sexual abuse perpetrated against older inmates by younger imprisoned adults. The older inmates who have the highest risk of older adult abuse are disabled inmates and those older inmates experiencing dementia (see Chapter 4). Alternative solutions to incarceration that need to be developed include halfway houses, specialized geriatric centers, and other ways to accommodate older adult inmates who are frail and no longer a threat to society.

REFERENCES

Abolfathi Momtaz, Y., Hamid, T. A., & Ibrahim, R. (2013). Theories and measures of elder abuse. *Psychogeriatrics, 13*(3), 182–188.

Abrams, R. C., Lachs, M., McAvay, G., Keohane, D. J., & Bruce, M. L. (2002). Predictors of self-neglect in community-dwelling elders. *American Journal of Psychiatry, 159*(10), 1724–1730.

Acierno, R., Hernandez, M. A., Arnstadter, A. B., Resnick, H. S., Steve, K., Muzzy, W., & Kilpatrick, D. G. (2010). Prevalence and correlates of emotional, physical, sexual, and financial abuse and potential neglect in the United States: The National Elder Mistreatment Study. *American Journal of Public Health, 100*(2), 292–297.

Anetzberger, G. J. (2012). An update on the nature and scope of elder abuse. *Generations, 36*(3), 12–20.

Ayalon, L. (2011). Abuse is in the eyes of the beholder: Using multiple perspectives to evaluate elder mistreatment under round-the-clock foreign home carers in Israel. *Ageing and Society, 31*(3), 499–520. doi:10.1017/S0144686X1000108X

Baker, M. W., & Heitkemper, M. M. (2005). The roles of nurses on interprofessional teams to combat elder mistreatment. *Nursing Outlook, 53*(5), 253–259.

Barry, R., Sallah, M., & Miller, C. M. (2011). Neglected to death: Part 1: Once pride of Florida; now scenes of neglect. *Miami Herald.* Retrieved from http://www.miamiherald.com/2011/04/30/2194842/once-pride-of-florida-now-scenes.html

Blackman, M. R., Sorkin, J. D., Munzer, T., Bellantoni, M. F., Busby-Whitehead, J., Stevens, T. E., . . . Harman, S. M. (2002). Growth hormone and sex steroid administration in healthy aged women and men: A randomized control trial. *JAMA, 288*(18), 282–292.

Brandl, B., & Raymond, J. A. (2012). Policy implications of recognizing that caregiver stress is not the primary cause of elder abuse. *Generations, 36*(3), 32–39.

Brintnall-Peterson, M. (2012). *Caregiving is different for everyone.* Madison, WI: University of Wisconsin Extension.

Brownell, P., & Berman, J. (2004). Homicides of older women in New York City. In A. R. Roberts & K. R. Yeager (Eds.), *Evidence-based practice manual* (pp. 771–778). New York, NY: Oxford University Press.

Brownridge, D. A. (2006). Partner violence against women with disabilities: Prevalence, risk, and explanations. *Violence Against Women*, *12*(9), 805–822.

Burnett, J., Achenbaum, W. A., Hayes, L., Flores, D. V., Hochschild, A. E., Kao, D., . . . Dyer, C. B. (2012). Increasing surveillance and prevention efforts for elder self-neglect in clinical settings. *Aging Health*, *8*(6), 647–655. doi:10.2217/ahe.12.67

Butler, R. N. (1975). *Why survive? Being old in America*. New York, NY: Harper & Row.

Casteel, C., Martin, S. L., Smith, J. B., Gurka, K. K., & Kupper, L. L. (2008). National study of physical and sexual assault among women with disabilities. *Injury Prevention*, *14*(2), 87–90.

Cohen, M., Halevy-Levin, S., Gagin, R., Priltuzky, D., & Friedman, G. (2010). Elder abuse in long-term care residences and the risk indicators. *Ageing and Society*, *30*(6), 1027–1040. doi:10.1017/S0144686X10000188

Crawley, E. (2005). Institutional thoughtlessness in prisons and its impacts on the day-to-day prison lives of elderly men. *Journal of Contemporary Criminal Justice*, *21*(4), 350.

Crystal, S. (1986). Social policy and elder abuse. In K. A. Pillemer & R. S. Wolf (Eds.), *Elder abuse: Conflict in the family* (pp. 331–340). Dover, MA: Auburn House.

Dienemann, J., Glass, N., & Hyman, R. (2005). Survivor preferences for response to IPV disclosure. *Clinical Nursing Research*, *14*(3), 215–233.

Dixon, J., Manthorpe, J., Biggs, S., Mowlam, A., Tennant, R., Tinker, A., & McCreadie, C. (2010). Defining elder mistreatment: Reflections on the United Kingdom study of abuse and neglect of older people. *Ageing and Society*, *30*(3), 403–420. doi:10.1017/S0144686X0999047X

Dong, X. (2005). Medical implication of elder abuse and neglect. *Clinical Geriatric Medicine*, *21*(2), 293–313.

Dong, X., Simon, M., Mendes de Leon, C. F., Fulmer, T., Beck, T., Hebert, L., . . . Evans, D. (2009). Elder self-neglect and abuse and mortality risk in a community-dwelling population. *JAMA*, *302*(5), 517–526.

Dong, X., & Simon, M. A. (2013). Association between elder abuse and use of ED: Findings from the Chicago Health and Aging Project. *American Journal of Emergency Medicine*, *31*(4), 693–698. doi:10.1016/j.ajem.2012.12.028

Gibbs, L. M., & Mosqueda, L. (2004). Confronting elder mistreatment in long-term care. *Annals of Long-Term Care*, *12*(4), 30–35.

Harwood, D., & Jacoby, R. (2000). Suicide behavior amongst the elderly. In K. Hawton & K. Van Heering (Eds.), *The international handbook of suicide and attempted suicide* (pp. 275–291). Chichester, England: John Wiley & Sons.

Hassouneh-Phillips, D. S., & McNeff, E. (2004). Understanding care-related abuse and neglect in the lives of women with SCI. *Spinal Cord Injury Nursing, 21*(2), 75–81.

Hawes, C. (2003). Elder abuse in residential long-term care settings: What is known and what information is needed? In R. J. Bonnie & R. B. Wallace (Eds.), *Elder mistreatment: Abuse, neglect, and exploitation in an aging America* (pp. 446–500). Washington, DC: National Academies Press.

Hoffman, G., & Mendez-Luck, C. (2011). *Stressed and strapped: Caregivers in California. Health policy brief for the Center for Health Policy Research.* Los Angeles, CA: University of California, Los Angeles.

Hooyman, N. R., & Kiyak, H. A. (2010). *Social gerontology: A multidisciplinary perspective.* Boston, MA: Pearson Allyn & Bacon.

Insel, K., Morrow, D., Brewer, B., & Figueredo, A. (2006). Executive function, working memory, and medication adherence among older adults. *Journal of Gerontology: Biomedical Sciences, 61*(B), 102–107.

Janssens, H., & Vanderschueren, D. M. O. I. (2000). Endocrinological aspects of aging in men: Is hormone replacement of benefit? *European Journal of Obstetrics and Gynecological Reproductive Biology, 92*, 7–12.

Jawahar, I. M., Stone, T. H., & Kisamore, J. L. (2007). Role conflict and burnout: The direct and moderating effects of political skill and perceived organizational support on burnout dimensions. *International Journal of Stress Management, 14*, 142–159.

Lachs, M. S., & Berman, J. (2011). *New York State Elder Abuse Prevalence Study. Self-reported prevalence and documented case surveys: Final report.* New York, NY: Lifespan of Greater Rochester, Inc., Weill Cornell University, New York City Department of Aging.

Lin, M.-C., & Giles, H. (2013). The dark side of family communication: A communication model of elder abuse and neglect. *International Psychogeriatrics, 25*(8), 1275–1290. doi:10.1159/000321881.2112400910.1300/J084v02n01_05http://dx.doi.org/10.1017/S1041610212002347

Maslach, C. S., Schaufeli, W. B., & Leiter, M. P. (2001). Job burnout. *Annual Review of Psychology, 52*, 397–422.

McCreadie, C. (2007). The mistreatment and abuse of older people. *Journal of Care Services, 1*(2), 173–179.

National Criminal Justice Reference Service. (2010). *The course of domestic abuse among Chicago's elderly: Risk factors, protective behaviors, and police intervention*. Retrieved from http://www.ncjrs.gov/pdffiles1/nij/grants/232623.pdf

Naughton, C., Drennan, J., Lyons, I., & Lafferty, A. (2013). The relationship between older people's awareness of the term elder abuse and actual experiences of elder abuse. *International Psychogeriatrics, 25*(8), 1257–1266. doi:10.1017/S1041610213000513

Page, C., Conner, T., Prokhorov, A., Fang, Y., & Post, L. (2009). The effect of care setting on elder abuse: Results from a Michigan survey. *Journal of Elder Abuse & Neglect, 21*(3), 239–252.

Patterson, M., & Malley-Morrison, K. (2006). Cognitive-ecological approach to elder abuse in five cultures: Human rights and education. *Educational Gerontology, 32*, 72–82.

Penhale, B. (2010). Responding and intervening in elder abuse and neglect. *Ageing International, 35*(3), 235–252. doi:10.1007/s12126-010-9065-0

Powers, L., Renker, P., Robinson-Whelen, S., Oschwald, M., Hughes, R. B. P., Swank, P., & Curry, M. A. (2009). Interpersonal violence and women with disabilities: Analysis of safety promoting behaviors. *Violence Against Women, 15*(9), 1040–1069.

Prince, M., Bryce, R., Albanese, E., Wimo, A., Ribeiro, W., & Ferri, C. P. (2013). The global prevalence of dementia: A systematic review and meta-analysis. *Alzheimer's & Dementia, 9*(1), 63–75.

Rose, M. H., & Killien, M. (1983). Risk and vulnerability: A case for differentiation. *Advances in Nursing Science, 5*(3), 60–73.

Schiamberg, L. B., Oehnmke, J., Zhang, Z., Barboza, G. E., Griffore, R. J., von Heydrich, L., . . . Maslin, T. (2012). Physical abuse of older adults in nursing homes: A random sample survey of adults with an elderly family member in a nursing home. *Journal of Elder Abuse & Neglect, 24*(1), 65–83.

Shumaker, S. A., Legault, C., Rapp, S. R., Thai, L., Wallace, R. B., Ockkene, J. K., . . . Wacatawski-Wende, J. (2003). Estrogen plus progestin and the incidence of dementia and mild cognitive impairment in postmenopausal women. The Women's Health Initiative Memory study: A randomized controlled trial. *JAMA, 289*(20), 2651–2662.

Smith, D. L. (2008). Disability, gender, and intimate partner violence: Relationships from the Behavioral Risk Factor Surveillance System. *Sexuality and Disability, 26*(1), 15–28.

Tanner, R., & Bercaw, L. (2005, December 31). Long-term care: Nursing home quality and safety. *Issue Brief Health Policy Tracking Service*, 1–17.

Tierney, M. C., Snow, W. G., Moineddin, C. J., & Kiss, A. (2007). Neuropsychological predictors of self-neglect in cognitively impaired older people who live alone. *American Journal of Geriatric Psychiatry*, 15(2), 140–148.

Turner, A., Hochschild, A., Burnett, J., Zulfiqar, A., & Dyer, C. B. (2012). High prevalence of medication non-adherence in a sample of community-dwelling older adults with Adult Protective Services validated self-neglect. *Drugs & Aging*, 29(9), 741–749.

von Heydrich, L., Schiamberg, L. B., & Chee, G. (2012). Social-relational risk factors for predicting elder physical abuse: An ecological bi-focal model. *International Journal of Aging and Human Development*, 75(1), 71–94.

Walsh, C. A., Olsen, J. L., Ploeg, J., Lohfield, L., & MacMillan, H. L. (2011). Elder abuse and oppression: Voices of marginalized elders. *Journal of Elder Abuse & Neglect*, 23(1), 17–42.

Whittaker, T. (1995). Violence, gender and elder abuse: Towards a feminist analysis and practice. *Journal of Gender Studies*, 4(1), 35–46.

Winnie, H. J. (2013, October 28). To combat elder abuse, doormen are enlisted to keep a watchful eye. *The New York Times*, p. A22.

Yan, E., & Kwok, T. (2011). Abuse of older Chinese with dementia by family caregivers: An inquiry into the role of caregiver burden. *International Journal of Geriatric Psychiatry*, 26(5), 527–535.

Youdin, R. (2014). *Clinical gerontological social work practice*. New York, NY: Springer Publishing Company.

Environmental Geropsychology

Thriving is a holistic, life-span perspective that considers the impact of environment as people age. Thriving is achieved when there is harmony among a person and his or her physical environment and personal relationships. Failure to thrive is because of discord among these three elements.

Haight, Barba, Tesh, and Courts (2002)

s described in Chapter 3, the theoretical focus of a strength-based orientation to psychological functioning of older adults is based on the *person-in-environment theory*. The person-in-environment theory was developed out of Lawton and Nahemow's *ecological model* (1973). When combined with Lewin's *field theory model* (1951), both theories form the foundation for environmental geropsychology.

Referring to Lewin's *field theory model* (Figure 8.1), Lewin indicates that in the case of an older adult, the older adult's behavior

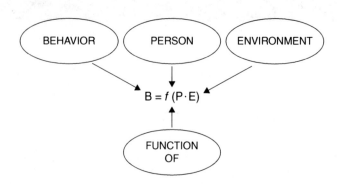

FIGURE 8.1 Lewin's conceptual equation of field theory.

reflects the interaction between the older adult and his or her environment. Contemporary psychotherapy addresses behavioral issues of an older adult by focusing on the degree to which an older adult is able to cope positively (*resilience*) with the environmental stressors converging on him or her. Psychopathology is viewed as the degree of *reduction in resilience* to these environmental stressors that is reflected by symptoms. A psychologist using the medical model (see Chapter 3) aggregates these symptoms into a symptom constellation that is transformed into a diagnosis based on the current version of the *Diagnostic and Statistical Manual of Mental Disorders* (5th ed.; *DSM-5*; American Psychiatric Association [APA], 2013). An environmental geropsychologist focuses on the environment component of Lewin's equation and develops interventions to change older adults' interpersonal and intrapersonal experiences with psychosocial stressors with interventions aimed at the environment (Gifford, 2007).

THE HUMAN–ENVIRONMENT INTERFACE

Ittelson (Ittelson, 1995; Ittelson, Rivlin, & Proshansky, 1976) coined the term *environmental psychology* as a distinct subdivision in the field of psychology. Environmental geropsychology is a growing

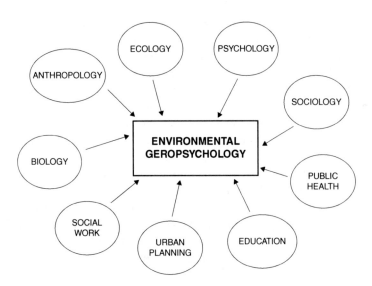

FIGURE 8.2 Environmental geropsychology is integrative, incorporating theories and techniques from allied fields.

subspecialty of environmental psychology solely devoted to the study of the interaction between older adults and their environments. An environmental geropsychologist intervenes in the area of older adults' environments for the purpose of changing their behaviors and enhancing their sense of well-being. Environmental geropsychology is integrative, incorporating theories and techniques from numerous allied fields (Figure 8.2). An environmental geropsychologist uses these converging theoretical and technical influences to inform decisions about what changes in the behaviors of older adults are needed. These environmental changes include those institutions that affect older adults by policy and physical environments that occur within the constraints of naturally occurring and fixed aspects of older adults' environments (De Young, 2010). An older adult's environment is composed of natural and constructed environments. Natural environments include geography and climate. Constructed environments include communities; institutions, such as hospitals and nursing homes; roads, sidewalks, and monuments; and policies—all of which are made by human construction.

Older adults are affected by many aspects of their environments, all of which are assessed, and at times become the focus of interventions by environmental geropsychologists. This is important because older adults constantly process and interact with the elements of their environments in order to develop a sense of self, and self in place. When older adults are treated with psychotherapy, the focus of treatment is on solving their problems, restoring resilience to environmental stressors, and building on existing strengths within them to facilitate problem solving (see Chapter 3). Unlike psychotherapy, an environmental psychologist facilitates change in older adults through the modification of their environments. By improving the interaction between older adults and their environments, environmental geropsychologists facilitate change within older adults, as well as among older adults, and between older adults and younger people.

THEORETICAL MODELS UNDERLYING ENVIRONMENTAL GEROPSYCHOLOGY

To date, there is no unifying theory of environmental geropsychology. As illustrated in Figure 8.2, environmental geropsychology borrows theories from a variety of related fields. Although environmental geropsychology uses the person-in-environment theory as a foundational theory, its focus is interactional in nature, and it has many lenses through which to view the interaction between an older adult and his or her environment. The following sections describe some theoretical models that are useful when trying to understand the complexity of the interaction between an older adult and his or her environment.

The Theory of Affordances

The *theory of affordances* states that the perceptions that older adults have of their physical environments have functional significance for older adults, and shape older adults' behaviors (Heft, 2010). This lends an opportunity for psychologists to change environmental factors for the purpose of creating functional significances to older adults, which in turn change their behaviors for a beneficial purpose or many beneficial purposes. Such changes may be used to motivate older adults to increase their movement by walking, to increase interpersonal communication, to increase intergenerational communication, or to facilitate an enhanced quality of life. This is often achieved by enhancing an older adult's environment with decorative landscaping and enhancing interior designs of buildings used by older adults with artwork, comfortable furniture, and handicapped-accessible features created by using techniques of *universal design*. Universal design enables modification of an older adult's home to keep the older adult aging in place in a safe and accessible environment without the living space appearing institutional or intimidating to an older adult and relatives/caregivers.

The Reasonable Person Model

The *reasonable person model* is a theoretical model stating that older people will act more positively in an environment that provides information to support positive behaviors (Kaplan & Kaplan, 2005). Kaplan and Kaplan (2005) indicate that in order for reasonableness to occur within an individual, a mental model that understands and explains human needs for understanding and exploration is essential for a psychologist. Once these needs for understanding and exploring the environment are met, an older adult needs to be assisted with a clear understanding of the aspects of his or her environment to respond appropriately to the environmental interventions initiated by a psychologist with the goal of facilitating an enhanced quality of life. The final stage of this model is the maintenance of meaningful actions by the older adult to bring about a consistent and endurable change in behavior.

This is achieved, for example, by placing informational signs in communities where older adults live that direct them to a clubhouse, areas for walking, available restrooms, recreational areas, dining areas, and so forth. In urban areas with older adult populations, similar signage can be developed with additional signs indicating historical locations and transportation hubs such as bus stops, subway or metro access, and taxi locations. All types of information provisions may cause older adults to actively feel an engagement with their environment, thus supporting positive behaviors such as increased movement, less isolation, and more interpersonal interaction.

The Theory of Social Settings

An early theoretical perspective is the *theory of social settings.* This theory states that social settings influence human behavior (Barker, 1968). Therefore, the social setting is the environmental target of the psychologist's interventions to improve and/or increase interpersonal interaction. In the case of an older adult, interpersonal interactions may be within his or her cohort or may be intergenerational, depending on the social goal determined by the social needs of the older adult, and the assessment of the psychologist of the elements in need of change in the social setting. An aspect of social settings that is often focused upon by environmental geropsychologists is the density and crowding of a social environment. As the density increases, an older adult's mood can be affected negatively, and an older adult's medical status can be compromised by the increased distress in the environment caused by overcrowding, noise, or inadequate physical accommodations (place to sit, private space, etc.).

The Tri-Dimensional Intervention Model

The *tri-dimensional intervention model* states that there is a comprehensive interaction among the *cognitive, conative,* and *affective* components in an older adult's environment (Shukla, 2008). All three components are the targets for intervention by an environmental geropsychologist. In interventions targeting the cognitive component, a psychologist may use cognitive behavioral therapy techniques to help an older adult change his or her attitude toward an environmental stressor through active problem solving and cognitive reframing. For many older adults, these techniques facilitate a more positive experience and outlook when interfacing with environmental stressors. More information on cognitive behavioral therapy can be found on the Beck Institute's website (www.beckinstitute.org).

The conative component is the aspect of the brain that acts on one's thoughts and feelings. A psychologist who teaches behaviors to an older adult that enable an older adult to exercise more ecologically friendly behavior toward his or her environment addresses this component. An example would be supporting an older adult to tend to a garden. By making such efforts, the older adult improves his or her environment, developing a sense of empowerment from the positive improvements made and the subsequent joy and satisfaction from the environmental change.

The affective component borrows from biology. All biological systems that have opposing components seek to keep the respective system in balance. For example, populations of people remain in balance with their environment when there is a steady rate of births and deaths. This balance of births and deaths is called *homeostasis*. When modifying an older adult's environment, an environmental geropsychologist facilitates a balance (homeostasis) between an older adult and positive aspects of his or her environment that support positive behaviors in the older adult.

IMPLICIT AGEISM: ENVIRONMENTAL AGEISM AND ITS EFFECTS ON OLDER ADULTS

Institutions are a significant component of an older adult's environment. The phenomenon of institutional ageism (see Chapter 2), also called *implicit ageism* (Levy & Banajo, 2002), has a profound effect on an older adult's quality of life. Institutional ageism is evidenced by discrimination in housing, discrimination in employment, mandatory employment policies, public policies that have negative effects on older adults, and inappropriate care and/or abuse by institutional staff (see Chapter 7) (Palmore, 2004). Examples of institutional ageism that oppress an older adult are ageist language, patronizing attitudes toward older adults, and age segregation (Butler, 2009). A classic example of ageist patronizing language occurs when nursing home staff members address older residents using *baby talk* (Levy & Banajo, 2002).

ENVIRONMENTAL INTERVENTIONS

Environmental Interventions to Increase Medical and Psychological Health

Physical exercise, mostly walking, proves to be beneficial to older adults by increasing their feelings of well-being, improving their health status, and improving cognitive functioning, especially executive functioning (Eggermont, Milber, Lipsitz, Scherder, & Leveille, 2009; Windle, Hughes, Linck, Russell, & Woods, 2010). Older adults experiencing chronic diseases may decrease their morbidity (sickness) and increase the probability of not experiencing sudden death if they engage in walking a minimum of 30 minutes per day, at least 5 days per week (Murray et al., 2012). In addition, this type of moderate exercise reduces the probability of developing a chronic illness (Murray et al., 2012). Therefore, an exercise regimen as simple as walking several times per week will increase the overall quality of life for older adults (Balboa-Castillo, Leon-Munoz, Graciani, Rodtiquez-Artalejo, & Guallar-Castillon, 2011). In this case, walking is seen as an environmental intervention that a psychologist can introduce to an older adult suffering from a chronic illness and/or experiencing psychological problems. Having a psychologist participate in interventions targeting an older adult's walking ability is important because of the complexity of feelings, conflicts, and issues the older adult may be experiencing that co-occur with his or her deficient amount of movement. A psychologist then has the opportunity to address the issues that have caused the older adult to remain mostly sedentary. This is often done in collaboration with the physician(s) treating the older adult for co-occurring medical and/or psychological problems.

Psychologists specializing in environmental geropsychology often advise communities and developers of urban design components that will facilitate walking for older adults within their community. Alfonzo (2005) recommends the environmental interventions listed in Table 8.1.

TABLE 8.1 Physical Environmental Factors and Interventions to Facilitate Older Adults Walking in the Community

Environmental Factors		Interventions		
Distance	Keeping destinations as close as possible to where older adults live	Presence of a sidewalk		
Comfort	Sidewalk evenness	Walking areas separate from traffic	Benches available throughout walking routes	
Safety and crime prevention	Closed circuit television monitors (CCTV)	Elimination of hiding places for perpetrators		
Pleasantness	Decorative vegetation	Historic information elements	Mixed land use	

Adapted from Alfonzo (2005).

Environmental Interventions to Encourage Social Connectedness and Intergenerational Communication and Socialization

Historically, as Cumming and Henry (1961) proposed, older adults engage in *voluntary social disengagement*, indicating that this is an irreversible process that leads to profound isolation. This theory was challenged by proponents of the *activity theory*, which states that older adults who remain socially active are more satisfied with their lives and aging, and are healthier than those older adults who disengage and isolate (Lemon, Bengtson, & Peterson, 1972). The activity theory dispels the notion that older adults engage in voluntary social disengagement with consequential irreversible isolation. Cumming's and Henry's theory of voluntary social disengagement supports a common stereotype of older adult isolation (see Chapter 2) that is still believed by some today.

Influenced by activity theory, environmental geropsychologists recognize that creating or expanding social networks is an essential environmental intervention to counteract the shrinking of social networks that occurs as people age when family members and friends die, or when an older adult is relocated to a new neighborhood because of the need for placement in an assisted living facility or a restricted older adult community (McPherson, Miller, & Cook, 2001; Schnittker, 2007). Environmental geropsychology research indicates that the shrinking of social networks is a paradoxical effect of older adults valuing higher-quality social relationships while leaving less-valued relationships (McPherson et al., 2001; Schnittker, 2007; Shaw, Krause, Liang, & Bennett, 2007). These high-quality relationships include kin and supportive friends, each having a strong emotional connection to an older adult. The less-valued relationships are acquaintances and dysfunctional kin, each being devoid of positive emotional connections. Confounding factors that strain and make maintaining high-quality social relationships difficult are retirement, relocation, medical illness, and psychological problems an older adult may be experiencing.

Environmental geropsychologists, recognizing the importance of social networks, work to facilitate communities to involve older adults in activities through community organizations and interorganizational interactions (Cornwell & Harrison, 2004). Community environmental resources are a ready-made environmental social construction that facilitates social interaction and social activity. Community organizations, faith-based communities and organizations, and volunteer organizations provide an opportunity for older adults to increase the probability of social interaction and the development of emotional ties that arise from shared interests.

Within residential communities, psychologists can help community members join one another in informal networks to provide mutual aid to older adults who, for health conditions and disability status, may not be able to participate in the community organizations and volunteer organizations. In communities where there are young, middle-aged, and older adults, such community aid facilitates intergenerational communication by providing opportunities for older adults to extend their social networks intergenerationally (Li & Ferraro, 2006; Shaw et al., 2007) (Vignette 8.1).

VIGNETTE 8.1   Creating a Community Garden to Facilitate Intergenerational Communication and Possible Intergenerational Social Networks

(*Note:* Names and other identifying information have been changed to preserve confidentiality.)

The board of directors of a condominium community of 600 homes enlisted the help of an environmental geropsychologist to solve a problem regarding the social isolation of many older adults living in this mixed-age community. Of the 600 homes, older adults live in 20% of these homes, and are 70 years old and older. Some of these older adults reported to the board of directors their concerns that

(continued)

VIGNETTE 8.1 (*continued*)

many of their fellow older residents are isolating themselves from social contact with younger residents and, surprisingly, with residents in their age cohorts. Some of these older adults are disabled, some have chronic medical problems, and some are suspected of being depressed.

The consulting environmental geropsychologist spent a considerable amount of time visiting most of these older adult residents to determine what, if any, environmental interventions could be employed to address the concerns brought to the board of directors. Many of the older adult residents shared similar concerns with the psychologist. They indicated that even though many of their neighbors are similar in age, they do not have much of a relationship with one another, aside from greeting each other in passing within the community walking areas. Many indicated that some residents are too ill to go to the clubhouse for the various social activities. Others indicated that the clubhouse social activities were dominated by younger residents who tended to shun them the few times they tried to participate in a social activity such as bridge playing, Scrabble tournaments, and book discussions. They said that they felt that younger people did not seem to share the same interests and, consequently, they felt out of place when they tried to join the younger residents in an activity. Many concluded, "It feels better to stay at home and watch television."

The psychologist met with the board of directors after completing her assessment of the older adults. She recommended a three-stage program to facilitate intergenerational contact that did not require participation in the social events at the clubhouse. The three-stage program comprised the following aspects:

1. A *senior watch* program in which residents, both young and old, would be encouraged to contact their older neighbors at least once a week to see if they needed any help with getting food, or possibly a ride to a physician appointment. As part of this initiative, an informal carpooling network would be set up whereby residents, young and old, would voluntarily offer an older neighbor a ride when they were going to local stores, giving

(continued)

VIGNETTE 8.1 (*continued*)

older residents who were unable to drive a chance to shop independently rather than depend on deliveries from stores, which are expensive and enable isolation.

2. The community would install benches at convenient intervals on public walkways so that older residents would have places to rest while increasing their amount of walking, which would benefit their psychological and physical health. In addition, older adults sitting on the benches would have more opportunities for socialization with neighbors either sitting or walking by the benches. The psychologists noted that this community had a loop road that many residents used for walks during the day and evening. Because this road was 2 miles in length, many older residents did not use it for walking because it did not have areas for resting.

3. A community garden would be established whereby a committee of residents would plan the garden during the upcoming winter, and the planting and maintenance of the garden would start in the spring. All planting activities and maintenance work would be accomplished by residents, not the maintenance staff or landscaping staff of the community.

To the surprise of the board of directors, older residents dominated the first garden-planning meeting. Some younger residents attended, but they were in the minority. When the psychologist debriefed the older adults who attended the meeting, she was told that this was the first time they felt a sense of importance in the community. They also said that they enjoyed interacting with the younger members and felt a degree of acceptance by them, correcting many misconceptions they had about why they were being rejected (e.g., "they think we are stupid because we are old," "we are too sick to enjoy anything," "most of us are senile").

At the end of the summer, the psychologist returned to the community and attended a meeting of the garden community. Over the summer, more older adults started participating in the work in the garden. Of the 20% who were originally seen as isolating, at least 60% were engaging in socialization both intergenerationally and within the older cohorts. Many of the older adults formed friendships

(continued)

> **VIGNETTE 8.1** (*continued*)
>
> with one another, but still preferred to socialize with one another in their homes rather than the clubhouse. The overall consensus was that the clubhouse was still a place for the younger residents. However, they were not as troubled by this as they were in the past because of their participation in the garden club and the increased socialization taking place within their homes.
>
> When questioned about walking, they indicated that the benches helped because they were able to rest. However, they reported that the only conversations that occurred were between older adults who would join each other on the benches, as the younger residents would either jog or walk by without stopping.
>
> The older adults felt that the carpooling idea was good, although the opportunities for carpooling were infrequent. However, they did indicate that fellow younger members of the garden club seemed to make themselves more available for carpooling than did others who were not members of the garden club.

Environment and Dementia: A Positive Approach

Late-life relocation to an assisted living facility, continuing care community, or a senior-only residential community is a significant life stressor affecting older adults and their relatives and caregivers (Mead, Eckert, Zimmerman, & Schumacher, 2005). Faced with a late-life relocation, many older adults react to this anticipated change in their environment with fear that is exacerbated by the anticipation of loss of their social support systems, familiar surroundings, and nearness of family members and friends (Lee, Woo, & Mackenzie, 2002).

Late-life relocation is worse for older adults experiencing dementia (see Chapter 4). Symptoms of older adults experiencing dementia are often exacerbated when they, because of their symptoms, are moved from a home environment to an assisted living facility or nursing home (Lee et al., 2002; Mead et al., 2005). These symptoms include increased impairment in their functioning, behavior disturbances, and the risk of elevated mortality.

To address these concerns, a unique community was established in Holland (see Vignette 8.2) that created an environment unlike any assisted living facility or nursing home, which are the usual destinations for older adults experiencing dementia and in need of late-life relocation. More information about this village can be found on its website (hogeweyk.dementiavillage.com/en).

VIGNETTE 8.2   A Fully Equipped Village Allows Dementia Patients Normal, Independent Lives

A village was created in Holland for older adults experiencing severe cases of dementia (Yam, 2015). Currently 152 residents are housed in 23 apartment units. Caregivers live with the residents in the apartment units. Therefore, there is not an immediate distinction between residents and caregivers on first sight. In addition, the caregivers help run the shops and provide services in the village. The village confines the residents to the village proper, allowing the residents to roam within the village and enjoy the activities and shops of the village. This gives the residents an approximation of normal living despite the fact of being confined. The developers of this village have been criticized by others who claim that they are providing a *fantasy life* for these residents experiencing severe dementia.

The creators of this village counter this criticism by claiming that providing a humanistic environment for the residents is a more ethical approach than the traditional confined hospital and assisted living environments. So far, indications are that these residents need less medication and live longer as compared with patients in traditional hospitals and assisted living environments.

Unlike in the humanistic village in Holland, older adults who live in assisted living facilities for Alzheimer's disease patients and patients experiencing other types of dementia (see Chapter 4) are subjected to an unfamiliar environment that is enclosed within a floor unit, has locked doors to prevent wandering, and has staff members attending to their needs without the ongoing presence of family members and/or friends. In addition, there are little, if any, physical aspects of the older adult's previous home environment, such as furniture, pictures, or the bed and bedding that he or she used for sleep. Access to dining is mostly communal or, in advanced cases, restricted to patient rooms, and eating occurs only at times controlled by the institution's schedules.

REFERENCES

Alfonzo, M. A. (2005). To walk or not to walk? The hierarchy of walking needs. *Environment and Behavior, 37*, 808–836.

American Psychiatric Association. (2013). *Diagnostic and statistical manual of mental disorders* (5th ed.). Washington, DC: Author.

Balboa-Castillo, T., Leon-Munoz, L. M., Graciani, A., Rodtiquez-Artalejo, F., & Guallar-Castillon, P. (2011). Longitudinal association of physical activity and sedentary behavior during leisure time with health-related quality of life in community-dwelling older adults. *Health and Quality of Life Outcomes, 9*, 47–57.

Barker, R. G. (1968). *Ecological psychology: Concepts and methods for studying the environment of human behavior*. Stanford, CA: Stanford University Press.

Butler, R. N. (2009). Combating ageism. *International Psychogeriatrics, 21*, 221.

Cornwell, B., & Harrison, J. A. (2004). Union members and voluntary associations: Membership overlap as a case of organizational embeddedness. *American Sociological Review, 69*, 862–881.

Cumming, E., & Henry, W. E. (1961). *Growing old: The process of disengagement*. New York, NY: Basic Books.

De Young, R. (2010). Restoring mental vitality in an endangered world. *Ecopsychology, 2*, 13–22.

Eggermont, L. H. P., Milber, W. P., Lipsitz, L. A., Scherder, E. J. A., & Leveille, S. G. (2009). Physical activity and executive function in aging: The Mobilize Boston study. *Journal of the American Geriatrics Society, 57*, 1750–1756.

Gifford, R. (2007). *Environmental psychology: Principles and practice* (4th ed.). Canada: Optimal Books.

Haight, B. K., Barba, B. E., Tesh, A. S., & Courts, N. F. (2002). Thriving: A life span theory. In K. L. Mauk (Ed.), *Gerontological nursing: Competencies for care* (3rd ed., p. 87). Burlington, MA: Jones & Bartlett Learning.

Heft, H. (2010). Affordances and the perception of landscape: An inquiry into environmental perception and aesthetics. In C. Ward Thompson, P. Aspinall, & S. Bell (Eds.), *Open spaces. People space 2: Innovative approaches to researching landscape and health* (pp. 9–32). London, England: Routledge.

Ittelson, W. H. (1995). Interview with Bill Ittelson. *Environmental Theory Atena, 3,* 1–7.

Ittelson, W. H., Rivlin, L. G., & Proshansky, H. H. (1976). The use of behavioral maps in environmental psychology. In H. H. Proshansky, W. H. Ittelson, & L. G. Rivlin (Eds.), *Environmental psychology: People and their physical settings* (2nd ed., pp. 340–351). New York, NY: Holt Rinehart & Winston.

Kaplan, R., & Kaplan, S. (2005). Preference, restoration, and meaningful action in the context of nearby nature. In P. F. Barlett (Ed.), *Urban place: Reconnecting with the natural world* (pp. 271–298). Cambridge, MA: MIT Press.

Lawton, M. P., & Nahemow, L. (1973). Ecology and the aging process. In C. Eisdorfer & M. P. Lawton (Eds.), *The psychology of adult development and aging* (pp. 619–674). Washington, DC: American Psychological Association.

Lee, D., Woo, J., & Mackenzie, A. E. (2002). The cultural context of adjusting to nursing home life: Chinese elders' perspectives. *The Gerontologist, 42,* 667–675.

Lemon, F. R., Bengtson, V. L., & Peterson, J. A. (1972). An exploration of activity theory of aging: Activity types and life satisfaction among in-movers to a retirement community. *Journal of Gerontology, 27,* 511–523.

Levy, B. R., & Banajo, M. R. (2002). Implicit ageism. In T. Nelson (Ed.), *Ageism: Stereotyping and prejudice against older persons* (pp. 49–75). Cambridge, MA: MIT Press.

Lewin, K. (1951). *Field theory in social science: Selected theoretical papers* (D. Cartwright, Ed.). Oxford, England: Harpers.

Li, Y., & Ferraro, K. F. (2006). Volunteering in middle and later life: Is health a benefit, barrier, or both? *Social Forces, 85,* 497–519.

McPherson, J., Miller, L. S.-L., & Cook, J. M. (2001). Birds of a feather: Homophily in social networks. *Annual Review of Sociology, 27,* 415–444.

Mead, L. C., Eckert, J. K., Zimmerman, S., & Schumacher, J. G. (2005). Sociocultural aspects of transitions from assisted living for residents with dementia. *The Gerontologist, 45,* 115–123.

Murray, C. J., Vos, T., Lozano, R., Naghavi, M., Flaxman, A. D., Michaud, C., . . . Lopez, A. D. (2012). Disability-adjusted life years (days) for 291 diseases and injuries in 21 regions. 1990–2010: A systematic analysis for the Global Burden of Disease Study 2010. *The Lancet, 380,* 2197–2223.

Palmore, E. B. (2004). Research note: Ageism in Canada and the United States. *Journal of Cross-Cultural Gerontology, 19,* 41–46.

Schnittker, J. (2007). Look (closely) at all the lonely people: Age and the social psychology of social support. *Journal of Aging and Health, 19,* 659–682.

Shaw, B. A., Krause, N., Liang, J., & Bennett, J. (2007). Tracking changes in social relations throughout late life. *Journal of Gerontology: Social Sciences, 62B,* S90–S99.

Shukla, M. (2008). Human environment interface: Effects and remedies. *Journal of Environmental Psychology and Development, 2*(4), 856–861.

Windle, C., Hughes, D., Linck, P., Russell, I., & Woods, B. (2010). Is exercise effective in promoting mental well-being in older age? A systematic review. *Aging & Mental Health, 14,* 652–669.

Yam, K. (2015). Fully equipped village allows dementia patients normal, independent lives. *Huffington Post.* Retrieved from http://www.huffingtonpost.com/2015/02/09/hogewey-dementia-village_n_6624376.html

Issues Surrounding Dying and Death

*Grief is a winding valley, time passes, the grief changes, but it is
not a straightforward working through of the stages.*

Lewis (1976, p. 5)

The heightened awareness of coming of death, and the anticipation of dying, results in many older adults experiencing an existential crisis. This existential crisis causes many older adults to lose their sense of purpose for their lives. This loss of purpose causes a loss of a sense of forward movement in their lives, creating an existential vacuum (Youdin, 2014). Cicirelli (2006) indicates that this existential crisis is greatest for older adults 75 to 84 years of age because this is the life stage when one's life expectancy is likely to end. Older adults 65 to 74 years of age and older adults 85 years of age and older experience this existential fear of dying and death to a lesser extent. Older adults who are 65 to 74 years of age tend to feel they have not reached the age zone of the end of their lives. Older adults who are 85 years of age and older tend to feel that they cheated death and are grateful for any further life they have. For those older adults who are experiencing disabilities and/or chronic health problems, the thought of death becomes a welcomed relief from the existential anguish they experience from their loss of functioning (Gott, Small, Barnes, Payne, & Seamark, 2008; Ternestedt & Franklin, 2006).

Therefore, dying and death, although a difficult phenomenon for most people, is a phenomenon that is not generic to all older adults; it is a heterogeneous experience, determined by multiple variables. For younger people and middle-aged adults, the concept of dying and death is feared. This fear is explained by *terror management theory* (Greenberg, Solomon, & Pyszczynski, 1997), which is based on the theory of *generative death anxiety* (Becker, 1973) and is the source of ageism and stigmatized views of older adults held by these younger people (see Chapter 2). Therefore, for younger people, older adults are symbols of dying and death.

DYING

A psychologist plays an important role in helping an older adult in the process of dying, and in giving support to the older adult's relatives and caregivers. This helping role includes providing assistance with end-of-life planning, addressing feelings and conflicts arising from the anticipated death of an older adult, addressing issues arising from the grieving process in family members and caregivers after an older adult dies, and, in some cases, participating in a hospice team that is helping an older adult as he or she dies. A psychologist may also play a role in helping an older adult make a decision about physician-assisted suicide. In the case of an older adult dying while experiencing dementia, a psychologist assumes a more prominent role with family members and caregivers in end-of-life planning issues due to the disorientation the dying older adult is experiencing from his or her dementia.

End-of-Life Planning (Advance Care Planning)

For some older adults approaching or in the age bracket of 75 to 84 years of age, the expectation of death becomes acute and triggers a need for *end-of-life planning*, also referred to as *advance care planning*. For other older adults who are experiencing a late-life physical disability or a terminal illness, a consequence of being given a prognosis of a limited time of living often instigates end-of-life planning, which may include the making of wills, a power of attorney, and an advance directive, and greater involvement in medical decision making (Carey, Walter, Lindquist, & Covinsky, 2004; Clayton, Butow, & Tattersall, 2005; Lee, Lindquist, Segal, & Covinsky, 2006). Another consequence of this type of prognosis is the impact it has on family members and caregivers. The older adult and his or her family members and caregivers often consult a psychologist for the provision of advice, supportive psychotherapy, and, in some cases, treatment of psychological problems (see Chapter 3), which are often exacerbated by the distress of the dying process.

Advance care directives formalize an older adult's wishes for medical care while dying and arrangements for death. End-of-life planning helps an older adult and his or her family members increase their quality of life and ensure a reduction in unnecessary or unwanted intensive life-sustaining medical interventions. When family members are active participants in end-of-life planning with an older adult, unnecessary distress and family discord are avoided.

When older adults consider end-of-life planning, socioeconomic status may affect such planning. Kwak and Haley (2005) find that older adults who are highly educated, White, and of European descent tend to prioritize end-of-life planning, and that non-White minorities and older adults with lower economic status tend not to initiate advance care plans (Kwak & Haley, 2005; Washington, Demiris, Parker Oliver, Wittenberg-Lyles, & Crumb,

2012). Since the findings of Kwak and Haley (2005), most hospitals have taken initiatives to introduce to older adults on admission to a hospital the importance of assigning a health proxy and having an advance care directive. These initiatives are proving to have positive results. Approximately one third to one half of older adults now make end-of-life plans (Silveira, Kim, & Langa, 2010). Currently, psychologists are involved in initiating psychoeducational interventions with older adults, their family members, and caregivers that are designed to encourage and support end-of-life planning (Moorman, Carr, Hammes, & Kirchhoff, 2012). These psychoeducational initiatives target older adults who, due to death anxiety, discourage themselves from initiating end-of-life planning. This is especially true of older adults who are 65 to 74 years of age.

The consequences that older adults who do not engage in end-of-life planning may experience are unwanted costly and potentially painful medical interventions, and/or withdrawal of medical treatment that may be desired (Silveira et al., 2010). For example, by not having a *do-not-resuscitate* (DNR) order, an older adult may have his or her life saved only to be maintained in a vegetative state without any positive quality of life. Alternatively, when no advance care directive is made, an older adult becomes vulnerable to medical procedures that he or she, given the chance, would not have given consent for such procedures.

Lack of end-of-life planning creates psychological conflicts that often bring family members for consultations with a psychologist. A psychologist plays a vital role in helping older adults and their family members initiate end-of-life planning. When end-of-life planning is achieved, health care team members along with family members perceive advance care directives as helpful to themselves as well as for the older adult (Buiting, Clayton, Butrow, van Delden, & van der Heide, 2011; Detering, Hancock, Reade, & Silvester, 2010). Recognizing this, Medicare recently began reimbursing physicians for their time when advising older adults on end-of-life planning (Pear, 2010).

In addition to formal advance care directives, older adults and their families engage in informal end-of-life planning.

Examples are advance funeral arrangements, giving away belongings while still alive, and designating belongings to be given to others after death. Supplementary to formal directives, many older adults may construct wills to further eliminate burdens on family members. This is especially true of wealthy older adults, who tend to acutely focus on financial planning and estate planning for the end of their lives, sometimes with greater vigor than their focus on end-of-life medical planning (Street & Desai, 2011).

End-of-Life Palliative Care

Palliative care is considered a *good death* because it keeps an older adult comfortable, provides counseling, and is a means to control pain that a dying older adult would otherwise experience (Broom & Cavenaugh, 2010; Steinhauser et al., 2000). A frequently used health service that provides palliative care is hospice service. Hospice care is a service that provides physical, psychological, social, and spiritual care for dying persons, their families, and their caregivers. Hospice teams are often composed of nurses, psychologists, social workers, physicians, and clergy. Hospice care requires that a physician must certify an older adult with a prognosis of dying within 6 months in order for the older adult to receive hospice services. Hospice professionals are well versed and skilled in addressing end-of-life issues with older adults and extend positive attitudes about the dying process. The increased frequency seen today in older adults' use of hospice services is a positive consequence of end-of-life planning (Nicholas et al., 2011).

Not engaging in end-of-life planning or not participating in a palliative approach to care for dying makes older adults vulnerable, within the last 3 months of their lives, to ending up in a hospital emergency room, consequently being hospitalized unnecessarily, and dying in the hospital (Abel, Rich, & Griffin, 2009; Baxter et al., 2013; Gott et al., 2013). Therefore, an opportunity arises for psychologists to provide psychoeducational programs to physicians to facilitate older adults' use of hospice services, and to encourage older adult patients to initiate end-of-life planning. The benefits of such programs would include enabling more older adults to experience a humanistic death in their homes, and a reduction in the high cost of end-of-life medical care.

Intensive Care and Terminal Illness

When palliative care is not an option, many older adults are treated for terminal care in a hospital intensive care unit. Contrary to many older adults' desires to die at home, 20% of their deaths occur in a hospital setting, or within a short period after being discharged (Angus et al., 2004). The care provided in intensive care units lacks the humanistic qualities of palliative care in an older adult's home. Many older adults in intensive care units experience pain and discomfort in an environment where there is little communication between the physician and the older adult, the physician and family members, or family members and the hospitalized older adult. This makes an older adult vulnerable to immediate decision making for procedures that may be unwanted (Curtis, Engelberg, Bensink, & Ramsey, 2012; Detering et al., 2010). This is especially true for older adults who neglected to appoint a health proxy designate, or who do not have advance care directives (Curtis et al., 2012; Curtis, Engelberg, Nielsen, Au, & Patrick, 2004; Lorenz et al., 2008).

Euthanasia: Physician-Assisted Suicide

Euthanasia is a term used when an older adult decides to intentionally end his or her life. This is accomplished by an older adult's request to his or her physician based on the intention of ending pain and suffering when terminally ill. Oregon was the first state to legalize *physician-assisted suicide* (Kaspers, Pasman, Onwuteaka-Philipsen, & Deeg, 2013) in the fall of 1994 through the Death with Dignity Act. This act legalized *active euthanasia*, or the intentional termination of a life through the direct action of a physician in response to a request from the person wishing to die. This is in direct contrast to *passive euthanasia*, which occurs when life-prolonging support is withheld or withdrawn.

Although physician-assisted suicide may be legal, it may provoke an intrapersonal conflict for a psychologist treating an older adult who is exploring this option to end his or her life. A psychologist needs to be empathic and nonjudgmental toward an older adult, and not impose his or her personal or religious beliefs in the decision process the older adult patient is exploring (Shallcross, 2010). If this is not possible for the psychologist, then he or she must assist the transition of care to another psychologist so that the older adult may explore this end-of-life decision without bias, judgment, or imposition of the personal morals and values of another. Some psychologists have religious values that forbid physician-assisted suicide. Examples of religions that oppose active euthanasia are listed in Table 9.1.

TABLE 9.1 Religions That Oppose the Practice of Euthanasia

Religion	Stated Opposition
Christianity	Dying is viewed as a natural process and a time for reflection and repentance and there should be no intervention. Active euthanasia is prohibited; however, passive euthanasia may be considered acceptable (Engelhardt & Ittis, 2005).
Jewish	The preservation of life is considered to be an irrevocable moral value; therefore, euthanasia is forbidden. As in Christianity, passive euthanasia is acceptable (Kinzbrunner, 2004).
Islam	All human life is sacred, and only Allah may determine when a person dies; therefore, active euthanasia, or any form of suicide, is unacceptable. As in Christianity and the Jewish religion, passive euthanasia is acceptable because an individual is not artificially attempting to extend his or her life (Hussein, 2004).
Buddhism	The transition process from one life to the next life should not be interrupted. One's suffering improves karma and increases the probability of a successful reincarnation. As with the other religions in this table, passive euthanasia is acceptable because it does not interfere with the transition process (Keown, 2005).

Dying With Dementia

Golan, Ligumsky, and Brezis (2007) found that physicians treating older adults experiencing dementia often order painful medical interventions and/or withdrawal of medical treatment when the older adult does not have an end-of-life plan. This, in turn, causes unnecessary anguish and conflicts in family members who find such interventions unacceptable. This finding is confirmed by other researchers who indicate that palliative care delivered to dementia patients is less than optimal (Mitchell, 2009; Sachs, Shega, & Cox-Hayley, 2004). Not providing adequate palliative care to an older adult experiencing dementia is an ethical concern that is experienced by many physicians and would be properly addressed by end-of-life planning initiatives initiated by the very same physicians antecedent to an older adult experiencing dementia (Brooks, 2011). Recognizing this, a critical role for psychologists emerges. Psychologists working with older adults experiencing dementia and their family members and caregivers can facilitate decision-making roles for the family members and caregivers to facilitate proper care and end-of-life planning for dementia patients. The ideal time for this end-of-life planning is at an early stage of the older adult's dementia so that the older adult may participate in the planning. This would eliminate the problem, as found by Meeussen et al. (2012), that most dementia patients' end-of-life preferences are not known, nor are health proxy relatives or caregivers designated by dementia patients before their symptoms and disabilities from their dementias make such appointments impossible.

DEATH, GRIEF, AND BEREAVEMENT

Place of Death

When curative treatment for an older adult is no longer effective, palliative care is often initiated (Gott et al., 2008). Because older adults prefer to die at home, not in a hospital or nursing home, hospice care is a preferred choice of an older adult. Hospice care enables an older adult to experience a humanistic death. In turn, family members and caregivers have a humanistic experience of their loved one dying as compared with the experience they would have if their loved one was dying in an intensive care unit or while institutionalized in a nursing home.

An advantage of hospice care at an older adult's home is that it gives the opportunity for some older adults to have a means of holding on so that family members and caregivers may experience a *good death* of their loved one rather than the distressful experience of dying in a hospital with poor end-of-life care. Another reason for wanting to die at home is the higher probability of having family members and/or friends experience a communal death with the older adult, which provides an opportunity for farewell communications (Clarke & Seymour, 2010) (Vignette 9.1).

VIGNETTE 9.1   A Funeral at Home (Zanierewski, 2015)

A new trend is developing whereby people choose to have a funeral at home, rather than more expensive options when one uses the services of a funeral home. A contributing factor to funerals at home is the growing trend for cremation of loved ones. This enables families to avoid the necessity of embalming services provided by funeral homes and enables a family to have a more intimate closing experience around the death of a loved one. Another advantage of home funerals when a loved one is cremated is that they are environmentally friendly and consistent with the new consciousness of respecting one's environment.

Many states still require a funeral director and a doctor or a medical examiner to sign a death certificate, and a funeral director is still needed to sign a permit when the deceased body is moved to a cemetery or crematorium. Nevertheless, funerals at home are cost-effective and humanistic.

Grief

A normal reaction to the loss of a loved one is called *bereavement* (Table 9.2). As discussed in Chapter 3, the new edition of

TABLE 9.2 Normal Grief Reactions Versus Complicated Grief Reactions

Normal Grief Reaction	Complicated Grief Reaction
Major depression is ruled out if the older adult's symptoms can be better accounted for by a reaction to a loved one's death (bereavement).	Increased probability that an older adult may experience a major depression. Often co-occurs with a mood disorder
The intensity and duration of symptoms do not match the severity, duration, and clinically significant distress or impairment of major depression.	
The time frame of the grief reaction is less than 2 months.	Repetitive symptoms may last 6 months or longer.
Symptom relief occurs in 6–10 weeks.	
Symptoms are depressed mood, sleep disturbance, and crying.	Overwhelming thoughts of disbelief, a preoccupation with the lost loved one, an intense feeling of searching and yearning, frequent memories causing distress, and feeling stuck and unable to move on with one's life
Secondary symptoms may occur, including difficulty concentrating, loss of interest in pleasurable things or activities, and weight loss.	Preoccupation or avoidance of things or activities related to the deceased loved one

Adapted from Clayton (2010); Lamb, Pies, and Zisook (2010); Newson et al. (2011); Wakefield, Schmitz, First, and Horowitz (2007).

the *Diagnostic and Statistical Manual of Mental Disorders* (5th ed.; *DSM-5*; American Psychiatric Association [APA], 2013) removed the bereavement exclusion that, in prior versions of the *DSM*, helped psychologists differentiate between a normal grief reaction (bereavement) and major depression that may occur in an older adult after the death of a loved one (APA, 2015). Unfortunately, with this removal of the bereavement exclusion in the *DSM-5*, a previously recognized reaction to the death of a loved one that was considered a normal grief reaction is now considered a case of depression, putting older adults at risk for inappropriate psychopharmacological treatment. This is unfortunate, because bereavement can be treated with supportive psychotherapy, enabling an older adult to experience the feelings of loss and go through a normal process of grieving his or her deceased loved one. Prior to the *DSM-5*, the bereavement exclusion intention was to exclude individuals experiencing symptoms of depression lasting less than 2 months after the death of a loved one from a diagnosis of major depression. The loss of the bereavement exclusion is another aspect of how the *DSM*, throughout all of its previous versions, contributes to the medicalization of normal aspects of one's life experience and, in this case, contributes to the possibility of increased cases of overdiagnosis of major depression (Frances, 2010).

Complicated Grief, an Abnormal Reaction to Loss of a Loved One

Complicated grief is a phenomenon in which an older adult, after the loss of a loved one, will experience symptoms that are atypical of a normal grief reaction (bereavement) (Newson, Boelen, Hek, Hofman, & Tiemeier, 2011). This symptom constellation includes overwhelming thoughts of disbelief, a preoccupation with the lost loved one, an intense feeling of searching and yearning for the deceased, frequent memories causing distress, and feeling stuck and unable to move on with one's life. This type of severe grief reaction increases the probability that an older adult may experience major depression, and may co-occur with preexisting mood disorders (Sung et al., 2011). A psychologist treating an older adult experiencing a difficult reaction to the loss of a loved one must discriminate between major depression and complicated grief (Vignette 9.2). Major depression (see Chapter 3) is ruled out if the symptoms of grief are focused solely on the separation and loss of a loved one.

VIGNETTE 9.2   A Case of a Complicated Grief Reaction

(*Note:* Names and other identifying information have been changed to preserve confidentiality.)

Barbara is a 74-year-old retired oncology nurse. She worked at a university hospital oncology unit for 42 years and has been in retirement for the past 9 years. Barbara's husband of 39 years died after complications of chronic lymphocytic leukemia that he was diagnosed with 6 years ago.

Barbara's husband's illness was the same as those she had encountered hundreds of times during her career as an oncology nurse. She had witnessed many deaths from this illness and always felt that she had a good understanding of dying and death. Because of this understanding, she had been able to help numerous relatives and caregivers of patients who died, showing compassion, empathy, and caring. While these patients were dying, Barbara was able to help them with the process of dying, making it as humanistic as possible. Often she grieved for the patients whom she felt especially close to, but she was always able to continue her responsibilities at the hospital and at home. She would feel a sadness and a sense of loss but felt a sense of comfort in the fact that she made a positive contribution to the dying process that her patients experienced, and to the help she gave to the relatives and caregivers while their loved ones were dying. She also felt good about her experiences volunteering in the outpatient counseling center's program for relatives and caregivers of patients who died while in the hospital's care.

The death of Barbara's husband had a different, unexpected consequence for Barbara. Based on her prior experience with death and dying, Barbara initially felt that she would grieve for a few weeks and feel sad on and off for a few months, but that the intensity of the feelings would subside and, because of her prior experiences, she would be able to cope in a positive manner. To Barbara's surprise, after the initial 4 or 5 weeks of her mourning, she began to experience several painful symptoms. She experienced unrelenting feelings of yearning for her deceased husband and episodically panicked when worrying about how she would be able to cope with moving on with her life without her deceased husband. When not

(*continued*)

VIGNETTE 9.2 (*continued*)

panicking, Barbara would felt numb and disconnected from her world. It was as if she had been traveling on a train, got off at the next depot for a break from traveling, and then found that the train left without her, leaving her stranded in a place that was unfamiliar, lonely, and isolating.

Barbara's feelings of disconnection increased in intensity. She felt no connection to her children when they would visit. She rejected offers from friends to join them in activities. Barbara preferred to be alone and fantasize about her husband, often feeling that he was by her side on the couch they would share, or sleeping with her in bed at night. One day, she found herself fighting these fantasies by ridding the house of any reminders of her husband. She stopped watching television because this was an activity she and her husband shared each evening.

Trying to not associate with anything that reminded her of her husband was now replaced with episodic feelings of anger for hm. "How could David do this to me?" she would often say to herself. Her anger began to turn on herself. She felt that it would have been better if she died and not her husband. "Then he would feel the pain, not me. I would not have to worry about how I would have to continue my life," she thought to herself. She started to think that if she did not wake up the next morning, that would be all right because the pain would be over. This thought of not waking up the next day began to intensify, happening several times a day.

Fortunately, Barbara recognized that, based on her prior experiences as a nurse, these thoughts were a beginning process of suicidal ideation that put her at risk of finding the means to kill herself and to construct a plan for her death. This scared Barbara enough to contact a psychologist she knew from her work at the outpatient clinic at the hospital. The next day, she presented herself for treatment.

Disenfranchised Grief

Disenfranchised grief is a type of grief an older adult may experience that is often not socially recognized by an older adult's relatives or friends (Attig, 2004; Doka, 2002, 2008). Examples of events that cause a disenfranchised grief reaction are the death of an older adult's pet, the end of an extramarital affair, or the death by suicide of a loved one. As a consequence of the nature of the loss, there is no formal public mourning, social support, or acknowledgment by others of the older adult's grieving experience. Often, as in the case of the loss of a pet, extended grief or publically painful symptoms are not considered legitimate (Packman, Field, Carmack, & Ronen, 2011). There is a significant need for psychologists to provide counseling to older adults experiencing disenfranchised grief because adults experiencing this type of grief suffer from difficulty experiencing their loss when it is not validated by others (Worden, 2008).

THEORETICAL MODELS OF GRIEF

The following are examples of theoretical models of grief. It must be understood that none of these models is all encompassing for all older adults. Each theory is merely a hypothesis of what an individual experiences during the grief process. The five stages of grief model is also applicable to the stages a person experiences when dying. A psychologist must recognize that these theories are guidelines to understanding the dying and grief process. When an older adult does not complete, or fit, any of these models, it does not necessarily indicate that there is something pathological about his or her grief experience.

Five Stages of Grief

Kübler-Ross (1969) describes the *five stages of grief* an older adult undergoes when grieving a loved one: *denial, anger, bargaining, depression,* and *acceptance.* In addition, these five stages of grief are now considered to be the *five stages of dying* an older adult experiences before death, which are also experienced by those grieving the loss of a loved one. A common misconception is that an older adult who is dying will go through each stage in linear order. In reality, these stages are not sequential, may occur in any order, and may recur, and some stages may not be experienced at all. Completion of all stages experienced heralds a successful dying process (Kübler-Ross, 1969; Leming & Dickinson, 2007; Youdin, 2014).

Four Tasks of Mourning

Worden (2008) proposes that there are *four tasks of mourning* that need to be experienced in order for mourning to be complete. These tasks are (1) *accepting the reality of the loss*, (2) *working through the pain of grief*, (3) *adjusting to an environment in which the deceased is missing*, and (4) *finding and maintaining an enduring connection with the deceased while embarking on a new life* (Worden, 2008). As with the Kübler-Ross *five-stage model* (Kübler-Ross, 1969), these tasks are not necessarily completed in a linear order. However, unlike the Kübler-Ross model, in which some stages may not be experienced, Worden feels that in order to regain equilibrium, all tasks must be completed. Worden does not give a timeline for the completion of the five tasks, indicating that completion is unique to the grieving individual and may take a considerable amount of time to complete, perhaps months, or perhaps years.

Dual-Process Model of Coping With Bereavement

The *dual-process model of coping with bereavement* (Stroebe & Schut, 2001; Stroebe, Schut, & Stroebe, 2005) is a dichotomous model consisting of the processes of *loss orientation* and *restoration orientation*. These are interactive processes that facilitate normal grieving until the older adult completes his or her experience of bereavement.

When an older adult experiences loss orientation, he or she experiences conflicting feelings of relief and disturbing feelings of loss and yearning for his or her deceased loved one. A psychologist helps the older adult understand his or her experience with these competing phenomena. An older adult learns that feelings of relief bring an absence of pain and anguish. These time-out periods help the older adult endure the pain that occurs when yearning for the deceased loved one, facilitating the understanding that yearning is a psychological mechanism for feeling an emotional bond for the deceased loved one despite the fact that he or she is no longer physically available.

The other side to the competing phenomena is restoration orientation. This is a process of the grieving older adult reestablishing his or her role and activities that were present prior to the loved one's death.

Three Stages of Grieving

Martin and Doka (2000) describe three stages of grieving: *intuitive, instrumental,* and *intuitive-instrumental.* Grieving is a universal experience, yet the ways in which older adults grieve can be observed from these three different perspectives. The intuitive type of grieving is an emotive type of grieving whereby the older adult vocalizes expressions of grief, cries, and displays a depressed posture. The instrumental type of grieving causes an older adult to engage in grieving through interpersonal activities. These include joining a self-help bereavement group or consulting a psychologist for psychotherapy support and treatment. The last type, the intuitive-instrumental type of grieving, finds an older adult reminiscing about times with the deceased loved one, engaging in activities that he or she enjoyed with the loved one, or engaging in any other experience that was previously shared with his or her loved one.

REFERENCES

Abel, J., Rich, A., & Griffin, T. (2009). End of life care in hospital: A descriptive study of all inpatient deaths in 1 year. *Palliative Medicine, 23,* 616–622.

American Psychiatric Association. (2013). *Diagnostic and statistical manual of mental disorders* (5th ed.). Washington, DC: Author.

American Psychiatric Association. (2015). *DSM: History of the manual.* Retrieved from http://www.psychiatry.org/practice/dsm/dsm-history-of-the-manual

Angus, D. C., Barnato, A. E., Linde-Zwirble, W. T., Weissfeld, L. A., Watson, R. S., Rickert, T., & Rubenfeld, G. D. (2004). Use of intensive care at the end of life in the United States: An epidemiologic study. *Critical Care Medicine, 32*, 638–643.

Attig, T. (2004). Disenfranchised grief revisited: Discounting hope and love. *Omega, 49*, 197–215.

Baxter, S. K., Baird, W. O., Thompson, S., Bianchi, S. M., Walters, S. J., Lee, E., . . . McDermott, C. J. (2013). The use of non-invasive ventilation at end of life in patients with motor neurone disease: A qualitative exploration of family carer and health professional experiences. *Palliative Medicine, 27*(6), 516–523. doi:10.1177/0269216313478449

Becker, E. (1973). *The denial of death*. New York, NY: Free Press.

Brooks, C. L. (2011). Considering elderly competence when consenting to treatment. *Holistic Nursing Practice, 16*, 1678–1686.

Broom, A., & Cavenaugh, J. (2010). Masculinity, moralities, and being cared for: An exploration of experiences of living and dying in hospice. *Social Science & Medicine, 71*(5), 869–876.

Buiting, H. M., Clayton, J. M., Butrow, P. N., van Delden, J. J., & van der Heide, A. (2011). Artificial nutrition and hydration for patients with advanced dementia: Perspectives from medical practitioners in the Netherlands and Australia. *Palliative Medicine, 25*, 83–91.

Carey, E. C., Walter, L. C., Lindquist, K., & Covinsky, K. E. (2004). Development and validation of a functional morbidity index to predict mortality in community-dwelling elders. *Journal of General Internal Medicine, 18*(10), 1027–1033.

Cicirelli, V. G. (2006). Fear of death in mid-old age. *Journal of Gerontology: Psychological Sciences, 61B*(2), P75–P81.

Clarke, D., & Seymour, J. (2010). "At the foot of a very long ladder." Discussing the end of life with older adults and informed caregivers. *Journal of Pain and Symptom Management, 40*(6), 857–869.

Clayton, J. M., Butow, P. N., & Tattersall, M. H. (2005). When and how to initiate discussion about prognosis and end-of-life issues with terminally ill patients. *Journal of Pain Symptom Management, 30*(2), 132–144.

Clayton, P. (2010). V code for bereavement. *Journal of Clinical Psychiatry, 71*, 359–360.

Curtis, J. R., Engelberg, R. A., Bensink, M. E., & Ramsey, S. D. (2012). End-of-life care in the intensive care unit: Can we simultaneously increase quality and reduce costs? *American Journal of Respiratory and Critical Care Medicine, 186*(7), 587–592.

Curtis, J. R., Engelberg, R. A., Nielsen, E. L., Au, D. H., & Patrick, D. L. (2004). Patient-physician communication about end-of-life care for patients with severe COPD. *European Respiratory Journal, 24*(2), 200–205.

Death with Dignity Act, Ore. Rev. Stat. § 127.800-99 C.F.R. (1994).

Detering, K. M., Hancock, A. D., Reade, M. C., & Silvester, W. (2010). The impact of advance care planning on end of life care in elderly patients: Randomised controlled trial. *British Medical Journal (Clinical Research Education), 340,* 1345–1354.

Doka, K. (2002). *Disenfranchised grief: New challenges, directions, and strategies for practice.* Champaign, IL: Research Press.

Doka, K. (2008). Disenfranchised grief in a historical and cultural perspective. In M. S. Stroebe, H. Hansson, H. Schut, & W. Stroebe (Eds.), *Handbook of bereavement research and practice: Advances in theory and intervention* (pp. 223–240). Washington, DC: American Psychological Association.

Engelhardt, H. T., & Ittis, A. S. (2005). End-of-life: The traditional Christian view. *The Lancet, 366,* 1045–1049.

Frances, A. (2010). Opening Pandoras box: The 19 worst suggestions for DSM5. *Psychiatric Times.* Retrieved from http://www.janusonline.it/sites/default/files/allegati_news/FrancesA_PsychiatricTimes110210.pdf

Gallo, W. T., Baker, M. J., & Bradley, E. H. (2001). Factors associated with home versus institutional death among cancer patients in Connecticut. *Journal of the American Geriatrics Society, 49,* 771–777.

Golan, I., Ligumsky, M., & Brezis, M. (2007). Percutaneous endoscopic gastrostomy in hospitalized incompetent geriatric patients: Poorly informed, constrained and paradoxical decisions. *Israeli Medical Association Journal, 9,* 839–842.

Gott, M., Frey, R., Robinson, J., Boyd, M., O'Callaghan, A., Richards, N., & Snow, B. (2013). The nature of, and reasons for, "inappropriate" hospitalisations among patients with palliative care needs: A qualitative exploration of the views of generalist palliative care providers. *Palliative Medicine, 27*(8), 747–756. doi:10.1177/0269216312469263

Gott, M., Small, N., Barnes, S., Payne, S., & Seamark, D. (2008). Older people's views of a good death in heart failure: Implications for palliative care provision. *Social Science and Medicine, 97*(7), 1113–1121.

Greenberg, J., Solomon, S., & Pyszczynski, T. (1997). Terror management theory of self-esteem and cultural worldviews: Empirical assessments and conceptual refinements. In M. P. Zanna (Ed.), *Advances in experimental social psychology* (Vol. 29, pp. 61–139). San Diego, CA: Academic Press.

Hussein, R. G. (2004). Philosophical and ethical issues: An Islamic perspective. *Journal of Advanced Nursing, 46,* 251–283.

Kaspers, P. J., Pasman, H. R. W., Onwuteaka-Philipsen, B. D., & Deeg, D. J. H. (2013). Changes over a decade in end-of-life care and transfers during the last 3 months of life: A repeated survey among proxies of deceased older people. *Palliative Medicine, 27*(6), 544–552.

Keown, D. (2005). End of life: The Buddhist view. *The Lancet, 366,* 952–955.

Kinzbrunner, B. M. (2004). Jewish medical ethics and end-of-life care. *Journal of Palliative Medicine, 7,* 558–573.

Kübler-Ross, E. (1969). *On death and dying.* New York, NY: Scribner.

Kwak, J., & Haley, W. E. (2005). Current research findings on end of life decision making among racially or ethnically diverse groups. *The Gerontologist, 45*(5), 634–641.

Lamb, K., Pies, R., & Zisook, S. (2010). The bereavement exclusion for the diagnosis of major depression: To be, or not to be. *Psychiatry, 7,* 19–25.

Lee, S. J., Lindquist, K., Segal, M. R., & Covinsky, K. E. (2006). Development and validation of a prognostic index for 4-year mortality in older adults. *JAMA, 295*(7), 801–808.

Leming, M. R., & Dickinson, G. E. (2007). *Understanding death, dying, and bereavement* (6th ed.). New York, NY: Wadsworth.

Lewis, C. S. (1976). *A grief observed.* New York, NY: Bantam Books.

Lorenz, K. A., Lynn, J., Dy, S. M., Shugarman, L. R., Wilkinson, A., Mularski, R. A., . . . Shekelle, P. G. (2008). Evidence for improving palliative care at the end of life: A systematic review. *American Internal Medicine, 148*(2), 147–159.

Martin, T., & Doka, K. (2000). *Men don't cry...women do: Transcending gender stereotypes of grief.* Philadelphia, PA: Brunner/Mazel.

Meeussen, K., Van den Block, L., Echteld, M., Boffin, N., Bilsen, J., Van Casteren, V., & Deliens, L. (2012). Older people dying with dementia: A nationwide study. *International Psychogeriatrics, 24*(10), 1581–1591. doi:10.1017/S1041610212000865

Mitchell, S. L. (2009). The clinical course of advanced dementia. *New England Journal of Medicine, 361,* 1529–1538.

Moorman, S., Carr, D., Hammes, B. J., & Kirchhoff, K. T. (2012). Evaluating the Respecting Choices® Advance Care Planning Program: An indirect assessment. *Death Studies, 36*(4), 301–323.

Newson, R. S., Boelen, P. A., Hek, K., Hofman, A., & Tiemeier, H. (2011). The prevalence and characteristics of complicated grief in older adults. *Journal of Affective Disorders, 132*(1–2), 231–238.

Nicholas, L. H., Langa, K. M., Iwashyna, J., & Weir, D. R. (2011). Regional variation in the association between advance directives and end-of-life expenditures. *JAMA, 306*(13), 1447–1453.

Packman, W., Field, N. P., Carmack, B. J., & Ronen, R. (2011). Continuing bonds and psychosocial adjustment in pet loss. *Journal of Loss and Trauma, 16*, 341–357.

Pear, R. (2010). *Obama returns to end-of-life plan that caused stir*. Retrieved from http://www.nytimes.com/2010/12/26/us/politics/26death.html?r=2&nl=todaysheadlines&emc=a2

Sachs, G. A., Shega, J. W., & Cox-Hayley, D. (2004). Barriers to excellent end-of-life care for patients with dementia. *Journal of General Internal Medicine, 19*, 1057–1063.

Shallcross, L. (2010). Putting clients ahead of personal values. *Counseling Today, 53*, 32–34.

Silveira, M. J., Kim, S. Y., & Langa, K. M. (2010). Advance directives and outcomes of surrogate decision making before death. *New England Journal of Medicine, 362*(13), 1211–1218.

Steinhauser, K. E., Clipp, E. C., McNeilly, M., Christakis, N. A., McIntyre, L. M., & Tulsky, J. A. (2000). In search of a good death: Observations of patients, families, and providers. *Annals of Internal Medicine, 132*(10), 825–832.

Street, D., & Desai, S. (2011). Planning for old age. In R. A. Settersten, Jr., & J. L. Angel (Eds.), *Handbook of sociology of aging* (pp. 3–15). New York, NY: Springer.

Stroebe, M. S., & Schut, H. (2001). Meaning making in the dual process model of coping with bereavement. In R. A. Neimeyer (Ed.), *Meaning reconstruction and the experience of loss* (pp. 55–73). Washington, DC: American Psychological Association.

Stroebe, M. S., Schut, H., & Stroebe, W. (2005). Attachment in coping with bereavement: A theoretical integration. *Review of General Psychology, 9*, 48–66.

Sung, S. C., Dryman, M. T., Marks, E., Shear, M. K., Ghequiere, A., Fava, M., & Simon, N. M. (2011). Complicated grief among individuals with major depression: Prevalence, comorbidity, and associated features. *Journal of Affective Disorders, 134*, 453–458.

Ternestedt, B. M., & Franklin, L. L. (2006). Ways of relating to death: Views of older people resident in nursing homes. *International Journal of Palliative Nursing, 12*(7), 334–340.

Tiernann, E., O'Connor, M. O., O'Siorain, L., & Kearney, M. (2002). A prospective study of preferred versus actual place of death among patients referred to a palliative care home-care service. *Irish Medical Journal, 95*, 232–235.

Wakefield, J., Schmitz, M., First, M., & Horowitz, A. (2007). Extending the bereavement exclusion for major depression to other losses: Evidence from the National Comorbidity Survey. *Archives of General Psychiatry, 64*, 433–440.

Washington, K. T., Demiris, G., Parker Oliver, D., Wittenberg-Lyles, E., & Crumb, E. (2012). Qualitative evaluation of a problem-solving intervention for informal hospice caregivers. *Palliative Medicine, 26*(8), 1018–1024. doi:10.1177/0269216311427191

Worden, J. W. (2008). *Grief counseling and grief therapy: A handbook for the mental health practitioner* (4th ed.). New York, NY: Springer Publishing Company.

Youdin, R. (2014). *Clinical gerontological social work practice*. New York, NY: Springer Publishing Company.

Zanierewski, A. (2015). Having a funeral at home, not at a funeral home. *Detroit Free Press*. Retrieved from http://www.usatoday.com/story/news/nation/2015/01/12/more-choosing-at-home-funerals/21622039/

Future Areas for Psychologists Interested in the Psychology of Aging

The road is everything, the destination nothing.
Bertha Pappenheim (Freeman, 1972)

Writing this book has been quite a journey. It took me to past experiences with patients in my practice, patients I have seen in hospital emergency rooms, the many relatives and caregivers of older adults I have worked with, and the health professionals who treat older adults whom I have encountered and collaborated with over many years. I have also learned a great deal while researching this text. It is my hope that you will find inspiration from this book about the exciting field of the psychology of aging. This is an incredible field for psychologists, offering many career opportunities in a field that is highly diversified. Following are suggestions I have for future paths you may wish to travel in the field of aging. Some of you may find inspiration from these suggestions and initiate your own path of discovery and adventure in aging. Or, perhaps, these inroads my pique your interest in some inquiry that is tangential to the ideas I have put forward. Whatever the case, I encourage you to consider making a contribution to the field of the psychology of aging.

PERSON-IN-ENVIRONMENT PERSPECTIVE

First and foremost is the need for a better diagnostic system for older adults that is humanistic and anchored in the person-in-environment perspective. This is necessary due to the inherent problems with the current version of the *Diagnostic and Statistical Manual of Mental Disorders* (5th ed.; *DSM-5*; American Psychiatric Association [APA], 2013) described in Chapter 3. Creating a person-in-environment diagnostic manual would remove psychologists from contributing to the medicalization of the psychological problems older adults experience that is promoted by the APA and the pharmaceutical industry (Healy, 2013).

COGNITIVE DECLINE AND DEMENTIA

Older adults experiencing cognitive decline and any of the dementias are suffering in ever increasing numbers. With the aging of the baby-boom generation, the incidence of cognitive decline and dementia will exponentially escalate over the coming years. With this coming *tsunami of dementia*, older adults experiencing dementia, as well as their family members and caregivers, will need the services of psychologists. These services include supportive psychotherapy and psychoeducation about cognitive decline and dementia. In addition, psychologists treat the co-occurring psychological problems experienced by relatives and caregivers that are exacerbated by the distress of caring for an older adult experiencing dementia.

As indicated in this book, health care professionals often underserve older adults experiencing dementia. Psychologists are needed to help families recognize the importance of end-of-life planning for an older adult when first diagnosed with a dementia. Supportive psychotherapy helps break through the denial many older adults and their families have about the consequences that occur from a dementia diagnosis. By initiating and developing early-intervention programs, a psychologist creates an opportunity for an older adult with a dementia diagnosis to express his or her wishes for end-of-life care before he or she suffers a profound loss of cognitive functions.

OLDER ADULT SUBSTANCE ABUSE

There is a promising trend in substance abuse treatment supporting the contention that the etiology of addiction is not a disease but is a maladaptive choice by an older adult to cope with problems and conflicts that were antecedent to his or her addiction. This trend is seen in neuroscience and clinical psychology (Lewis, 2015). When an older adult understands that he or she has responsibility for and choice in the decision to abuse a psychoactive substance, there is a greater probability of successful treatment and recovery from a substance abuse problem. In addition, the development of psychoeducational programs by psychologists to teach older adults, their relatives, and caregivers proper medication compliance strategies will help lessen the problem of psychoactive substance *misuse* that initiates the consequent addiction problem for many older adults.

OLDER ADULT ABUSE

Older adult abuse is an unacceptable problem in today's society. Older adult abuse is mostly hidden, and many health professionals are unaware of its devastating consequences. Psychologists are in a unique position to assess whether older abuse is occurring and, when discovered, to intervene with advocacy initiatives. Another opportunity for psychologists to help older adults is in an advisory role to government agencies and elected officials. With the use of psychoeducational initiatives to heighten awareness of older adult abuse, policy changes and development of new laws for intervention with perpetrators of older adult abuse may be accomplished. Psychologists participating in *think tanks* help heighten the awareness of the general public, media, and government officials about the extent and consequences of older adult abuse. Such heightened awareness facilitates the allocation of resources to agencies and nonprofit organizations that are actively engaged in combating older adult abuse.

In addition, greater emphasis needs to be placed on the identification of and intervention with perpetrators of older adult abuse. By creating research initiatives focusing on perpetrators of older adult abuse, psychologists may develop interventions that forestall older adult abuse; cause early intervention with an older adult abuser; and, from a therapeutic standpoint, rehabilitate an older adult abuser so stop the cycle of abuse he or she has been perpetrating on older adults.

ENVIRONMENTAL PSYCHOLOGY

The field of environmental psychology is a gateway opportunity for psychologists to implement interventions targeting an older adult's environment as a means for behavioral change. This contributes to a sense of empowerment instead of the pathological view of older adults found in traditional psychiatric diagnoses and treatments. More research is needed to develop environmental interventions to improve the quality of life for older adults, and to maintain a healthy balance between the interactions of older adults and their environments. In addition, psychologists assist architects and urban planners to develop environments that facilitate interaction among older adults to lessen isolation, as well as among older adults and younger people. Such initiatives help reduce the prevalence of ageism driven by younger people's lack of interaction with older adults. Instead of viewing older adults through a lens of stereotype and stigma, younger people will then have the opportunity to see older adults for their strengths, their knowledge, and the helpful guidance that they may offer.

DYING AND DEATH

Psychologists may face, at an increasing frequency, an older adult who desires to end his or her life via physician-assisted suicide. This decision by an older adult often causes conflict with his or her family members and caregivers. A psychologist's support and assistance in facilitating the family system's acceptance of the loved one's wishes is a critically needed psychological service. In addition, many physicians are in need of psychoeducation regarding physician-assisted suicide to dispel misinformation and help work through the personal values and judgments experienced by a physician when opposing an older adult's wish to end pain and suffering with assistance from his or her treating physician.

DISENFRANCHISED GRIEF

Many psychologists are not knowledgeable about disenfranchised grief and devalue its significance to older adults. Becoming informed and acknowledging the significance of losses that are not acknowledged by a suffering older adult's friends or relatives will facilitate a psychologist's empathic understanding and will not only help a grieving older adult, but will serve as a catalyst to others, creating a much-needed social change in an older adult's environment.

Disenfranchised grief is a phenomenon that is often overlooked by psychologists. Many older adults experience various types of loss that are not considered significant by others, leaving these older adults to grieve alone, and at times to devalue the grief that they are experiencing. The lack of others validating their grief as well as their own devaluation may lead to depression, or to the exacerbation of preexisting psychological problems. Examples of such losses are the death of a pet; relocation; loss of a home lived in for many years complicated by the loss of a social network and a familiar environment; loss of a lover who is not a spouse; loss of a partner in a lesbian, gay, bisexual, or transgender (LGBT) relationship; and loss of functioning in an active aspect of one's life due to a physical disability or medical illness. A psychologist's intervention is such cases validates the loss the older adult is grieving and may in some instances be an opportunity for psychoeducation for relatives and caregivers of the grieving older adult.

It is now time for you to start your journey into the field of aging. With the exponential increase of older adults now occurring, limitless opportunities exist for a rewarding professional career in the psychology of aging.

REFERENCES

American Psychiatric Association. (2013). *Diagnostic and statistical manual of mental disorders* (5th ed.). Washington, DC: Author.

Freeman, L. (1972). *The story of Anna O.* New York, NY: Walker and Company.

Healy, D. (2013). *Pharmageddon.* Berkeley, CA: University of California Press.

Lewis, M. (2015). *The biology of desire: Why addiction is not a disease.* New York, NY: PublicAffairs.

Index

vascular cognitive
impairment (VCI), 90
vascular dementia (VaD), 90–91
verbal abuse, 31, 32
virility surveillance, 115
visual hallucinations
and dementia with Lewy
bodies, 93
and Parkinson's disease
dementia, 94

voluntary social
disengagement, 200
vulnerability and risk model,
172, 173

women, older adult, sexuality
of, 113–114

yoga, 63
young-old adults, 11–13